Rising Star, Setting Sun

Rising Star, Setting Sun

DWIGHT D. EISENHOWER, JOHN F. KENNEDY, AND
THE PRESIDENTIAL TRANSITION THAT CHANGED AMERICA

JOHN T. SHAW

PEGASUS BOOKS
NEW YORK LONDON

RISING STAR, SETTING SUN

Pegasus Books Ltd.
148 W 37th Street, 13th Floor
New York, NY 10018

First Pegasus Books cloth edition May 2018

Interior design by Maria Fernandez

Library of Congress Cataloging-in-Publication Data is available.

ISBN: 978-1-68177-732-0

10 9 8 7 6 5 4 3 2 1

Printed in the United States of America
Distributed by W. W. Norton & Company
www.pegasusbooks.us

For Mindy

Contents

Introduction

This book is about two men and a transition of presidential power that ushered in a new age in American politics and culture. Dwight David Eisenhower, the thirty-fourth president of the United States, and John Fitzgerald Kennedy, the thirty-fifth president, are two of the most intriguing and compelling political figures of the twentieth century. Both were singular personalities who were eager and confident to stand before what Kennedy once referred to as "the High Court of History."[1] But Eisenhower and Kennedy can be seen more vividly and understood more clearly when considered in tandem, as sharply contrasting political leaders and as generational rivals.

The striking contrast between these two men is captured best by examining the complicated and poignant transfer of the presidency from one to the other at the end of 1960 and the beginning of 1961. This exchange of power from Eisenhower to Kennedy marked more than merely a succession of American presidents. It triggered a generational shift in American politics and culture. During this time, Eisenhower, long a dominant force in American life, reluctantly prepared to hand over the presidency to Kennedy, the upstart junior senator from Massachusetts whose successful presidential campaign ridiculed and repudiated the Eisenhower administration. Though the passing of Eisenhower's administration and the arrival of Kennedy's is a distinctly American story, it evokes timeless themes that can be found in Greek mythology, the Bible, and Shakespeare: the transitory nature of power, the allure of change, the wisdom of age, the impetuousness of youth, and the perpetual misunderstandings between generations.

Eisenhower and Kennedy are a study in contrasts; they had profoundly different personalities, interests, temperaments, family backgrounds, educations, skills, friendships, working styles, reading preferences, staffs, wives, and strategies for America. They came from different generations and different Americas. Eisenhower was, at the time of the transition, the oldest man ever to serve as president. He was from the rural Midwest, a Presbyterian, a graduate of West Point, a former five-star general and commanding officer during World War II, and the last American president born in the nineteenth century. Kennedy was twenty-seven years his junior and, in 1960, became the youngest man ever elected president, at the age of forty-three. He was from the urban East Coast, a Catholic, a graduate of Harvard, a former navy lieutenant during World War II, and the first American president born in the twentieth century. Eisenhower was an extrovert and highly organized. He was a man of routine who made decisions after carefully structured meetings and lengthy deliberations with his team. Kennedy was an introvert and highly disorganized. He was a man who avoided routines and preferred to make decisions after absorbing written briefings and informal conversations with his staff.

On November 4, 1952, Dwight Eisenhower was elected president of the United States, trouncing the Democratic candidate Adlai Stevenson. That same night, Congressman John F. Kennedy narrowly defeated Republican senator Henry Cabot Lodge Jr. to become only the third Democratic senator in the history of Massachusetts. Both were sworn into office in January of 1953, and during the next eight years Eisenhower and Kennedy lived and worked in close proximity in Washington, D.C. But they inhabited different worlds and their paths seldom crossed—at least directly. Eisenhower was the president who dominated American politics and Kennedy was an ambitious young senator who aspired to greater heights.

As he assumed the presidency in 1953, Dwight Eisenhower was already a global icon and an American hero, the military strategist who defeated Adolf Hitler. Revered by Middle America, Eisenhower projected a sunny, serene, modest, and confidence-inspiring persona. He exuded strength and authority and came to preside over what historians would call the Age of Eisenhower, the Eisenhower Era, and the Ike Age.

At the start of the Eisenhower presidency, John Kennedy was a back-bencher from the minority party with a middling record as a congressman. Reserved and sometimes aloof, he aspired to become a statesman-scholar who connected the worlds of ideas and action along the lines of his hero, Winston Churchill. An amalgam of wealth, privilege, and personal struggle, he projected an intellectual, skeptical, edgy, and devotion-inspiring persona. Respected by academics and political operatives, he exuded ambition and aspiration, and was determined to secure the keys to 1600 Pennsylvania Avenue without enduring a lengthy Senate apprenticeship.

During Eisenhower's first term there was a huge stature gap between the world-renowned president and the relatively unknown senator. However, the gap began to narrow in 1956. Eisenhower won reelection to a second term and his political career reached its zenith and at the same time Kennedy was emerging as the rising young star of the Democratic Party. He was propelled into prominence by his best-selling, Pulitzer Prize–winning book, *Profiles in Courage*; his narrow miss for his party's vice presidential nomination; and his role as the most popular Democratic surrogate for Illinois governor and Democratic presidential nominee Adlai Stevenson on the 1956 presidential campaign trail. Less than a month after the election in which Eisenhower once again trounced Stevenson, Kennedy was already preparing to run for the presidency in 1960—four years later. He became one of his party's fiercest critics of the Eisenhower administration and the opposition's most telegenic spokesman. He largely defined his political career in opposition to Eisenhower and his relentless attacks on the administration attracted the president's disdain and scorn. Kennedy's central campaign theme, refined over four years, was that the listless Eisenhower administration was hamstringing America and the nation needed a new, energetic leader to propel it forward.

Eisenhower was prohibited by the constitution from running for a third term in 1960 so he sought to solidify his legacy by championing the candidacy of his vice president, Richard Nixon. Eisenhower smoldered as Kennedy attacked his administration on the campaign trail as inept, and portrayed Nixon as a weak junior partner in a mediocre government. Ike initially tried to bolster Nixon's campaign by staying above the political fray while outlining and defending his administration's accomplishments. But disappointed by Nixon's faltering effort, Eisenhower aggressively joined the campaign in its final weeks, ridiculing Kennedy's New Frontier campaign slogan, deriding his legislative record, and questioning Kennedy's credentials to serve as president. Kennedy feared that Eisenhower's forceful advocacy for Nixon might lead to his own defeat. "With every word he utters, I can feel the votes leaving me," he told a friend a week before the election. "It's like standing on a mound of sand with the tide running out. I tell you he's knocking our block off. If the election was tomorrow, I'd win easily, but six days from now it's up for grabs," Kennedy said.[2]

Despite Eisenhower's efforts, Kennedy narrowly secured the presidency, winning the popular vote over Nixon by about 113,000 votes out of the 69 million that were cast. When Kennedy finally prevailed Eisenhower sent him a gracious note but was privately devastated, confiding to friends that Kennedy's election was a repudiation of his presidency.

The election of Kennedy set in motion a remarkable ten-week period in American history during which Eisenhower prepared to close down his presidency while still running the federal government and Kennedy geared up to take over the job he long sought, relentlessly pursued, and audaciously secured. The Eisenhower-Kennedy transition was a fascinating mix of dutiful cooperation, petty grievances, lofty sentiments, careful organization, ad hoc improvisations, hardball politics, poignant farewells, and elevated public statements. Eisenhower likened the interregnum to waiting for his own execution. For him, it was a time of sadness, regret, and farewells. Despite Ike's protestations that he was eager for retirement, he found leaving center stage a wrenching, even humiliating, ordeal. For Kennedy, Inauguration Day was the joyful culmination of a fifteen-year political quest that began when he first ran for the House of Representatives in 1946. Only vaguely aware of the scope and complexity of the presidential challenges he would face, Kennedy was triumphant after defeating Nixon. "For a moment it seemed, as if the entire country, the whole spinning globe, rested malleable and receptive in our beneficent hands," said one of his aides, Richard Goodwin.[3]

For Kennedy the transition began on election night as he nervously awaited the outcome at the family's Cape Cod compound. He later traveled to Palm Beach, Florida, to his family's Spanish revival mansion to rest following the grueling campaign. Then he shifted many of his activities to Washington and New York to create his administration. There were also trips to Key Biscayne, Florida, for an awkward meeting with Richard Nixon, to Johnson City, Texas, for a bizarre visit to Lyndon Johnson's ranch for a hunting excursion, to Boston for his farewell speech to the citizens of Massachusetts, and then back to Washington for his dramatic assumption of the presidency. During these weeks, Kennedy golfed, swam, watched movies, strategized with aides, worried about Republican threats to challenge the election results, pored over policy memos, read novels, assembled a cabinet, resigned from the Senate, prepared with his wife for their second child, fashioned a governing agenda, tried to figure out what to do with Lyndon Johnson, his vice president-to-be, and wrote an inaugural address that continues to resonate after more than half a century.

For Eisenhower, the transition began at the White House on election night as he nervously monitored the voting, hoping his vice president would succeed him and solidify his own legacy. Bitterly disappointed, Eisenhower briefly discussed with Nixon the possibility of contesting the election results. But then he quickly shifted gears, urged Nixon to accept the results, and prepared to wrap up his affairs. Eisenhower traveled to Augusta National Golf Club for a two-week vacation and then returned to Washington to close down his administration. He spent several weekends at Camp David to relax and took brief trips to Gettysburg to prepare for retirement. Eisenhower still had a government to oversee during what was a turbulent time and had to make several consequential economic and foreign policy decisions. He wasn't retired yet. He also received several reports from task forces he commissioned, submitted his final budget and economic report, said goodbye to friends and associates, posed for endless photos, and wrote his powerful and enduring farewell address.

Eisenhower's farewell and Kennedy's inaugural were the rhetorical culmination of the presidential transition and can be viewed as each man's plea both to his contemporaries and to the future. The addresses were indirect jabs at each other, coherent and conflicting grand strategies, and ultimately two of the most important state papers in American history.

On January 17, 1961, Eisenhower's farewell address, delivered from the Oval Office to a televised audience, drew comparisons to George

Washington's departing remarks. Speaking in direct and unadorned prose, Eisenhower urged Americans to live frugally, be responsible stewards of the nation, respond prudently to international and domestic challenges, and be mindful that a "military-industrial complex" threatened to dominate America's government and economy. Ike's speech was, among other things, a rebuke to the incoming Kennedy administration, especially its sweeping and he believed ruinously expensive agenda. He responded to themes Kennedy articulated during the presidential campaign and disputed Kennedy's central argument that America had fallen behind the Soviet Union. In his address, Eisenhower assumed the mantle of a wise and prudent elder statesman and adopted a surprising stance. The former war hero and conservative Republican president left the national stage with dovish warnings about the power of the military and large corporations to dominate the American economy.[4]

Just three days later, on January 20, Kennedy delivered his stirring inaugural from the east front of the United States Capitol before a crowd of up to one hundred thousand, with more than one hundred million more watching on television and listening to the radio in the U.S. and around the world. Often considered one of the best inaugural speeches in American history, Kennedy earned comparisons to Thomas Jefferson, Abraham Lincoln, and Franklin Roosevelt. In strong and poetic language, he urged Americans to become more civically active and confident. He warned the nation's adversaries that he would vigorously confront Cold War challenges and project strong American leadership. Kennedy's speech was, among other things, a repudiation of the Eisenhower administration. He indirectly rebuked Ike for allowing the nation to drift as America's international standing weakened. Kennedy assumed the mantle of a young, aggressive Cold Warrior, and the liberal Democrat began his presidency with a hawkish call to arms and action.[5]

The dueling visions of the world presented in Eisenhower's farewell and Kennedy's inaugural addresses divided their contemporaries and continue to intrigue historians. At the time, Eisenhower's views were respectfully received but most political leaders and the public focused primarily on his stellar service to the country. They did not linger over or ponder his departing admonishments about frugality, prudence, and stewardship. They were unsure on how to respond to his warnings about the military-industrial complex. By contrast, America, and much of the world, was captivated by Kennedy's meteoric political rise and mesmerized by the dramatic themes and images he conjured during his inaugural address. His call to arms and summons to service were powerful and inspiring.

The Eisenhower-Kennedy transition was also consequential in practical ways. The handover of government was relatively smooth. Kennedy publicly described it as one of the most effective transitions in American history but privately he had misgivings about its lack of federal financial support. As president, he would introduce a package of proposals to create more regular transition procedures financed with public funds that still exist in modified form to this day. For his part, Eisenhower took pride in his cooperation with his successor. "This is a question of the government of the United States. It is not a partisan question," the outgoing president said in response to Kennedy's expression of gratitude.[6] However, during this time, Eisenhower made preliminary foreign policy decisions that influenced future events such as the Bay of Pigs invasion and the United States' deepening military entanglement into Southeast Asia. As Kennedy prepared to dismantle Eisenhower's carefully constructed White House organization and staff system, Ike grew pained and peeved, filled with skepticism and doubt about what was to come. Americans watched with broad approval as one generation handed power to the next, and to a different party. "The changing of the guard in Washington has been achieved with more common sense than any in memory," wrote James Reston in the *New York Times*. "In no truly democratic country in the world is there such a contrast between the lives of the defeated and the lives of the victorious. In victory, Richard Nixon is the leader of the whole free world. In defeat, he is a lawyer. It is a cruel system, maybe not as cruel as in Russia where a man who loses power may lose his head, but it is cruel enough to bruise men's souls and debase their reason."[7]

More than half a century has passed since Dwight Eisenhower and John Kennedy competed on the political stage and then cooperated on the transfer of presidential power. Kennedy's victory and Eisenhower's retirement triggered a generational transformation in America. From the vantage point of January 1961, it surely appeared that Kennedy was the rising star and Eisenhower, the setting sun. But life and history can surprise and confound. Few would have imagined during that poignant transition that

Eisenhower would outlive Kennedy by half a decade or that their respective legacies would be fiercely contested into the next century.

The debate continues about these two presidents. Most of their successors have been shaped by the competing records and visions of Eisenhower and Kennedy, and absorbed the language and wrestled with the competing worldviews of the thirty-fourth and thirty-fifth American presidents. They have also pondered their mid-century predecessors' very different approaches to managing the presidency.

Few dispute that the transition from Dwight Eisenhower to John Kennedy was one of the singular moments of the twentieth century and perhaps in all American history. In the pages that follow, we shall return to the world of America in late 1960 and early 1961 and consider what happened in those pivotal weeks between Dwight Eisenhower and John Kennedy. To understand this watershed moment and its ramifications we must explore the political climate these two men lived in. We begin on November 8, 1960, Election Day, as Americans hovered in front of their TV sets and watched the nail-biting returns.

ONE

Election Day in America

I

November 8, 1960. Election Day. Americans descended on voting booths in churches, post offices, schools, libraries, and private homes to choose their next president. As they cast their votes, they were variously expectant, hopeful, tense, uncertain, and exhausted. Their votes were influenced by partisan loyalty, financial circumstances, family history, and sheer habit. Some voters were famous; most were not. Most Election Day experiences were routine; a few were not. But American voters were determined to register their verdicts on who should next occupy the White House come January 1961.

In Chicago, Gisella Gipson, fifty-eight, was seriously ill and was taken by an ambulance from Doctors Hospital to vote in her precinct polling place at 1241 Loyola Avenue. Gipson, with portable oxygen equipment strapped to her body, was wheeled into the polling place on a stretcher.

She selected an election judge who pulled the levers of the voting machine for her. Then she went back to the hospital to wait to see who her next president would be.[1]

In upstate New York, the last thing that Linn Young, ninety-five, did in his long life was vote on November 8, 1960. A retired farmer and lifelong Republican, he was driven by his daughter the five miles from his Baiting Hollow home to vote in the Riverhead Town Hall. After voting, he collapsed in the car and then died at a nearby hospital. His daughter said he had told her he voted for Richard Nixon.[2]

Across the country, in Ventura, California, an eighty-six-year-old woman cast her first-ever vote for president. Widowed two years earlier, Lucy Peddicord said her husband had previously taken care of the family's politics and had voted for both of them. "And now it's up to me," she said. When she arrived at the voting booth she was unable to read the entire ballot and asked if her son could help. "Where's the spot for John Fitzgerald Kennedy?" she queried. "Right there," her son responded. She later said she was relieved her voting obligation had been fulfilled. "It made me a little nervous," she said.[3]

Not far from Mrs. Peddicord, a famous American was eager to register his opinion. Actor Clark Gable, fifty-nine, was confined to Hollywood Presbyterian Medical Center as the result of a serious heart attack. His doctor signed an authorization so he could get an absentee ballot and vote from his bed. His wife, who was expecting the couple's first child, was close by. Sadly, Gable was to die before the next president took office.[4]

Former president Herbert Hoover, now eighty-six and living at the Waldorf Astoria hotel in Manhattan, voted at a high school on East 50th St. Prone to grumpiness, Hoover declined to predict for a reporter who would win the election. "I'm not a prophet," he groused. While at the polling station Hoover bumped into a former political rival. Voting at the same time and place as the former president was James Farley, seventy-two, once a Democratic national chairman who had served as Franklin Roosevelt's 1932 campaign manager when FDR defeated Hoover. Farley and Hoover shook hands and exchanged pleasantries.[5] Although he did not know this at the time, Hoover was the source of controversy at a polling place in Bergenfield, New Jersey. Jack Bodenstein cast his ballot at a school named after the former president but objected to the larger-than-life-size photograph of

Hoover displayed in the school. He called on the Bergen County Board of Elections to cover up the rendering of Hoover while the polls were open because he believed it constituted a form of electioneering. There is no record as to whether this request was complied with.[6]

Adlai Stevenson, a former Illinois governor and the Democratic presidential nominee in 1952 and 1956, was eager to cast his vote for president near his home in Libertyville, Illinois, on Election Day. But he had to wait in line for about forty minutes and was displeased. "This may be a Republican plot," he quipped.[7]

Election Day 1960 provided curious moments.

In Montebello, California, voters in Precinct 13 were initially frustrated. Their polling place, a private home owned by Ruby Sproul, was locked and no one answered the door. The police were called and eventually used a crowbar to enter. They found that Sproul, the election board inspector, had died in her home. In order for citizens to exercise their right to vote an alternative polling place was set up next door.[8]

Jose Lira, a naturalized American citizen, was determined to vote. He had returned to live in his native Spain the previous spring but came back to the United States to express his presidential preference. He arrived in Detroit in October and registered to vote. However, when he tried to cast his ballot on Election Day he learned he was not eligible to vote because he no longer met Michigan's six-month residency requirement.[9]

Voters at a firehouse in Fieldale, Virginia, were briefly distracted by a peculiar incident. A woman filled out her ballot and then inexplicably placed it in a slot in the back of a television set. Election Judge E. S. McCombs struggled to understand her mistake, observing the TV was turned to the wall and was 30 feet from the ballot box. There is no record of whether the ballot was retrieved and, if so, which presidential candidate was selected.[10]

Although subsequent controversies in ensuing weeks would come to challenge this view, America's voting day processes were widely seen as a model for the world. More than fifty foreign missions accepted Secretary of State Christian Herter's invitation for Washington-based diplomats to observe Americans going to the polls in November of 1960. Diplomats from Brazil, Bolivia, Japan, and Jordan watched voting in Maryland and Virginia; India, Paraguay, and Burma dispatched diplomats to Baltimore.

Liberia had a representative in Atlanta, New Zealand sent an observer to Nashville, Italy to New Orleans, Spain to Whittier, California, and the United Arab Republic to Houston. Yugoslavia was the only Communist bloc nation to take up Herter's offer to observe the American election.[11]

European royalty was also intrigued by America's civic ritual. Two Swedish princesses, Birgitta and Desiree, were in New York on Election Day. It was the first visit to the United States for the two sisters who were granddaughters of Sweden's King Gustav Adolf. On their first full day in New York, they made the typical tourist stops: Central Park, Radio City Music Hall, and the Empire State Building. But they also visited the Gramercy Park Hotel to observe the polling place in the hotel's lobby. That evening they attended a private dinner hosted by Sweden's counsel general, and then watched the returns on his television.[12]

On previous Election Days, Americans often congregated in public places, such as Times Square, to watch the returns. But the arrival of the television culture had altered that ritual. So on election night, 1960, Times Square had only its usual weekday crowd. Theatergoers glanced at updates as they hurried from shows to the subway to go home. There were some groups of election watchers reading electronic signs that were substituting election news for their usual commercials, or watching TV screens in store windows. But the crowd was sparse and the twenty New York City mounted policemen and 114 foot patrolmen had little to do as the returns from America drifted in.[13] While most Americans watched the returns at home, election night parties were popular as well. A party hosted by Mr. and Mrs. Oscar Samuelson in Brentwood, California, was probably only a little more elaborate than the norm. They offered their guests a buffet supper to enjoy in front of the television. Their home was decorated with American flags and displayed posters of both Senator Kennedy and Vice President Nixon.[14]

Democrats and Republicans in Washington held dueling election night parties. Republicans were ensconced at the Sheraton Park. Party officials occupied suites throughout the hotel, with the chairman of the Republican National Committee, Senator Thruston Morton, working from the sixth floor and Henry Cabot Lodge Jr., the Republican vice presidential nominee, on the seventh. Rank and file party members and supporters gathered in a large ballroom to watch the results on TV screens and to study a giant scoreboard that tallied election results.

Democrats gathered at the Mayflower Hotel where the crowd was building by 10:00 P.M. Junior staffers and young party supporters circulated on the first floor; party leaders worked out of upstairs suites. Senator Henry Jackson, the chairman of the Democratic National Committee, held hourly briefings that resembled pep rallies. Early in the evening, Jackson began predicting a Kennedy victory. Party stalwarts sang, "Happy Days Are Here Again," "Hail, Hail, the Gang's All Here," and "When Irish Eyes Are Smiling." But Jackson's proclamations of an impending victory seemed based as much on hope as on concrete evidence.[15]

II

The long, punishing American presidential campaign was ending and a new generation of leadership was poised to come to power. Dwight D. Eisenhower, the first president to be limited to two terms in office by the 22nd Amendment to the U.S. Constitution, was to depart the White House in January. He would be replaced either by forty-seven-year-old Republican Richard Nixon, his vice president, or forty-three-year-old Democrat John F. Kennedy, the junior senator from Massachusetts. While the two men were relatively close in age, Nixon's serious demeanor and lengthy experience as vice president made him appear older than he was, and Kennedy's obvious elder. Either way, NBC News anchor Chet Huntley observed that Americans would have to adjust to the jarring reality that the next American president was not going to be a father figure like Eisenhower had been for eight years, but more like a brother or uncle.

The 1960 campaign had been dominated by relentless cross-country travel, dramatic debates covered by the increasingly important television, and energetic candidates with formidable campaign operations. This had been a long campaign. Kennedy began running for president in the fall of 1956 and Nixon, for all practical purposes, since his election as vice president in 1952.

As Election Day approached, *U.S. News & World Report* dissected what it called "the most intensive campaign in history," and said the frenzy of the race should trigger reassessment of the very nature of presidential campaigns. "Out of the 1960 campaign for the Presidency comes this conclusion: Either there must be a change in future campaign methods, or only young men in the pink of condition can expect to be nominated," the magazine mused. "The nation," it added, "had never seen anything like the campaign that was just ending. It has been almost unbelievably hectic and wearing on everyone concerned." Kennedy and Nixon were physical wrecks by early November—exhausted and hoarse, with hands swollen and bruised from countless handshakes. The magazine suggested the contemporary presidential candidate required "the hands and arms of a boilermaker and the durable voice of a carnival spieler." The candidates routinely worked around the clock and drove themselves and their staffs to the brink of collapse. "Sleep was all but forgotten. Meals were irregular and often skipped. Colds and illness plagued the campaign parties. Doctoring had to be done on the fly in fifteen-minute stopovers," the magazine reported, adding that at the end of one twenty-two-hour campaign day, one veteran reporter snapped, "This is utter madness."[16]

In addition to being intense, the 1960 campaign was also contentious, occurring against the backdrop of deep economic and political uncertainty. Eisenhower had hoped for a triumphant final year in which peace and prosperity were in full display and without dispute. However, the economy sputtered and fell into recession. The much-anticipated summer summit with the leading Western powers and the Soviet Union collapsed after a U.S. spy plane was shot down over the skies of Russia, leaving American officials dissembling about what happened. Eisenhower refused to apologize to the Soviet Union for the American incursion into its air space, and Nikita Khrushchev, the Soviet leader, decided to undermine this long-planned and much-anticipated summit in Paris, fearing that hard-line critics at home would accuse him of being weak and a pushover for Eisenhower.

Newsweek declared the American election was taking place "at a time of world tension such as mankind had seldom known, when two mighty coalitions, one headed by the United States, the other by Soviet Russia, faced each other with weapons at the ready—the most frightful weapons of modern times. The threatening world was something that every American voter could plainly see."[17]

The stakes for the presidential election could not be higher, for the world was troubled and America needed a leader of the highest quality. "Leadership is an art, not a science or a business, and what our people need and instinctively want is an artist," declared Eric Sevareid of CBS. "They have need now of a very great artist; for the immense canvas of our national life, our mirror to ourselves and our world, is frayed and obscured with a thousand tiny cracks. The American portrait is growing dim, and only the boldest strokes from the boldest hand will restore the original in its strong and vivid colors."[18]

Neither Richard Nixon nor John Kennedy was regarded as a political artist by the American public. But each was a tough and skilled politician who was able and willing to promote himself and thoroughly denounce his opponent. Their campaign was ending, according to one account, as "an old fashioned slugging match."[19] In the final months of their battle for the White House, Kennedy and Nixon traveled nearly 100,000 miles between them, scrambling for themes and votes.

Most preelection polls showed Kennedy with a small but persistent lead over Nixon. In a *Newsweek* survey of fifty political experts a few weeks before the election, forty said they expected Kennedy to win. But these predictions were made before the campaign's final surge when Eisenhower stepped up his campaign for Nixon and Republicans spent lavishly on TV ads and special broadcasts. Some also wondered if the preelection polling was able to pick up intangible but important factors such as apprehension about Kennedy's Catholicism or the unarticulated concerns of young voters and new suburbanites. *Newsweek* pondered whether the U.S. was about to have an "iceberg election," in which the forces that determined the outcome were all under the surface. "It's a campaign filled with more imponderables than any other I've seen in twenty years of political reporting—the hardest of all of them to call," said Charles Whiteford of the *Baltimore Sun*.[20]

Americans were absorbed by the election. As many as 70 million of the nation's 180 million citizens watched the first televised presidential debate that autumn, and Americans voted in record numbers on November 8. Nearly 69 million voters cast ballots, almost 65% of those who were eligible to vote, higher than any election in a half-century and a larger percentage of voters than in any of Franklin Roosevelt's elections. Each candidate had passionate supporters, as was evident by the huge crowds that attended campaign events and followed the political jousting. But there were, of course, skeptics. "Be thankful only one can win," declared a car bumper sticker in Los Angeles.[21]

After casting their ballots on Election Day and settling in for the night, Americans turned on their black-and-white TVs and watched the returns. About two-thirds of American households watched some of the TV coverage that night, according to the AC Nielsen Company. David Brinkley and Chet Huntley anchored NBC's coverage; Huntley urged viewers to prepare for a "legendary night," but acknowledged there might be some "dial twisting" as viewers checked on the coverage of other two networks. CBS's coverage was led by Walter Cronkite and Eric Sevareid. ABC's broadcast was anchored by John Charles Daly.

To track the results, the networks built large tally boards, dispatched reporters to key locations, and used new computers that looked like barges and promised to calculate election returns quickly. NBC bragged that its RCA 301 computer could do the work of 60,000 clerks. CBS unveiled a special IBM 7090 computer that promised to see trends and project results earlier than had been possible before. ABC lauded its Remington Rand Univac computer as state-of-the-art technology. Before the night was over these new computers would manage to confuse and mislead nearly everyone—candidates, campaign teams, and the public. Kennedy's top pollster was skeptical of the new technology and made his calculations on a slide rule throughout the night. A leading Republican operative, Leonard Hall, said the computers were a public menace. "I think we should put all these electronic machines in the junk pile as far as the elections are concerned," he said.[22] Brinkley, the acerbic NBC newsman, expressed deep skepticism about the new technology. "The basic tools for reporting an election are still a reporter, a pencil, paper, and a telephone."[23]

As evening fell over America, the public was in for one of the most dramatic and suspenseful election nights in the country's political history. The hopes and fears of the two campaigns rose and sank dramatically, tension and uncertainty gripped the nation, and clarity and finality seemed elusive. "It was like having a ringside seat at the unfolding of a great drama," a media critic said, adding it was "better than a tight football game, the way the action see-sawed back and forth through the various states."

But, of course, anxiety was most acute for the leading players in this drama: Richard Nixon in Los Angeles, John Kennedy in Hyannis Port, and Dwight Eisenhower at the White House.

III

Vice President Richard Nixon returned to Los Angeles in the early hours of Election Day after a frenzied finish to his campaign. Trailing in most national polls for several weeks, Nixon made a frantic final push, even flying to Alaska over the final weekend of the campaign so he could honor his pledge to visit all fifty states before voters made their decisions. On election eve, November 7, Nixon flew more than eight hours to Wisconsin from Alaska, and gave speeches in Madison and Detroit, took part in a campaign telethon outside the Motor City, and then delivered his final TV address from Chicago. Nixon, his wife, and two daughters then wearily flew back to Los Angeles. They reached the Ambassador Hotel at about 4:00 A.M. on Election Day. In the final three days of the campaign, Nixon had slept only a handful of hours.

Richard and Pat Nixon rose early to vote at their polling place, a private house in East Whittier, California, so photographs of the ritual would run in the afternoon and evening newspapers and images would be broadcast on the evening television news. Mrs. Nixon returned to the Ambassador Hotel and spent the day with their two teenage daughters, Tricia and Julie. But the vice president was restless. So he; Don Hughes, a military aide; Jack Sherwood, a Secret Service agent; and John DiBetta, his driver from the Los Angeles Police Department, decided to go on an Election Day adventure. They ditched the press, changed cars, and opted for Southern California cruising. They drove a convertible down the Pacific Coast Highway toward San Diego and stopped in Oceanside to refuel, to the astonishment of unsuspecting fellow motorists. Nixon used his credit card to pay the $4.68 gas bill, shook hands with a truck driver, and told the station owner that his father had once run a service station.[24]

As they neared San Diego they decided to keep going south and have lunch in Tijuana at the Old Heidelberg Inn, which was, curiously, despite its name, known for its Mexican food. Word of the American vice president's visit spread across town, and he was soon joined by the mayor of Tijuana. Nixon ordered enchiladas, tacos, and German beer. His cohorts finally checked in with his political team back in Los Angeles who were incredulous about the trip. Nixon enjoyed the distinction of being the first—and probably last—presidential candidate in American history to have an Election Day meal in a foreign country. He viewed his impromptu road trip with irony. "If we win tonight, we will not be able to escape the press or the Secret Service for four years. If we lose—they won't care what happened to us," he told his traveling companions.

After lunch, the group drove the 140 miles back to Los Angeles. They stopped at the Mission San Juan Capistrano where Nixon showed his associates around and visited the chapel, possibly to request some divine intervention for the evening ahead. He later recalled strolling past a classroom of startled schoolchildren and nuns who were not expecting to see the vice president (and possibly the next president) of the United States walking by their school window. One nun flashed the V for Victory salute to Nixon, who returned the gesture. As they drove the rest of the way to Los Angeles, Nixon insisted on keeping the radio off. He did not want to hear any preliminary election reports.[25]

Nixon rejoined his family and friends in the Ambassador Hotel at about 5:00 P.M. Pacific time for what would be a long night waiting for the election returns. The party included the vice president's mother; his brothers Ed and Don and their spouses; his friend, Bebe Rebozo; and his long-time campaign aide, Murray Chotiner. The group watched the returns from the fifth floor royal suite of the hotel while Nixon watched alone from a room one floor below. He made notes, crunched numbers, and tried to envision an electoral path to victory. His was a mostly solitary vigil. Even before election night, Nixon had said that if he were to write a book about running for president it would be called *The Exquisite Agony*. Election night 1960 would not persuade him to change that title, except perhaps to remove the word "exquisite."

The early evening returns were ambiguous. Nixon jumped ahead very early but then Kennedy surged to a healthy lead after 8:00 P.M. eastern time—just as Nixon was tuning in. As he watched the TV, Nixon grew angry that the networks seemed eager to extrapolate a final result from partial returns, especially from precincts where Kennedy was expected to be strongest. He was furious when commentators began to speculate about a Kennedy victory well before the polls closed in the West, including California, which was a state Nixon needed to win. "The prospects were not encouraging but we were a long way from giving up," he later recalled. "There were still a lot of votes to be recorded. But the TV commentators were going all out in predicting a Kennedy victory—or perhaps the better word is 'conceding.' Eric Sevareid, just before eight, had said: 'A Kennedy victory is now beyond any reasonable doubt.'" Several TV commentators even ruminated about what Nixon would do in the aftermath of his impending defeat.[26]

But as the hours passed, and Tuesday night gave way to Wednesday morning, Kennedy's lead over Nixon in the popular vote dwindled, and the Democrat had still not secured the 269 votes he needed to win in the Electoral College.

IV

Senator John Kennedy was just as exhausted and tense on Election Day as his rival, although he did not have the same hankering for a driving diversion. Kennedy's final campaign swing had taken him through the Northeast, culminating in a nostalgic election eve rally at the Boston Garden and a final speech at the city's historic Faneuil Hall. This schedule spared Kennedy from a long Election Day trip back home to vote, but it increased the candidate's apprehension about whether his final days on the campaign trail might have been more profitably spent in the Midwest or on the West Coast, especially California, rather than in his native New England.

An aide woke Kennedy around 7:30 A.M. on Election Day at his room at Boston's Statler Hilton hotel. About an hour later, he met his wife, Jackie, who had driven in that morning from Hyannis Port and avoided the growing crowd at the hotel by entering through an airline ticket office at a side door. With dozens of photographers and reporters watching, the Kennedys voted at the West Branch of the Boston Public Library. "Your names?" they were asked by election officials. "John F. Kennedy, 122 Bowdoin Street," the candidate said. "Jacqueline," his wife answered. Both were done voting in less than thirty seconds. They were then driven to the airport and flew on their private plane to Hyannis Port to await the returns at the family compound on Nantucket Sound. During the short flight, the keyed-up Kennedy dictated good luck messages to several political allies, including the governor of Iowa, Herschel Loveless, and Arkansas senator

J. William Fulbright. Kennedy's cousin, Ann Gargan, met Jack and Jackie at the small Hyannis Airport and drove them to the family compound.[27]

Kennedy had breakfast with his father, conferred with aides, chatted with his family, tossed a football, tried to take a nap, had lunch with Jackie, and agonized. He took solace in a conversation with an aide, Cornelius Ryan, the author of *The Longest Day*, which chronicled the anguished anticipation before the D-Day invasion during World War II. Jackie called November 8 "the longest hours of my life."[28]

Following an afternoon and early evening of roaming between his own house and the homes of his father and his brother, Robert, the candidate and his wife had a quiet dinner with a friend at their residence. Then Kennedy walked across the lawn to Robert's house, which had been transformed into an election command center. The enclosed porch was dominated by several large tables where more than a dozen phone operators, all women, received voting updates from around the country. In the dining room, there was a tabulating machine, more phones, and four news service Teletype machines. Kennedy's top pollster, Lou Harris, worked in a makeshift office upstairs in the children's large bedroom. Cribs and playpens were pushed aside to make space for data sheets and election records. TV sets were spread around the house; sandwiches, soft drinks, and beer were served.

Between 8:00 P.M. and midnight eastern time, Kennedy surged to a substantial lead and a mood of impending triumph pervaded the compound. But Kennedy knew the race was ultimately going to be very close, and his political fate would hinge on the results in just a few states. Ted Sorensen, one of his top aides, recalled that Kennedy watched the returns on TV carefully and warily. By 2:00 A.M. eastern time, Kennedy's lead in the popular vote had shrunk from two million votes to about one million votes. He still had not secured the needed 269 electoral votes either. Four states hung in the balance: Michigan, Minnesota, Illinois, and California. Kennedy needed to win at least one of them to become the next president.

V

While President Eisenhower had a less direct stake in the election than did Nixon or Kennedy, he was hardly a disinterested bystander. He had campaigned forcefully for Nixon in the final weeks of the campaign and believed the election was a referendum on his own presidency. During the fall campaign, Nixon had portrayed himself as an active member of the Eisenhower administration who wanted to build on the president's achievements. Kennedy assailed the vice president as the embodiment of a listless and mediocre administration. While Eisenhower had complex, even conflicting, feelings about Nixon, he much preferred turning power over to him than to his Democratic opponent. It went beyond partisanship. Kennedy's campaign in particular had made him furious.

On Election Day, Eisenhower woke early at the White House and by 6:30 A.M. was on a helicopter to Gettysburg, Pennsylvania, where he and his wife had a farm and were registered to vote. The president cast his ballot at the Barlow Township Fire House just as the polls opened at 7:00 A.M., and he was on his way back to Washington within a half hour. Eisenhower was at his desk in the Oval Office before 8:00. The first half of his day was packed with meetings, including sessions with Richard Bissell from the Central Intelligence Agency; Ezra Taft Benson, secretary of agriculture; John McCone, head of the Atomic Energy Commission; and various members of his staff.[29]

Restless and anxious about the election results, Eisenhower had lunch and a light afternoon of appointments, and spent several hours in his residence. Then, joined by his press secretary, Jim Hagerty, Eisenhower left the White House at about 7:15 that evening for a Republican election party at the Sheraton Park Hotel. He met with the Republican vice-presidential nominee, Henry Cabot Lodge Jr., Republican Party officials, and several members of his cabinet. Ike confessed that he could not sit still and spoke for six minutes at a rally in the hotel's grand ballroom, imploring Republicans across the country to keep fighting to the last minute. He invoked lessons from his military career about the need to stay vigilant in battle until the very end.

The president returned to the White House about an hour later and watched the returns in the residence until about midnight with his son John, his daughter-in-law, Barbara, and one of her friends. He did not like what he was seeing; the early returns suggested the outcome he dreaded: a Kennedy victory.

★

VI

For Nixon, Kennedy, and Eisenhower, and for millions of Americans, election night was suspenseful and perplexing. There were confusing numbers, contradictory network projections, paper-thin voting margins, and scores of allegations about voting irregularities or even outright fraud.

For Americans trying to follow the returns and determine who was going to be their next president, the twelve hours from 7:00 P.M. Tuesday evening to 7:00 A.M. Wednesday morning were a roller coaster. Early Tuesday evening, ABC and CBS, relying on their much-celebrated computers, projected that Nixon would win. But within an hour, the networks completely reversed themselves and predicted Kennedy would win. In a landslide, no less. CBS's Eric Sevareid said at about 9:40 P.M. eastern time that CBS's computers were now "pretty confident" of a Kennedy victory.[30]

With the outcome still hanging in the balance, tense newspaper editors were agonizing over the next day's headlines and stories. Could they confidently say that Kennedy had won the election or did they need to equivocate? A headline in the second edition of the *New York Times* published at 12:36 A.M. Wednesday declared, "Kennedy Holds Wide Lead." About three hours later the late city edition went out with the headline, "Kennedy Elected," but then at 4:47 A.M. the *Times'* editors stopped the presses. At 7:17 A.M. Wednesday, an extra edition of the paper was published with the headline, "Kennedy is the Apparent Victor; Lead Cut in Two Key States." Scores of less prominent papers also struggled to inform their readers about the election's outcome.

Election night was agony for Nixon. There was nothing exquisite about it. He was like the runner who, starting out behind his opponent, relentlessly narrows the lead, but never quite overtakes him. "Any election night is an emotional roller-coaster, but election night in 1960 was the most tantalizing and frustrating I have experienced," Nixon said later. He was convinced the press was actively rooting for Kennedy and was determined to proclaim the Democrat the victor. He recalled that at 7:30 P.M. eastern time NBC calculated the odds of a Kennedy victory to be 250 to 1, and that a little later NBC's computer predicted a Kennedy electoral landslide, with a final count of 401 electoral votes.

Around midnight Pacific time, Nixon conferred with his advisers Len Hall, Cliff Folger, Robert Finch, Fred Seaton, and Herb Klein in Los Angeles. They reviewed the situation by phone with Senate Republican leader Everett Dirksen and Senator Thruston Morton, the RNC chairman. Nixon admitted he was likely to lose but the outcome was not absolutely certain. About twenty minutes later, Nixon and his wife went to the ball-room of the Ambassador Hotel. He told several hundred supporters that if "the present trend continues Senator Kennedy will be the next president of the United States."[31] He smiled tightly as his supporters booed and shouted, "We Want Nixon! We Want Nixon!"

Nixon's equivocal statement did not add clarity or bring closure to the election. After listening to the vice president, Huntley of NBC said, "I don't know whether that was a concession or not," and his partner Brinkley responded, "I suppose it was, but I never heard one just like it before. You can choose your own name for it." Kennedy officials said they did not regard Nixon's comments as a concession.

The vice president decided that he wanted to sleep for a few hours and study the returns again Wednesday morning. He went to bed thinking there was some chance that he still might win. But when he woke, his twelve-year-old daughter Julie asked about the outcome of the election and Nixon told her that he had lost. She immediately fired off questions about their postelection lives: where they were going to live, what kind of job would he get, and where she would go to school.

Nixon instructed his press aide, Herb Klein, to read his concession telegram to Kennedy before TV cameras, which he did at about 9:45 A.M. Pacific time. "I want to repeat through this wire the congratulations and best wishes I extended to you on television last night. I know that you will have the united support of all Americans as you lead the nation in the cause of peace and freedom during the next four years." Nixon then spoke to Eisenhower on the phone and later recalled the president "did his best to try and buck me up, but he could not hide his own disappointment. I had never heard him sound more depressed. But he still had a lot of fight left; he had heard early reports of fraud charges in Illinois and Texas and urged me to do everything possible to check them out."

Later Wednesday, Nixon and his family flew back to Washington and landed in a dreary rain. They were met by a group of Republican loyalists, staffers, and friends, including John Eisenhower, representing his father. The Nixons returned to their home in northwest Washington. After the others had gone to bed, Nixon went to his library, built a fire, and considered his options. "In the quiet of my own home, I tried not to think of the past, but of the future. I knew that the next few days and weeks would probably present me with the greatest test of my life," he later recalled.[32]

Kennedy also endured a night of enormous tension, but his fears eased by Wednesday morning. Kennedy had watched Nixon's quasi-concession speech at 3:20 A.M. eastern time with his family and aides. Kennedy's supporters were angry that Nixon did not make an unequivocal concession but Kennedy was more understanding of Nixon's predicament, saying, "Why should he concede? I wouldn't." Kennedy then walked back to his house in the family compound and most of his aides retired to their rooms at the Yachtsman Hotel. His secretary, Evelyn Lincoln, walked across the toy-strewn lawn of the Kennedy compound and saw Kennedy in his house, sitting alone in an easy chair, under a light, trying to read a book.[33]

About 9:30 A.M. Wednesday, Kennedy's aide, Ted Sorensen, greeted him with the news that he had been elected president. Kennedy celebrated by soaking in the bathtub, inviting Sorensen and his press aide, Pierre Salinger, into the bathroom as he eased into the tub. They reviewed the latest returns, recapped the campaign and wondered when Kennedy would receive an official concession from Nixon.

Shortly before noon eastern time, Salinger received a call from Eisenhower's press secretary—who said the president would send Kennedy an official wire of congratulations after Nixon conceded, which was expected soon. Ike's press secretary had accidentally sent a congratulatory cable to Kennedy many hours earlier in Eisenhower's name but Salinger agreed to set it aside when he was informed that it was a mistake. Kennedy now watched Herb Klein read Nixon's concession on TV; Kennedy's aides grumbled that Nixon did not read the statement himself. "He went out the same way he came in—no class," Kennedy snapped.[34]

The Kennedy family gathered for a photo in Joseph Kennedy's residence, then drove in a convoy to the Hyannis Armory. The winning candidate sat in the front seat of a white Lincoln, waving wearily to those standing by the road. At the Armory, he received a standing ovation from supporters and the press, went to the dais, and read telegrams he received from Eisenhower and Nixon, as well as his responses to them. Almost always stoic, reporters now detected tears in his eyes. He offered a few impromptu words. "It is a satisfying moment for me. I want to express my appreciation to the citizens of this country and to Mr. Nixon personally," he said. "The next four years will be difficult and challenging. There is general agreement by all our citizens that a supreme national effort is needed to move this country safely through the 1960s. We need your help. All our energies will be devoted to the interests of the United States and the cause of freedom around the world." Then, ending on a more personal note, he said: "My wife and I now prepare for a new administration—and a new baby."[35]

Kennedy met later that afternoon with his campaign team to go over the most current election results and review the procedures by which the election would be certified. They discussed potential challenges Republicans might lodge about alleged voting irregularities. Later that night, Jack and Jackie had dinner with their friend, Bill Walton, the journalist Ben Bradlee, and Bradlee's pregnant wife, Tony. Looking at the two pregnant women, Kennedy quipped, "Okay girls, you can take out the pillows now. We won."[36]

On Thursday, November 10, Kennedy met with his top aides to begin planning for the transition. Months earlier, he had commissioned Clark Clifford, a wily and respected Democratic political operative, and Richard Neustadt, a Columbia professor and expert on the presidency, to develop plans on how organize a transition and build an administration. He did not want to see them until after the election. Both reports were now ready for his inspection. Kennedy was now ready to start thinking concretely about building a government.

Eisenhower went to bed Tuesday night about midnight before the election's outcome was certain, but it seemed likely that Kennedy was going to win. By the next morning, his fears were confirmed. Eisenhower's son John, a White House aide, recalled entering the Oval Office and seeing his father staring outside, looking dejectedly at the south grounds. "All I've been trying to do for eight years has gone down the drain. I might just as well have been having fun," the despondent president told his son.[37]

Eisenhower sent Kennedy a brief telegram. "My congratulations to you for the victory you have just won at the polls. I will be sending you promptly a more comprehensive telegram suggesting certain measures that may commend themselves to you as you prepare to take over next January the responsibilities of the Presidency." Ike also sent a telegram of congratulation to Lyndon Johnson, the incoming vice president, and consolation wires to both Nixon and Lodge.

The president conducted several meetings at the White House, including a nearly hour-long session with his cabinet and top administration officials in which he instructed them to assist the new administration. Eisenhower then sent Kennedy a longer telegram, saying he was committed to a smooth transfer of power and pledged his administration would cooperate fully with Kennedy's team.

Eisenhower left the White House that afternoon to fly to Augusta, Georgia, for a long-planned golf vacation. During the flight, he told his friend Ellis Slater that Nixon's loss was "the biggest defeat of my life." The president second-guessed many aspects of Nixon's campaign, wondering why Nixon did not use him more prominently. Later in the day, he continued to talk with Slater about what he might have done differently to alter the outcome. "You know if I had written an article for the [*Reader's*] *Digest*, it might have won us enough votes, but by the time I thought of it, it was too late."[38]

Kennedy won the presidency by 303 to 219 votes in the Electoral College, but only by about 113,000 votes out of the 69 million popular votes cast. The popular vote was astonishingly close: 49.7% to 49.6% in Kennedy's favor. Fewer than 30,000 votes distributed differently in Illinois and Texas would have made Nixon the thirty-fifth president of the United States. Nixon won more states and more congressional districts than did Kennedy.

The debate about which candidate actually won the election would continue for the next ten weeks—and beyond—but Kennedy emerged as the victor and Nixon as the vanquished. Eisenhower had prepared an elaborate process to turn power over to his successor and ordered it to commence. There was a lot to do in a short period as one presidency gave way to another. Following a remarkable year in American life and a riveting campaign for the presidency, a historic transfer of power was about to begin.

TWO

DAWN OF THE NEW DECADE

I

N early a year before that fraught election night in November of 1960, Americans greeted the start of the decade with swagger and uncertainty, hope and trepidation, confidence and concern. As the New Year and the new decade began, Americans remembered their past, lived in the present, and pondered the future.

Throughout the United States people ushered in 1960 with parties, celebrations, and church services. While most of official Washington took time off for the holidays, Ezra Benson, Eisenhower's combative and controversial secretary of agriculture, decided to hold a press conference on New Year's Eve. Benson was, according to one reporter, "unwontedly roguish" about the timing of his briefing. The secretary said he scheduled his press conference early enough in the day so it would not interfere with the celebration plans of reporters. With an election year about to begin and with reporters anxious to bring in the New Year, Benson's briefing elicited little interest in, or news about, farming or agricultural policy. Instead, the secretary was asked to comment on the presidential campaigns of Hubert Humphrey and Richard Nixon, whether he had any desire to stay in his job in the next administration, and how he gauged the mood of the American public. He dodged the questions on Humphrey and Nixon. On the question regarding how he assessed the national mood, Benson said he talked with people from all walks of life, read his mail, and met with members of Congress, "some of whom have been in Washington since the summer—off and on." This was an apparent jab at Congress's limited legislative schedule that year.[1] As Benson was holding his press conference in Washington, crowds were already gathering in New York City's Times Square. Nearby, there was plenty of activity at Madison Square Garden that was fully booked with New Year's Eve events: a New York Knicks basketball game against the Minneapolis Lakers, a tennis match between Althea Gibson and Karol Fageros, an exhibition game by the Harlem Globetrotters, and a Japanese "Ballet on Bicycle" performance. The next day the Garden hosted three ten-round boxing matches.[2]

Americans celebrated New Year's Eve at home, private parties, restaurants, and bars. In Chicago, the city's best establishments charged between $20 and $50 per couple for an evening of entertainment. In Kansas City, the Hotel Muehlebach charged a $7.00 minimum—dinner and drinks were extra. At the Arlington Hotel in Hot Springs, Arkansas, each guest paid a minimum of $12.50.[3]

Bars were, of course, popular across America as the clock ticked toward midnight, January 1, 1960. In Boston, bars were required to issue their last calls at 1:00 A.M. but revelers were allowed to stay until 4:00 A.M. The city's transit system ran all night. In Milwaukee, L. V. Barnes, a middle-aged businessman, stepped out of a party to get something from his car and returned with a remarkable story. He had just witnessed a black bear inside a car, blowing the horn in a nearby parking lot. His report, not surprisingly, was treated with skepticism by his party. Later, seeking confirmation, Barnes placed a personal ad in a Milwaukee newspaper asking if anyone else had also seen a black bear blowing a car horn in a parking lot on East Capitol Drive about 2:30 A.M. "Confound it, I know a big, black hairy bear when I see one and I saw one," he told a curious reporter. Barnes was relieved when Mrs. Theodore Weissinger from Mequon, a Milwaukee suburb, responded. She said that she and her husband had indeed brought their fifty-pound black bear cub, Booboo, into the city on New Year's Eve, had left him alone in their car, and he may have been blowing a horn. "Booboo loves to blow horns," Mrs. Weissinger observed.[4]

About the same time Booboo was blowing the car horn, two sixteen-year-old boys in Spruce Pine, North Carolina, decided to celebrate 1960 with a bang. They set off an explosion with ninety-nine sticks of dynamite that rocked their mountain mining town. Douglas Green and Joe McKinney left a party on New Year's Eve and planted dynamite in the center of a football field. Their blast created a crater large enough to contain a truck. The explosion shattered glass in nearly every store along two main streets in the business district. Damage to the stores and homes was estimated at $10,000. The boys were released on a $1,000 bond to presumably displeased parents.[5]

Other dangers surrounded the New Year weekend in the United States. During the holiday weekend, from 6:00 P.M. Thursday, December 31, until midnight on Sunday, January 3, 374 people were killed in car, bus, and truck accidents. A spokesman for the National Safety Council issued a stern admonishment to Americans. "The nation should not need this grim reminder that accidents never take a holiday. Certainly this is not the way America prefers to start a new year and a new decade dedicated to better living. We can only hope that out of this will come increased determination by public officials and private citizens alike to put a stop to such wholesale slaughter on highways." Nearly five hundred Americans were killed on the nation's roads during the Christmas weekend the week before.[6]

But most Americans had a safe and celebratory New Year. In Laguna Beach, California, the fifty members of the Polar Bear Club emerged from their trailers and cabanas at Treasure Island at noon for their annual New Year's Day plunge into the Pacific Ocean. According to club rules, the men were required to jump into the water all the way while the women were only required to submerge themselves up to their necks. Fred Hodge, the seventy-nine-year-old club founder, was designated Father Polar Bear and observed a test plunge on New Year's Eve by Mrs. Roy Wilbur, with a *Los Angeles Times* photographer chronicling the partial submersion.[7]

As Americans relaxed on January 1, probably few were aware the symbolic Doomsday Clock on the cover of the *Bulletin of the Atomic Scientists* magazine was moved back five minutes. Rather than being set at two minutes to midnight where it had been since 1953 the clock now showed seven minutes before midnight, an indication of a slightly less dangerous world.[8] This improvement was largely due to the scheduled spring summit in Paris in which global leaders were expected to find ways to further defuse tensions and cooperate more extensiviely. It was also probably due to President Eisenhower's repeated vow to work relentlessly for peace during his final year in office.

Eisenhower brought in the New Year at his vacation home on the edge of Augusta National Golf Club in Georgia in the middle of a ten-day golf and bridge holiday. On New Year's Eve, the president spent a few hours doing routine paperwork, then golfed in sunny fifty-degree weather with his friends George Allen, Barry Leithead, and Ellis Slater. That evening, he relaxed with friends in the trophy room of Augusta National. On New Year's Day, the president worked for a few hours in the morning and then took the rest of the day off.[9]

Vice President Richard Nixon began the New Year in Southern California serving as the grand marshal for the Rose Bowl parade in Pasadena. That afternoon he spoke at a Kiwanis luncheon celebrating the Rose Bowl and touting the competitive qualities encouraged by football. "We need competitive spirit in our young people both on and off the athletic field," he intoned. "And football at its best provides this as well as anything I know. This is good for the country." Nixon then flew to the East Coast on a jet that set a commercial record for coast-to-coast travel. His plane, with a capacity load of 112 passengers, traveled from Los Angeles to Baltimore's Friendship Airport in three hours and thirty-nine minutes, breaking the previous record of four hours.[10]

Another ambitious American politician, Senator John F. Kennedy, was ending a vacation in Jamaica as the New Year began. He returned to Washington around 8:15 P.M. on New Year's Day to prepare for the next day's official announcement of his presidential candidacy. When he arrived at his Georgetown home, he called his secretary, Evelyn Lincoln, and told her to make sure that his barber, Dave, would be at his office at 10:00 A.M. the next day so the senator could get a trim before his Saturday afternoon press conference at the Senate Caucus Room.[11]

As 1960 began, America's columnists and newspaper editorialists expressed both the hope and the ambivalence that was prevalent in the United States. "And now begins the decade of the dynamic dream," declared columnist J. A. Livingston, predicting the "soaring sixties" would seamlessly follow the "fabulous fifties." Livingston saw a world of endless possibilities. "Nuclear energy and space probes quicken minds, widen horizons, raise hopes. Nineteen-sixty becomes the red carpet to an unlimited expanse of prosperity—the promise of rising standards of living in America and throughout the world. Electronic brains will replace human impulses in factories and offices. Men will have greater leisure. Even peace is a possibility," he wrote.[12]

A January 1 editorial in the *New York Herald Tribune* argued that man's adventurous spirit was exemplified by the exploration of outer space. "Standing on the verge of explorations almost beyond imagination, he should perhaps gain a new sense of proportion for problems both terrestrial and personal." The editorial acknowledged there was much uncertainty on earth but eagerly anticipated the Paris summit of world leaders scheduled for May. "Millions of persons in all earth's lands earnestly desire that this may be the most fruitful of all Springtimes in Paris."[13]

The *New York Times* was also thinking about the coming Paris summit, insisting that inconclusive discussions were far preferable to surly silence. "It is impossible to talk, even in these often wearisome international marathons, without getting acquainted." The essay then shifted into a mystical meditation on the nation, the world, and the universe. "We shall not pass this way again. Astronomically, we cannot. The whole solar system is believed to be moving at the rate of about twelve miles a second in the direction of the constellation Hercules. And just as we leave behind forever a portion of the wilderness of space, so we leave behind, also, some of our thoughts, some of our hopes, and perhaps with good luck some of our fears. Now let us raise the curtains and look up. This is another day."[14]

The *Hartford Courant* seized on the dawning of the new decade to urge Americans to reassess their priorities and become more public spirited and less materialistic. "Are we going to continue turning out gadgets and golf clubs, outboards and tail fins, barbeque sets and swimming pools? Or are we going to put our money and energy into schools and medical care, the roads and dams, the factories and universities, that are the real sources of wealth?" it asked. "We can look ahead without fear. But we could use a sobering sense of responsibility that has not always marked the '50s."[15]

A wide-ranging essay in the *Washington Post* called "The Fateful Decade" warned that the United States had fallen behind the Soviet Union in space, defense, and other manifestations of national power and prestige. "It is almost as if a deliberate decision has been taken to accept second class status. This continued slippage also affects starkly the challenges that lie ahead in the next year and decade," the essay scolded. Americans were appropriately concerned about immediate challenges such as inflation, the prolonged steel strike, political scandals, and misguided agricultural policies, but these problems should be subordinated to the overriding question of whether the United States would retain its primacy. "What then is our purpose? In the immediate present, defense is surely paramount. Some of the lag in military preparation and in space exploration may indeed be well-nigh irremediable. The deficiencies will place a heavy obligation upon the new President and Congress for the utmost candor and realism in acquainting the people with the hard facts as they relate to budgets and taxes." The essay then questioned the nation's most fundamental values, asking, "What is our aim? Two cars in every garage? A decent job for every breadwinner and a decent house for every family? More beneficial recreation? More leisure time to watch more ball games and television?" The essay concluded with the hope that the year's presidential campaign would offer "thoughtful and enterprising answers" to these important questions and challenges.[16]

II

As Americans looked backward from the vantage point of January 1960, the most obvious period of reflection was the decade that had just ended. Two competing narratives immediately emerged about the 1950s. As a general rule, Republicans saw the decade as a golden time of prosperity and peace. Economic growth combined with relative geopolitical calm to enhance American power. "Everything's booming but guns," Republicans declared. In the Republican view, Eisenhower had both presided over, and in fact created, a broad consensus in America life. This consensus posited that the American economy was vibrant and successful, the nation was the undisputed leader of the West, and the federal government could play a constructive role in solving social problems. But others, mostly Democrats, had a gloomier assessment of Eisenhower's legacy. They argued that the United States lost its way during the 1950s and was now stagnant and self-absorbed. America, these critics said, was soft and lost, and Eisenhower was at least partly to blame. Democrats told this joke. Question: How does an Eisenhower doll work? Answer: You wind it up and it does nothing for eight years. Columnist William Shannon called the Eisenhower years the "time of the great postponement."[17]

Less partisan observers were conflicted about the legacy of the 1950s. Arnold Toynbee, the celebrated British historian, observed that global tensions had eased during the decade, but warned this might be a temporary reprieve. "An accident might detonate the war to end the human race, even if the button was not deliberately pressed by any of the governments." Nuclear war had been averted so far and this should be the cause of modest celebration, or at least gratitude. "We may now allow ourselves to breathe a sigh of relief now that the 1950s have passed without seeing mankind commit race-suicide. But one such sigh is the most we can afford to allow ourselves. We certainly cannot afford to rest on our oars," he said. But the great historian posited that mankind was also on the cusp of amazing accomplishments. He described recent space exploration as "epoch-making achievements" that constituted "a triumph for the whole human race; they mark Man's bursting of the bounds of this planet." He also noted the pace of change had dramatically accelerated, and "has now become so rapid that there is now more change within a single lifetime than the human psyche can easily digest."[18]

Walter Lippmann, Washington's premier newspaper columnist, took a more negative view of the 1950s. In a column called, "The Second Best," he wrote that America was growing richer economically but weaker politically and strategically. He argued that the nation had fallen behind, and was not "holding our own in terms of national power, in overall military capacity, in the competition to pioneer in outer space, in the comparative rate of economic growth and in education, which is the life giver of national power." Lippmann said the United States was spending too much on private consumption and not enough for public investment. Stewardship and responsibility should take precedence over private indulgence. "The voices that will serve this country and indeed save it, will be those of stern men demanding hard things," he declared.[19]

Eric Goldman, a Princeton University history professor, viewed the 1950s as a largely wasted decade. In an essay in *Harper's Magazine* called, "Good Bye to the Fifties—and Good Riddance," Goldman said the United States had become stale, boring, and humorless. "We've grown unbelievably prosperous and we maunder along in a stupor of fat. We were badly scared by the Communists, so scared that we are leery of anybody who even so much as twits our ideas, our customs, and our leaders. We live in a heavy, humorless, sanctimonious, stultifying atmosphere, singularly lacking in the self-mockery that is self-criticism. Probably the climate of the late 'Fifties' was the dullest and dreariest in all our history," he wrote. Goldman said Americans needed to learn how to laugh and be playful again.[20]

A powerful critique of the 1950s was advanced by Lawrence Weiss in a *Denver Post* essay called "Has America Lost the Way?—An Appraisal of the National Mood in the Decade of the 1950s." Weiss argued that despite the surface prosperity of the 1950s, a "sense of uneasiness and fear has begun to afflict the American spirit." In his view, America's self-confidence had been eroded by the dangers of nuclear annihilation, the stalemate in Korea, the Soviet Union's apparent victory in the space race, the political agility and energy of Soviet leader Nikita Khrushchev, the allure of endless creature comforts, cultural and intellectual deadening brought on by the television age, pervasive crime and corruption, havoc caused by McCarthyism, and continuing struggles for civil rights and a fair society. But Weiss saw signs the nation was emerging from the malaise of the 1950s with a renewed sense of purpose. The new national spirit, he wrote, should be channeled into rebuilding the nation by clearing slums, revitalizing cities, improving schools, strengthening the military, providing better care for the elderly and sick, enriching the nation's culture and fighting for equal rights. America should also display its excellence for the rest of the world, especially the developing world.

America's progress during the 1950s would become a critical point of contention during the coming political year. Kennedy was planning to build his campaign on the premise that the Eisenhower administration had failed to provide vigorous leadership during the 1950s. Eisenhower and Vice President Nixon would depict this decade in a starkly different way. Where

Kennedy saw stagnation and sloth, Eisenhower and Nixon saw stability and steady progress.[21]

While it was natural to think back on the preceding decade with a critical eye, historically and socially inclined Americans responded to the arrival of 1960 with reflections on the centennial anniversary of Abraham Lincoln's election and the coming of the Civil War. The last presumed Civil War veteran, Confederate soldier Walter Williams, died near the end of 1959. Several years earlier the last known Union veteran, Albert Woolson, passed away. Texas senator Ralph Yarborough spoke on the Senate floor on January 6, 1960, and discussed "The War Between the States" and its legacy for the nation. He introduced a resolution observing the death of Williams and calling for memorials to honor all Civil War soldiers. He also submitted into the Congressional Record a half dozen newspaper articles about Williams and the bravery of the four million men who had fought in the Civil War.[22] Publishers anticipated a renewed interest in the conflict and prepared new books related to the war. Eisenhower and Congress created a special commission that planned events between 1961 and 1965 to commemorate the Civil War.

III

Americans naturally wondered what the 1960s would bring. Some focused on the country's immediate challenges and a tangible agenda for renewal and growth while others cast their gaze to more distant horizons, dreaming of space travel, cities built underwater, and the discovery of distant planets.

The New York Herald Tribune published a series of essays about the nation's agenda for the 1960s, examining defense, space, agriculture, education, and foreign aid. It called the nation's defense programs "the biggest question mark" and argued the United States needed to substantially ramp up its military spending and weapons systems. As for the space race, the paper said America needed to get serious and get moving. "Present indications are that unless we quickly and markedly accelerate our own efforts, the Soviets will be the first on the moon—and also, despite our dramatic Mercury astronaut program, the first man in orbit is quite likely to be a Russian. Whether we like it or not, we are in a race—a race that we cannot afford to lose." The essay warned that the Soviet Union was using its preeminence in space to enhance its reputation as the global leader of the future and concluded with a plea for action. "We can't win unless we start running. The free world has a right to demand more vigorous leadership than it has gotten from the United States in the competitive conquest of man's ultimate frontier." Education, the paper said, was central to America's future vitality and there was a desperate need for 140,000 additional classrooms to educate the large population of young children that became known as the Baby Boom. Moreover, the continuing stalemate in Congress over the appropriate roles of the federal and state governments was viewed as thwarting progress. Other essays insisted that more rational programs were necessary for both agriculture and foreign assistance. The current farm program resulted in massive surpluses and declining incomes for farmers. American foreign aid was needed to help the developing world grow and to prove that the United States supported its progress. The overarching theme of the *Herald Tribune*'s essays was that America needed vision, pragmatism, and vitality to reach its potential.[23]

There were American leaders who had been thinking about the challenges of the 1960s for several years. Eisenhower, in his 1959 State of the Union address, announced his intention to convene a panel of experts to identify national goals for the 1960s. This was partly a response to the fear, even panic, which swept the United States in the aftermath of the 1957 launching of the Sputnik satellite and assertions by some security experts that the Soviets were surging ahead of the United States in both bombers and missiles. When the president's eleven-member Commission on National Goals released its report at the end of 1960, it outlined recommendations to strengthen education, foster the arts and sciences, promote economic growth, expand the use of new technology, revitalize agriculture, bolster health and welfare, and modernize foreign policy, defense, arms control, and trade programs.[24]

Concern about America's future direction was reflected in major research projects undertaken by *Life* magazine, the *New York Times*, and the Rockefeller Brothers Fund. All began with the premise that America needed new energy and a clear direction. The essays published by *Life* and the *Times* became the basis for a book called *The National Purpose*, which compiled the views of leading public intellectuals including Adlai Stevenson, Archibald MacLeish, David Sarnoff, Billy Graham, John Gardner, Clinton Rossiter,

Albert Wohlstetter, and James Reston. The dominant theme of the essays was that the nation had grown wealthy but also uncertain of its mission in the world. MacLeish, one of the country's leading poets, said Americans had lost their confidence. "That something has gone wrong in America most of us know," he wrote. "We are prosperous, lively, successful, inventive, diligent—but nevertheless and notwithstanding, something is wrong and we know it. The trouble seems to be that we don't feel right with ourselves or with the country . . . It isn't just the Russians now: it's ourselves. It's about the way we feel about ourselves as Americans. We feel that we've lost our way in the woods, that we don't know where we are going—if anywhere." MacLeish said the nation should go back to its founding documents, especially the Declaration of Independence, to remind itself of its purpose. Reverend Billy Graham urged a spiritual renewal for the nation. "I am convinced that regardless of the outward appearance of prosperity within the corporate life of America there is present a form of moral and spiritual cancer which could ultimately lead to the country's destruction unless the disease is treated promptly and the trend reversed," he wrote. He said Americans had grown complacent and soft. "We play too much and work too little. We overeat, overdrink, oversex, and overplay, but few of us are ever overexercised . . . We need to recapture the love and dedication of hard work," he said. Several of the essayists argued that strong and forceful presidential leadership could pull the nation out of its lethargy and they hoped the 1960 campaign would provide such a leader.[25]

The Senate Foreign Relations Committee commissioned more than a dozen studies in 1959 and 1960 on the future of American foreign policy. The panel received and reviewed reports on America's policies toward Western Europe, Eastern Europe, Africa, and Asia, as well as the broad goals of American foreign policy and the challenge of formulating and implementing successful national security programs. All of these reports reflected a deep uncertainty and unease about the path the nation was on.

But while concerns about the future were in the air, so were feelings of optimism. There was a palpable fascination with exploring the unknown. At one end of the cultural scale, hundreds of comic books and science fiction books published in 1960 speculated about the universe and possible distant worlds. Major journals, organizations, and analysts also gazed at their crystal balls and tried to imagine the future. A team of analysts from

Douglas Aircraft developed a plan for a three-man expedition to Mars that they claimed could be accomplished within the decade. They described a space vehicle that was 330 feet high and weighed 734,000 pounds. Their proposed mission would take exactly 421 days: 125 days in transit, 50 days in Mars orbit for exploration and refueling from unmanned tankers sent up from the earth, and then 246 days to return to Earth. The crew would perform reconnaissance and conduct experiments from the orbiting space-craft and, if deemed advisable, one crew member would explore the planet's surface with a small, maneuverable, chemically powered vehicle that would return to the orbiting mother ship. The small vehicle would be used for exploring Mars by one astronaut at a time and would also serve as the earth reentry capsule. The study noted that should the astronaut and vehicle be lost on Mars, the other two astronauts could return toward earth and establish an orbit from which they could be retrieved by a shuttle vehicle.[26]

Focusing on the challenges of daily life on earth, Dexter Keezer, director of the economics department of the McGraw-Hill Publishing Company, detailed his vision for the coming decade in a *Baltimore Sun* article, arguing that America by 1970 would be very different from 1960. The lives of indi-vidual Americans would be "radically changed for the better in a thousand ways," he insisted. Drawing from what he called "responsible reports by scientists, industrial leaders and technical editors on products and services which are now definitely in prospect," Keezer described revolutionary changes in travel, communications, and daily living. He predicted the home of the future would be a manufactured house with collapsible panels that would allow its owners to change its shape, move it to another part of the country, trade it in at a used house lot, or even just trade one room at a time. These homes would have plastic plumbing and an ultrasonic dishwasher and spray-on carpeting. Much of the building material would be plastic and aluminum. Keezer predicted light bulbs would become a relic of the past and future lighting would come from colored electroluminescent panels that occupied most of the ceilings and side walls of the home. The illumina-tion would be ten to twenty times as bright as the norm in 1960 but the glare would be eliminated by a technology called "polarization." Some household appliances would work without moving parts. The house of 1970 would be completely air-conditioned; using a heat pump, the same system would heat the house in the winter as cool it in the summer. "The air indoors is mountain fresh, electrostatically stripped of every particle of dust. If you insist on opening a window, you just push a button or point a finger in the right direction," Keezer wrote. "The house is so completely soundproofed that the loudest bellow isn't heard two rooms away. A built-in intercom system is the substitute for shouting."

He also conceived of a small box about a foot square in the front hall that would serve as the electronic control room for the house. "It turns on the panel lighting when you enter a room, maintains a comfortable temperature in every room and figures out your monthly bills. It turns on the heat conductors under your driveway when it snows, waters the lawn, and changes your swimming pool water. It wakes you up with your own kind of music, starts the coffee, warms the car, and lets the cat in." Keezer envisioned a four-day workweek, radar systems in cars, commuters who traveled by air bus with a helicopter attachment, or on a commuter train that moved on a cushion of air. He also contemplated phones that had TVs within them and didn't require dialing and a mostly cashless economy in which small cards would replace cash or checks and would transmit transaction data to the bank. He imagined a personal health machine in every house. Before going to bed at night, Americans could step on this machine and it would instantly record weight, blood pressure, pulse, and nervous reactions. A red light would flash if the machine determined a person needed to see his or her doctor immediately.[27]

IV

As Americans looked back and gazed ahead, they were understandably preoccupied with the world and the country they lived in. The 1960 census and a series of Gallup polls provide a telling snapshot of the United States at the dawn of the new decade.

The United States' eighteenth decennial census began on April 1, 1960, when, after a preliminary mailing to every known mailbox to outline procedures, 160,000 enumerators went door to door across America to conduct interviews and pick up the surveys. Their worksheets were eventually sent to Washington and tabulated by four massive mainframe computers. The results were sent to the White House on November 15, two weeks before the December 1 statutory deadline. While the census was primarily designed to get an updated population count to apportion seats in the House of Representatives, it also solicited additional information. Americans were asked where they worked and how they got to their jobs. The census also asked about the fuel they used for heating their homes and how many cars, household air conditioning units, washing machines, clothes dryers, food freezers, and radio and TV sets they had. For the first time, parents were asked about whether their children attended private or public schools.

According to the 1960 census, the country's population had grown to 179 million, almost 28 million more than in 1950, an increase of 18.5% over the previous decade. About two-thirds of the population growth took place in the suburbs while eight of the ten largest American cities lost population. More than half of the nation's 3,072 counties lost population, primarily in rural areas. New York City retained its position as the nation's largest city with 7.8 million followed by Chicago (3.5 million), Los Angeles (2.5 million), Philadelphia (2 million), and Detroit (1.6 million). America was growing. Regionally, the West experienced the largest rate of growth, increasing by almost 40% since 1950, while the South grew by 16.5%, the North Central region by 16.1%, and the Northeast by 13.2%.[28]

Four states now had populations of over 10 million: New York (16.8 million), California (15.8 million), Pennsylvania (11.3 million), and Illinois (10.1 million). Ohio and Texas fell just shy of 10 million. Population growth was uneven, however. More than 60% of the national population increase was accounted for by growth in eight states, led by California and Florida. Three states—Arkansas, Mississippi, and West Virginia—lost population, as did the District of Columbia.

Reflecting this shift in population, the West was set to secure added political strength. For the coming congressional elections in 1962, the West gained ten seats in the House, the Northeast lost seven, the North Central lost four, and the South lost one. In terms of big changes in representation California gained eight seats and Florida gained four. Pennsylvania lost three seats and Arkansas, Massachusetts, and New York each lost two seats. The House of Representatives had expanded from 435 to 437 members in 1959 to accommodate the admission of Hawaii and Alaska into the United States, but it was reduced back to 435 for the 1962 congressional elections.

In a long-established practice to help Americans visualize the distribution of the nation's population, the Census Bureau identified the nation's population center. This is the point through which a straight line could be drawn north to south and east to west dividing the country's population into quarters. As many people lived on one side of the line as the other. The first census in 1790 placed the nation's population center near Baltimore, Maryland. In 1960, the nation's center of population moved to just northwest of Centralia, Illinois, which was 63 miles west of Olney, Illinois, the population center in 1950. According to the Census Bureau, about 47 miles of the 63-mile shift west was due to the admission of Alaska and Hawaii. But the other 16 miles were due to the growing population in the West.

The census also tallied age and by 1960 Americans were younger on average than they had been in 1950. The median age of the population declined for the first time in 170 years, falling from 30.2 years to 29.5 years. The American family was larger than ever but households had become smaller because of the decline of three generations living under the one roof. Households were increasingly comprised of two, and sometimes only one generation. The census revealed that during the 1950s median family income jumped by 86%, from $3,083 in 1949 to $5,657 in 1959. However, the nonwhite national median income of $3,161 was only 54% of the national median for whites. In 1960, one American in nine was nonwhite.

The 1960 census was studied by demographers, professors, business leaders, and, of course, politicians. Much of the analysis and discussion focused on its central findings: substantial growth in the country, especially in the West and in the suburbs, and declining population in many of the nation's large central cities, especially in the Northeast and Midwest. Substantial attention was paid to the fact that for the first time less than half of the labor force was engaged in the production of physical goods, so-called blue collar workers. America was becoming a service-oriented economy.

If the census provided a snapshot of America in 1960 so did a raft of surveys conducted by Gallup throughout the year that revealed striking themes. President Eisenhower's popularity with the American people was enduring. The president was well liked and highly respected. In January of 1960 Eisenhower's approval rating was 71% and it remained above 60% for the rest of the year, as it had throughout his eight-year presidency. Gallup polls confirmed Eisenhower was the most admired man in America in

1960 and the most respected world leader of the 1950s. While far more American voters identified themselves as Democrats than Republicans, the nation was evenly divided between liberals and conservatives. In July, respondents said that if the congressional elections were held then, 60% preferred Democrats and 40% preferred Republicans. But that same month, 45% identified themselves as conservatives and 43% as liberals. Also, 41% of the respondents said the Democrats were best for American prestige while 25% said Republicans would improve America's image.

Gallup polls showed the country was hopeful but wary. Two-thirds of the respondents believed a peace agreement between the United States and the Soviet Union was possible. But nearly one-third of Americans said another world war was also possible in the next five years. Respondents to surveys in several European nations said the United States was falling behind the Soviet Union in science. Despite the heavy religious overtones that persisted in American life and culture, only about half of the country went to church regularly. About 70% of the respondents said they belonged to a church and nearly everyone believed in a God. On a less spiritual level, Gallup polls showed the presidential race between Richard Nixon and John F. Kennedy was very tight. The two spent most of 1960 in a near tie; when one surged slightly, the other would almost immediately respond and retake the lead.[29]

V

Looking out at the world in 1960, Americans saw an international scene that was deeply divided and in unmistakable transition. The capitalist and communist worlds were at loggerheads but neither was monolithic. There were fissures within the West, as the United States and France differed over security strategy and nuclear policy. In February of that year France tested an atomic bomb in the Sahara, becoming the world's fourth nuclear power. America and her allies were also seeking a coherent strategy to retain their position in Berlin. There were also growing tensions between the Soviet Union and China, with Chinese leaders embracing a harder, more unyielding brand of Marxism. Throughout the year American leaders tried to manage a seemingly endless cascade of crises—in Berlin, the Belgian Congo, Cambodia, Cuba, Laos, and South Vietnam.

During the first months of 1960, millions of people around the world eagerly awaited the Paris summit of great powers that was scheduled for May. The leaders of France, Great Britain, the United States, and the Soviet Union were preparing to meet for the first major summit since Geneva in 1955 and many hoped Cold War tensions would ease. However about two weeks before the start of the conference, the Soviet Union shot down an American spy plane deep inside Soviet territory and captured the plane's pilot, Francis Gary Powers. The summit unraveled amid bitter accusations about spying, charges of American deception, strong evidence of misleading statements by the Eisenhower administration, and Soviet demands for an American apology that Ike rejected. The collapse of the summit stunned and saddened many around the world and seemed to portend a Cold War without end. Soviet leaders withdrew their invitation to Eisenhower to visit the Soviet Union and the president's scheduled visit to Japan was later canceled in the summer of 1960 due to rising anti-American protests there.

Nationalism was a powerful, pulsating force throughout the world, especially in Africa where seventeen new nations came into being in 1960 as Europe's colonial empires either collapsed or were dismantled. From the first day of the year until its end, nationalism and the plea for a new political order echoed across Africa, Asia, and Latin America.

The United Nations was the central venue of global diplomacy in 1960. Created in 1945, the UN was praised by nations around the world and by most Americans. Both Republicans and Democrats supported the world body. The UN's General Assembly met in late September for a remarkable—and remarkably contentious—session in which more than twenty heads of government attended meetings or gave formal addresses. Nikita Khrushchev gave fiery remarks about American and Western intransigence, and banged his shoe in a raw display of displeasure. By year's end, Khrushchev and other Soviet leaders seemed determined to undermine the UN and depose its celebrated secretary general, Dag Hammarskjöld. The Soviets found much to dislike about the UN, including its handling of the civil war in the Belgian Congo, where Soviets alleged the world body was supporting Western interests rather than serving as an honest broker.[30]

The world of 1960 was dominated by large and intriguing personalities: Chou En-Lai and Mao Tse-tung (contemporary spellings are now Zhou Enlai and Mao Zedong) in China, Chiang Kai-shek in Formosa (present day Taiwan), Fidel Castro in Cuba, Haile Selassie in Ethiopia, Konrad Adenauer in West Germany, Queen Elizabeth and Harold Macmillan in the United Kingdom, Jawaharlal Nehru in India, President Sukarno in Indonesia, Charles de Gaulle in France, David Ben-Gurion in Israel, Emperor Hirohito in Japan, King Hussein I in Jordan, Luis Somoza in Nicaragua, Nikita Khrushchev in the Soviet Union, King Saud of Saudi Arabia, Gamal Abdel Nasser of Egypt, Pope John XXIII in Vatican City, Ho Chi Minh in North Vietnam, Ngo Dinh Diem in South Vietnam, and Josip Broz Tito in Yugoslavia.

Other countries viewed the United States more skeptically than they had in the immediate aftermath of World War II. A survey conducted in twenty-three nations by the United States Information Agency, made public in early November, showed that West Europeans regarded the United States as trailing the Soviet Union in military strength, space exploration, and economic growth. A Gallup poll also showed that respect for the United States had fallen in France, Great Britain, and Norway during 1960, probably due to the perception that it was falling behind the Soviet Union in a number of areas. Meanwhile, polling in the United States revealed that Americans believed that respect for their country had declined abroad. "The agonizing over the national purpose and declining national prestige would be an integral part of the campaign of 1960s," one historian was to write.[31]

VI

Most Americans accepted the Cold War as a given and did not ruminate about geopolitics. Instead they spent their time immersed in the day to day challenges of life: raising families, going to work and school, attending churches, enjoying vacations, reading books, watching television, going to movies, and joining civic clubs.

The American economy was doing well at the beginning of 1960 but then slowed and fell into a recession near the end of the year. Still the United States' total goods and services exceeded $500 billion for the first time. But the nation suffered from a balance of payments deficit with a serious drain on gold reserves that perplexed and troubled the Eisenhower administration. The annual federal budget was $78 billion and the public debt was $286 billion, up from $258 billion in 1945. The size of the debt was a concern especially for conservatives. The nation's 16 million farmers produced more than enough food for all Americans and also generated ample surpluses. More than 3 million Americans lived on the free pork, beans, and eggs given out by the federal government to those in need. Wages rose during the year, reaching an average of $2.29 an hour for manufacturing jobs. About 66 million Americans had jobs, but almost 7% of the workforce was unemployed by the end of the year. Industrial strife eased; there were fewer strikes in 1960 than in any year since 1945.

The Department of Labor projected the coming decade would offer promising careers in medicine, dentistry, nursing, and library science. Engineers of all kinds would be in high demand with starting salaries ranging from $4,350 to $7,400. New college graduates could expect to earn about $6,000 in accounting, $5,400 in retail, $5,100 in sales and management, $4,800 in advertising and government service, $4,560 in journalism, and $4,500 in teaching.[32]

While Americans were flocking to the suburbs, the nation's premier cities were undergoing a striking facelift. In New York City, twenty-five new skyscrapers appeared on the Manhattan skyline in 1960 and another fifteen were planned for 1961. Notable new buildings included the forty-eight-story Time & Life Building and the sixty-story One Chase Manhattan Plaza. The razing of Ebbets Field in Brooklyn began in February, to the consternation of sentimental Dodgers fans who had seen their team move west to Los Angeles. In Chicago, the ground was broken for the sixty-story twin towers of Marina City that was designed for residential and commercial purposes. The massive McCormick Place convention center opened in 1960 as did the full length of the Congress Expressway. Northwest of the city, the O'Hare Hilton opened that year as part of a thirty-two-acre complex with a golf course, 1,200-seat convention hall, radio-press room, and swimming pool. In Los Angeles, the recent removal of height limits allowed for the construction of skyscrapers. Buildings of more than twenty stories began to spread across Los Angeles, and work continued near Chavez Ravine on Dodgers Stadium that was scheduled to cost $15 million and seat 56,000. Construction of Century City was set to begin in 1961. Across America, the new interstate highway system was coming to life, reshaping the look and the transportation patterns of the nation. This system was spearheaded by the president and would come to be seen as one of his historic achievements.[33]

Yet for all the growth, America's racial situation remained tense and uneasy, especially in the South, heightening the poignancy of the approaching centennial of the Civil War. In February, four freshmen at the all-black North Carolina Agricultural and Technical College in Greensboro sat at the "Whites Only" lunch counter at Woolworths and requested service. The store was willing to sell products to African Americans but did not allow Blacks and Whites to eat together. There was a standoff. The next day more than twenty black students joined the sit-in and the following day sixty additional students took part. Within three months there were similar sit-ins in more than seventy-five cities with two thousand arrests. Attorney General William Rogers eventually brokered talks between store owners and civic leaders. An agreement was reached and previously segregated store lunch counters were quietly opened to Blacks in 112 communities in ten Southern and Border states by the end of the year. A new civil rights activist group emerged from this struggle—the Student Nonviolent Coordinating Committee. But racial progress remained tenuous. Only 765 of the South's more than 7,000 school districts were integrated in 1960 and only 7% of black children in the South attended an integrated school. And segregation and Jim Crow laws were still widely applied throughout the South, which included everything from public transportation to restaurants, restrooms, and movie theaters.[34]

Even with the rise of TV and the continuing importance of radio, Americans read books, magazines, and newspapers. Major cities often had several newspapers; some had both afternoon and morning papers. The *San Francisco Chronicle* and the *Washington Star* had circulations of more than 200,000, the *Boston Globe* and the *New York Post* more than 300,000, the *Baltimore Sun* and the *Washington Post* more than 400,000, the *Chicago Sun-Times* and the *Los Angeles Times* more than 500,000, the *New York Times* and the *Wall Street Journal* more than 800,000, and the New York *Daily News* had more than 2 million readers.

Americans loved magazines. *Reader's Digest* topped the list with 12 million subscribers, followed by *TV Guide* (6.8 million), *Life* (6.5 million), the *Saturday Evening Post* (6.2 million), *Ladies' Home Journal* (5.9 million), and *Look* (5.8 million). Women's magazines also had large circulations. The most popular were *McCall's, Everywoman's Family Circle, Better Homes and Gardens, Good Housekeeping, Woman's Day, American Home, Coronet,* and *Redbook.*[35]

Among the most popular books were *Hawaii* by James Michener, *The Leopard* by Giuseppe di Lampedusa, *The Lovely Ambition* by Mary Ellen Chase, and *Dean's Watch* by Elizabeth Goudge. Americans also read Vance Packard's *The Waste Makers, The Liberal Hour* by John Kenneth Galbraith, *Mr. Citizen* by Harry Truman, William Shirer's *The Rise and Fall of the Third Reich, Born Free* by Joy Adamson, and *The Complete War Memoirs of Charles de Gaulle.* A renewed interest in the Civil War was evident by the success of the *Picture History of the Civil War* and *Grant Moves South,* both by Bruce Catton. Margaret Leech was awarded the Pulitzer Prize in history for *In the Days of McKinley,* and Samuel Eliot Morison received the coveted award in biography for *John Paul Jones.*[36]

The Pulitzer Prize in fiction was awarded to Allen Drury for his political thriller, *Advise and Consent,* a book heavy with Cold War and McCarthy-era themes. It was a *New York Times* best seller for more than one hundred weeks and later became the basis for a Broadway play and a movie. A fictionalized account of Cold War Washington, the book included characters based on recognizable politicians, including Franklin Roosevelt and Harry Truman. It depicted an America that was embattled, fearful of the communist threat and deeply concerned about internal subversives. Drury's work described an America that was losing its verve. His narrator posits, "Everywhere, in every phase of her life, there was a slowing down, an acceptance of second-best, an almost hopeless complacence and compliance with all the things that devious people wanted to do, an unwillingness to come to grips with anything unpleasant, a desire to lean back and sleep; and sleep."[37]

Presidential Power was written by a young Columbia University political scientist named Richard Neustadt. The book attracted the interest of many academics and some politicians, especially John Kennedy, who agreed with the author's emphasis on the variability of presidential power and the importance of persuasion in the White House. "Presidential power is the power to persuade," Neustadt argued, saying the formal powers of the office could be expanded by a creative and resourceful president. The book primarily examined the presidencies of Franklin Roosevelt, Harry

Truman, and Dwight Eisenhower in the context of presidential power and found FDR's presidency stellar, Truman's solid but uneven, and Eisenhower's disappointing and often lackluster. Neustadt was highly critical of Eisenhower's presidency, depicting him as passive, detached, and often ineffective.[38] The book helped shape the arguments Senator Kennedy used during his quest for the presidency, specifically his attacks on the Eisenhower administration.

The Conscience of a Conservative by Republican senator Barry Goldwater detailed the conservative position on government regulation, taxes, spending, welfare, education, and foreign policy, and became an improbable sensation. The first printing of the book was just 10,000 copies but within a month of its publication it jumped to number ten on *Time* magazine's bestseller list. By November, 500,000 copies of the book were in print. The book's success influenced the conservative movement in the United States and also revealed the fissures in the Republican Party between those who wanted to slow the growth of the New Deal and those who wanted to dismantle it, showing that Eisenhower's effort to create a moderate, middle of the road party was less than a complete success.

Less politically oriented than the others, but more powerful socially and culturally, was a book published in July 1960 written by a young Alabama woman and first-time author Harper Lee. *To Kill a Mockingbird* was the story of a small-town lawyer and his defense of a black man who was wrongly accused and convicted of raping a white woman. The book struck a profound nerve in the nation as it continued to struggle with race. The book was a national best seller and critical success within weeks. "A hundred pounds of sermons on tolerance, or an equal measure of invective deploring the lack of it, will weigh far less in the scale of enlightenment than a mere eighteen ounces of new fiction bearing the title, *To Kill a Mockingbird*," began a review in the *Washington Post*.[39]

When it came to relaxation, Americans turned to sports, both as players and spectators. The most popular participatory sports in the United States in 1960 were fishing, bowling, hunting, boating, and golfing. For fans, there was a seasonal flow to the world of sports that all were accustomed to: college and professional basketball in the winter, horse racing in the spring, baseball and golf in the summer, baseball's pennant race followed by the World Series in the fall, the National

Football League championship game in late December and the college football bowls at the start of the new year.

Baseball remained the national pastime and the eight teams of the American League combined with the eight teams of the National League together drew about twenty million fans. At the start of the year, there were some high-profile contract signings for the coming season: Stan Musial was to earn $80,000 playing for the St. Louis Cardinals, Willie Mays the same amount for the San Francisco Giants, Ted Williams $60,000 for the Boston Red Sox, and Yogi Berra $50,000 for the New York Yankees. The 1960 World Series was a crazy, madcap event, eventually won by the Pittsburgh Pirates over the New York Yankees with a dramatic game seven, final inning home run by Bill Mazeroski. The Yankees then surprised and saddened the sports world by firing legendary manager Casey Stengel, citing his advanced age. He was seventy. Several weeks earlier Ted Williams retired from the Red Sox. He was forty-two, and in his last game he hit his 521st homer.[40]

The United States hosted the 1960 Winter Olympics in Squaw Valley, California, from February 18 to February 28. The games were opened by Vice President Nixon and were attended by nearly 400,000 fans. The Soviet Union won the overall medal count followed by Sweden and then the United States. The Summer Olympics were held in Rome from August 25 to September 11. Once again the Soviet Union dominated the Americans. Arthur Daley of the *New York Times* lamented that the United States was losing its prowess as a sports power. "The world is stirring not only politically. It is stirring athletically too," he wrote. "The U.S. scares not a soul now. Once, the Americans dominated the show. They don't any more, nor are they likely to again," he said, adding that the Rome Olympics "represented a resounding victory for Soviet Russia."[41] But there were some bright moments for the Americans in Rome. Rafer Johnson became the first African American flag bearer for the U.S. team and won a gold medal in the decathlon. Wilma Rudolph won three gold medals in track and Cassius Clay earned a gold medal in boxing. The Associated Press later voted Johnson as Athlete of the Year while the UPI selected Rudolph.

Of course, in addition to sports there were many other leisure activities for Americans in 1960. According to the *Los Angeles Times*, Americans were spending $40 billion a year on leisure in a $500 billion economy. This included about $2 billion for magazines; $1.2 billion on movies and about the same for books; $500 million for musical instruments; $313 million for theater, opera, and concerts; and $225 million for bathing suits for which, the paper said, "American women paid more and more for less and less." The essay also reported that Americans spent $30 million for amateur art supplies and a whopping $2.6 billion for fishing related expenses—from licenses to suntan lotion. Americans also spent $40 million for inflatable water toys and floats for backyard swimming pools and beaches.[42]

Broadway was busy and bustling as the new decade began. Popular new plays in the 1959-1960 season included *My Fair Lady*, *A Raisin in the Sun*, *Gypsy*, *Bye Bye Birdie*, a revival of *The King and I*, *The World of Carl Sandburg*, and *Advise and Consent*. There were also celebrated long-running musicals on Broadway that were still drawing large audiences such as *Oklahoma*, *South Pacific*, *The Music Man*, *Guys and Dolls*, *Annie Get Your Gun*, *Kiss Me Kate*, and *Damn Yankees*.

Americans still loved going to movies. *Ben-Hur* was released in late 1959 but it remained hugely popular in 1960 and won eleven Academy Awards. People went to the cinema to watch *Elmer Gantry*, *The Entertainer*, *Man in a Cocked Hat*, *Once More, with Feeling!*, *Pollyanna*, *Psycho*, *Sons and Lovers*, *Spartacus*, *Sunrise at Campobello*, and *The Unforgiven*. Americans also continued to watch a lot of TV including *The Andy Griffith Show*, *Gunsmoke*, *Bonanza*, *Leave it to Beaver*, *My Three Sons*, *The Ed Sullivan Show*, *Father Knows Best*, *The Adventures of Ozzie and Harriet*, *American Bandstand*, and *The Lucy-Desi Comedy Hour*.[43]

That same year, Clark Gable died at the age of fifty-nine, Oscar Hammerstein at sixty-five, and Emily Post at eighty-six. Lucille Ball divorced Desi Arnaz, and Arthur Miller and Marilyn Monroe announced the end of their four-year marriage. The fifty-star American flag was unveiled in Philadelphia on July 4, heralding the addition of Alaska and Hawaii. Elvis Presley returned from military service in West Germany. Betty Friedan wrote an article called "Women Are People Too" in the September issue of *Good Housekeeping*. The U.S. Food and Drug Administration approved the oral contraceptive, Enovid, in May, the first ever birth control pill. Roger Woodward, a seven-year-old, was swept from a boat and went over Niagara Falls—and was rescued with only a few bruises. Americans celebrated the centennial of the Pony Express, the historic mail route from St. Joseph,

Missouri, to Sacramento, California. In April, eighty riders rode in 75-mile relays across the nearly 2,000-mile route. Later that year the U.S. Post Office sponsored a second reenactment of the Pony Express run.

The nation remained religious, but more in attitude than regular church attendance. According to the *Yearbook of American Churches*, there were 41 million Catholics, 20 million Baptists, 12 million Methodists, 8 million Lutherans, 5.5 million Jews, 4 million Presbyterians, and 3.3 million Episcopalians.[44]

Americans made major advances in space and scientific research in 1960. There was a bipartisan consensus in Congress supporting greater federal support for scientific research and one report noted that "achievements tumbled out of laboratories in breath-taking profusion." Among the accomplishments of American science were successful launchings of U.S. satellites capable of transmitting weather information, and boosters to launch a capsule with human travelers; the Hale Telescope's photographs of the most distant identifiable celestial object, which was thought to be a galaxy or a pair of galaxies in collision; a genetic cross between a Cornish chicken and a turkey that was the first known case in which two families of birds were hybridized; discovery of chemical predecessors of living matter in stony meteorites from outer space that suggested there might be life elsewhere in the universe; the U.S. Public Health Service's approval for wide use of a polio vaccine that could be taken orally; the high-altitude Project Excelsior balloon flight and parachute jump that demonstrated man's ability to withstand exposure to conditions in outer space; brain waves picked up from a single nerve cell grown in tissue culture; advances in the amplification of light beams by means of an optical laser that was expected to have applications for TV, astronomy, and X-rays; and the launching of a radio-telescope to pick up signals generated in space by possible inhabitants of other solar systems.[45]

The United States began to embrace and then became fixated with the space race. The Soviets appeared ahead of the Americans in rocketry but the United States was competitive in other areas. During 1960, the U.S. program celebrated several accomplishments: the launching of the Pioneer 5 into orbit between Earth and Venus that led to the deepest radio space probe so far; the launching of Tiros-1, the forerunner of a group of weather satellites; the launching of Midas II, a spy satellite that was designed to detect with infrared sensors the heat trail of an enemy rocket; the launching of Transit I-B that was the forerunner of a system that sought to revolutionize space navigation by enabling ships and planes to fix their position; and the launching of Echo I, the first experimental communication satellite that was seen as the precursor of a system of space communication in which all types of electronic signals, including TV, would be bounced around the world. Based on this research and more, American leaders were hopeful that they would be able to send a man into space as early as April of 1961.[46]

In addition to these major scientific advances that took place in laboratories and government research facilities, American entrepreneurs tinkered in their garages and basements and came up with intriguing gadgets. U.S. patents recorded in 1960 included devices to control and eliminate exhaust fumes from motor vehicles; an infant pacifier that produced a mild vibration and buzzing sound; a burglar alarm that sounded a horn continuously if a car was broken into; an automatic umpire that photographed a baseball batter with three cameras to register the exact passage of a ball; a compact radio transmitter that fit into the metal housing of a parking meter and transmitted a signal when the coin box was opened; a device that registered radioactivity while being flown over ground to help identify minerals from the air; a high heel that could be adjusted to the height desired; a bowler's stance indicator that directed the bowler where to stand to strike specific pins; and a motion picture method that produced a panoramic picture around a circular room. This last patent was not filed by a random garage entrepreneur but by an ambitious entertainment company based in Anaheim, California, called Walt Disney Productions.[47]

While there were concerns about crime, especially juvenile delinquency and communist subversion, this was also a trusting time at least as it pertained to personal privacy and security. The 1960 congressional directory, for example, provided the Washington-area home addresses of senators and House members[48] and the home addresses of the president's cabinet, as well as those of the Supreme Court justices were there for all to see too.

The second session of the 86th Congress convened at noon on January 6, 1960, and recessed on July 3 for the Democratic and Republican national conventions. The Senate returned on August 8 and the House on August 15; both chambers adjourned for the year on September 1 as lawmakers returned home for the fall campaign. At the start of the year, there were 65 Democrats and 35 Republicans in the Senate and 280 Democrats and 153 Republicans (with four vacancies) in the House.

As the Eisenhower administration entered its last year, the president offered a balanced budget and a lengthy list of legislation he wanted passed. Congress ultimately approved only 56 of the president's 183 proposals. Medical care for the aged was a major point of contention between Congress and the president and became a significant campaign issue. Congress approved modest civil rights legislation in May after one of the longest filibusters in Senate history. The new law provided additional safeguards for African American voting rights; states were required to keep voting records for twenty-two months after elections and to open them to inspection by Department of Justice. The Senate also ratified two important treaties in 1960: one demilitarized Antarctica and another updated the U.S.-Japan security relationship. Congress and the administration battled over Eisenhower's request for authority to end American imports of Cuban sugar. They reached a compromise that allowed the president to revise the sugar quota.[49]

Congressional Quarterly described the 86th Congress as having left "behind a record of indifferent accomplishment and spirited partisanship." Moreover, it said, "The sixth year of divided government has been the least rewarding for the nation, for President Eisenhower, and for the Democratic majority in Congress. Weighed against the slim fruits of the 1960 session were acres of un-harvested production, blighted by the rust of political schism."[50]

Campaign politics, especially the battle for the White House, dominated American political life in 1960, and the clamor for change was in the air. Columnist Walter Lippmann put it succinctly: "1960 marks the passage of the old political generation and the appearance of the new."[51] For many, Dwight Eisenhower represented the passing political generation and John Kennedy the rising one.

THREE

THE SHADOW CAMPAIGN

I

Less than two weeks after he officially announced his candidacy, Senator John F. Kennedy prepared to address the National Press Club on January 14, 1960, and explain why he was running for president. The speech was the product of weeks of discussion and deliberation within the campaign and also drew upon ideas offered by several presidential scholars. Kennedy aspired to be both high-minded and sharp-tongued. "I don't mind sticking it to old Ike," Kennedy told his aides Ted Sorensen and Richard Goodwin as they put the final touches on the speech in the deserted Butler Aviation terminal at Washington National Airport, where the senator had just returned from a campaign trip. His address was designed to be an indictment of the Eisenhower presidency and an explanation about why Kennedy was running for the White House.[1]

The central issue for the 1960 campaign, he declared at the Press Club, was neither foreign nor domestic policy but rather the presidency itself. While barely uttering the name of President Dwight Eisenhower, Kennedy ripped into the incumbent. In a skewering that the president must have regarded as patronizing, presumptuous, and even preposterous, Kennedy said American voters may have preferred a "detached, limited concept of the presidency" in the elections of 1952 and 1956. But according to Kennedy, this style of leadership was inadequate to the challenges of the coming decade. The times now required a "vigorous proponent of the national interest—not a passive broker for conflicting private interests." They demanded a man capable of acting as the leader of the western world, "not merely a bookkeeper who feels that his work is done when the numbers on the balance sheet come out even."

The junior senator from Massachusetts insisted the world was dangerous and that under Eisenhower's restricted concept of the presidency, America had not kept pace with mounting threats. He argued that "beneath today's surface gloss of peace and prosperity are increasingly dangerous, unsolved, long postponed problems—problems that will inevitably explode to the surface during the next four years of the next administration." The United States faced a growing missile gap with the Soviet Union, the rise of Communist China, the soaring hopes of the developing world, explosive crises in Berlin and the Formosa Straits, the deterioration of NATO which at this point, was about a dozen years old, the lack of an arms control agreement with the Soviet Union, and a raft of domestic problems related to agriculture, the cities, and education. The coming decade that Kennedy called "the challenging revolutionary sixties" required vigorous leadership, not "ringing manifestoes issued from the rear of the battle." The next president must be willing to "place himself in the very thick of the fight" and lead without regard to personal popularity.

Kennedy vowed to bring energy and intensity to the White House. He pledged to use the full powers of the presidency, master the nuances of complex issues, marry the worlds of ideas and power—and act decisively. Drawing from American history, Kennedy said the nation desperately required an activist Democrat who envisioned the presidency as a "vital center of action" rather than another passive Republican. The senator declared a Democratic leader along the lines of Andrew Jackson, Woodrow

Wilson, and Franklin Roosevelt was far preferable to a Republican president who descended from the political lineage of James Buchanan, Warren Harding, or Calvin Coolidge. In his only direct reference to Eisenhower, Kennedy said Ike sought to stay above the fray and out of politics. But Kennedy insisted that no president can hover above the political realm and cited the example of Abraham Lincoln as someone who relished the art of politics. "We will need . . . a president who is willing and able to summon his national constituency to its finest hour—to alert the people to our dangers and our opportunities—to demand of them the sacrifices that will be necessary," he warned.[2]

Kennedy signaled that he was running against the kind of president that the incumbent was—or at least as he was depicted by his critics. Political pundits took notice of Kennedy's speech. Some called it bold, even audacious. James Reston, the influential columnist for the *New York Times*, said the senator's remarks were "the first really serious political speech of the formal campaign" and applauded Kennedy for challenging Eisenhower's conception of the presidency and offering an alternative paradigm. The columnist said Kennedy "dealt with the primary issue. He dealt with the future," adding it was both appropriate and necessary to begin a presidential campaign with a candidate defining this vision of the presidency.[3] Speaking a few days later in Miami, Vice President Nixon dismissed Kennedy's speech as simplistic and naïve. He derided it as the perspective of someone who had never been near the seat of power. Kennedy and Nixon would have much more to say about the presidency—and each other—throughout the year.

II

What would follow after Kennedy and Nixon declared their candidacies for president in January of 1960 was a bruising and bitter campaign. It directly involved three men who would ultimately serve as president of the United States—Kennedy, Nixon, and Lyndon Johnson—and dozens of others who would play a prominent role in American politics for the rest of the twentieth century. The most obvious lens through which to view the election is as a duel between Kennedy and Nixon. Another approach is to look at it as a battle between the two rival tickets: Democrats John Kennedy and Lyndon Johnson versus Republicans Richard Nixon and Henry Cabot Lodge. A less common but more instructive lens for our purposes is to see it as a confrontation between Kennedy and the Eisenhower administration.

Kennedy was a shrewd politician who knew it would be foolish to directly challenge Ike, the hugely popular and much revered president. But Kennedy believed it was not only possible but necessary to run against the Eisenhower administration as tired, timid, and lethargic, and to attack Nixon as its paradigmatic representative and heir. This line of attack was familiar and comfortable for Kennedy; one of the cardinal features of his Senate career was as a relentless critic of the Republican administration in power.

Dwight Eisenhower and John Kennedy were elected to high national office on the same day, November 4, 1952—Eisenhower as the thirty-fourth American president and Kennedy as the junior senator from Massachusetts. Kennedy was sworn into the Senate on January 3, 1953, two weeks before Eisenhower's January 20 inauguration. However, by the time Eisenhower entered the White House he was a national icon by virtue of his World War II heroics which propelled his political career and led to his landslide election in 1952 over Adlai Stevenson. By the time Kennedy began his Senate career he had achieved his own sort of fame as a man from a prominent and wealthy family with a well-known military record.

In 1953, as Eisenhower presided over Washington from the White House, Kennedy tried to find his way in a Senate where seniority determined power and stellar careers went to the patient and the deferential. Patience and deference were not Kennedy's strongest suits. He opposed much of the administration's domestic agenda, including labor and health policies, save for occasional issues such as building the Saint Lawrence Seaway. Kennedy's primary interest was foreign policy and he quickly and comfortably settled into the role of a persistent critic of the administration in this realm. In 1954 he was sharply critical of the administration's "New Look" national security strategy, which emphasized a smaller conventional force, greater air power, and the unabashed threat to use nuclear weapons. Kennedy argued this strategy lacked flexibility, failed to adequately fund conventional forces, and relied too heavily on the threat of using nuclear weapons.[4] He was also an early critic of the administration's strategy on

Indochina, saying it replicated the mistakes the French made in the region, gave more optimistic assessments than the facts warranted, and failed to grasp the power of anti-colonial sentiment in the developing world.

As Eisenhower sought a second term as president in 1956, Kennedy's political career began to soar, and as he grew in influence, he intensified his criticisms of the Eisenhower administration. His book, *Profiles in Courage*, published in 1956, became a national best seller, earning him a reputation as one of Congress's leading intellectuals and later, a Pulitzer Prize. With the Democratic National Convention approaching that summer, Kennedy's name was mentioned as a possible vice presidential candidate. He narrated the film *The Pursuit of Happiness*, which opened the convention and was asked by Adlai Stevenson to nominate him for president. In that nomination speech Kennedy scorched the Eisenhower administration for lethargy and disarray. "Each Republican year of indecision and hesitation has brought new communist advances—in Indochina, in the Middle East, in North Africa, in all the tense and troubled areas of the world. The Grand Alliance of the West—that chain for freedom forged by Truman and Marshall and the rest—is cracking, its unity deteriorating, its strength dissipating. We are hesitant on Suez, silent on colonialism, uncertain on disarmament, and contradictory on the other issues of the day . . . Once we are able to cut through the slogans and the press releases and the vague reassurances, we realize to our shock and dismay that the next four years of this hydrogen age represent the most dangerous and difficult period in the history of our nation." Kennedy believed that vigorous presidential leadership was needed, not a chief executive who relied heavily on his staff, cabinet, and special task forces. "The absence of new ideas, the lack of leadership, the failure to keep pace with new developments, have all contributed to the growth of gigantic economic and social problems—problems that can perhaps be postponed or explained away or ignored now, but the problems that during the next four years will burst forth with continuing velocity." Embracing his role as an advocate for Stevenson, Kennedy said the Democratic standard-bearer offered a clear agenda that stood in stark contrast to the "collection of broken promises, neglected problems, and dangerous blunders" of Eisenhower. Kennedy warned his fellow Democrats about a difficult autumn campaign against the Republican ticket. "Our party will be up against two of the toughest, most skillful campaigners in its history—one who takes the high road, and one who takes the low," he said, managing to deliver shots at both Eisenhower and Nixon with one phrase.[5] Kennedy's speech was well received by the convention and a few days later he nearly won the vice presidential nomination after Stevenson allowed the convention to choose his running mate. After several ballots, Senator Estes Kefauver of Tennessee narrowly defeated Kennedy.

Kennedy, then a thirty-nine-year-old freshman senator, was disappointed to lose the vice presidential nomination but was heartened by his emergence as a party star. He dutifully hit the campaign trail that fall as a surrogate for Stevenson, making about one hundred and fifty speeches in twenty-four states over five weeks. In those appearances, he lamented the failures of the Eisenhower administration and heralded the promise of Stevenson. Though Eisenhower coasted to reelection over Stevenson, Kennedy gained significant stature during that summer and fall and learned about what worked—and what did not work—in a presidential campaign. During the Thanksgiving weekend, just a few weeks after the 1956 election, Kennedy decided to run for president in 1960. His was the first four-year presidential campaign, even if it was officially unannounced for three years. Speaking invitations poured in for the rising politician and Kennedy traveled the nation over the next four years sketching out a traditional Democratic domestic agenda and hammering the Eisenhower administration for flawed defense and foreign policies.

Kennedy received 2,500 speaking invitations in 1957 and accepted nearly 150 of them. He was constantly on the road. He also used the Senate floor and a prized seat on the Senate Foreign Relations Committee as venues to critique the administration. He made broad points about global affairs and landed sharp jabs at the administration on specific policies and controversies. His criticisms intensified with the Soviet Union's launch of the Sputnik satellite in October 1957 and over the findings of an administration task force, the Gaither Committee, that warned that the United States faced grave threats from the Soviet Union. That year, he wrote a much noticed essay in *Foreign Affairs*, "A Democrat Looks at Foreign Policy," in which he charged that the administration did not understand the power of nationalism sweeping the world and also lacked a decisive foreign policy. Too often, he admonished, it substituted slogans for solutions.[6]

By 1958 Kennedy was battling the administration on multiple fronts, from labor legislation to foreign policy. He always seemed to be looking for a fight, or at least examples that showed the administration was failing to seize opportunities. Kennedy chided the Eisenhower White House for squandering an opportunity to showcase the American way of life at the World's Fair in Brussels. He felt the U.S. pavilion was lackluster and he proposed a more dramatic exhibit to highlight the country's technology and ingenuity. Far more consequentially, Kennedy delivered a major foreign policy address on the Senate floor on August 14, 1958, warning the United States was falling behind the Soviet Union in critical military areas. Most provocatively, the senator said the United States faced a missile gap in which American offensive and defensive missiles were poised to fall so far behind the Soviet Union that the nation's security was in peril. He warned this gap could open to the Soviets a new shortcut to world domination.[7]

Kennedy continued to travel the country in 1959, presenting an alternative Democratic agenda and blasting the administration. He was not alone. Several more senior, and similarly ambitious, Democratic senators also launched assaults on the GOP: Lyndon Johnson of Texas, Stuart Symington of Missouri, Henry Jackson of Washington, and Hubert Humphrey of Minnesota. In a speech to Milwaukee Democrats Kennedy accused the administration of lackluster leadership and adorned his critique in political poetry. "When we should have sailed hard into the wind, we too, drifted. When we should have planned anew, sacrificed, and marched ahead, we too, stood still, sought the easy way, and looked to the past." Reviewing the balance sheet between the United States and the Soviet Union, Kennedy said America had fallen behind in all realms: military, economic, agriculture, education, and trade. "Eight gray years—'years the locusts have eaten.' Years of drift, years of falling behind, of postponing decisions and crises. And as a result, the burdens that will face the next administration will be tremendous."[8]

III

As 1960 approached, Kennedy was in breakneck pursuit of the presidency. He presented a liberal domestic agenda on health care, a higher minimum wage, immigration reform, expanded Social Security, more housing, and increased federal support for education with a hawkish foreign policy that took sharp aim at the Eisenhower administration for inadequate defense spending. In a January 1 essay, Kennedy blasted the White House for presiding over diminishing American power. The nation, in Kennedy's view, was "trending toward a slide downhill into dust, dullness, languor, and decay." He accused the Eisenhower administration of being passive as the communist menace grew. "We have allowed the Communists to evict us from our rightful estate at the head of the worldwide revolution. We have been made to appear as defenders of the status quo, while the Communists have portrayed themselves as the vanguard force, pointing the way to a better, brighter, and braver order of life . . . Attitudes, platitudes, and beatitudes have taken the place of a critical and vigilant intelligence marching in advance of events," he wrote.[9]

Kennedy officially announced his candidacy for the presidency on January 2, 1960, at a crowded press conference in the Senate Caucus Room. Speaking before three hundred reporters and supporters, he said the United States faced massive challenges and it was in the executive branch that "the most crucial decisions of this century must be made in the next four years." The nation needed a strategy to compete with the Soviets in the arms race, and secure freedom and order in newly emerging nations. He also called on Americans to revive science and education, prevent the collapse of the farm economy and the decay of American cities, boost economic growth, and renew the nation's moral purpose.[10]

During the first half of 1960 Kennedy was consumed with primary battles and winning the Democratic nomination, and consequently focused largely on domestic issues. In May, during the year's first televised Democratic candidates debate in West Virginia opposite Hubert Humphrey, Kennedy emphasized state and national economic issues.

But Kennedy's critique of Eisenhower was always central to his argument for running for the presidency even in the primary stages. The administration, from his perspective, was passive and penurious, tired and timid. He declared that the new generation would take a stronger and more proactive stance. A few weeks before Kennedy officially secured the Democratic presidential nomination, he blasted the administration in the aftermath of the collapsed Paris summit. In a June 14 speech on the Senate floor,

Kennedy said the unraveling of the summit "marked the end of an era—an era of illusion—the illusion that platitudes and slogans are a substitute for strength and planning—the illusion that personal goodwill is a substitute for hard, carefully prepared bargaining on concrete issues—the illusion that good intentions and pious principles are substitutes for strong, creative leadership." The United States needed a new security strategy to deal with "the most critical period in our nation's history since the bleak winter at Valley Forge." He called for an invulnerable nuclear retaliatory power, more missiles to close the gap, enhanced conventional capacity to wage limited military actions, a stronger NATO alliance, a long range solution to Berlin, a new China policy, workable programs for arms control and peace, and expanded science, research, and space programs.[11]

When he accepted the Democratic nomination at the Los Angeles Coliseum on July 15 Kennedy declared that, "after eight years of drugged and fitful sleep, this nation needs strong creative Democratic leadership in the White House." America, Kennedy said, had faltered during the Eisenhower years, "a slippage—in our intellectual and moral strength. Seven lean years of drought and famine have withered a field of ideas. Blight has descended on our regulatory agencies, and a dry rot, beginning in Washington, is seeping into every corner of America—in the payola mentality, the expense account way of life, the confusion between what is legal and what is right. Too many Americans have lost their way, their will, and their sense of historic purpose." Embracing his New Frontier theme, Kennedy said the United States needed a new generation of leaders. "All over the world, particularly in the newer nations, young men are coming to power—men who are not bound by the traditions of the past—men who are not blinded by the old fears and hates and rivalries—young men who can cast off the old slogans and delusions and suspicions." The Democratic Party, he declared, must lead the United States into the future. "For the world is changing. The old era is ending. The old ways will not do. Abroad, the balance of power is shifting. There are new and more terrible weapons, new and uncertain nations, new pressures of population and deprivation . . . More energy is released by the awakening of these new nations than by the fission of the atom itself."[12]

In the fall campaign, Kennedy was personally respectful of Eisenhower, stipulating the president had good intentions and was a man of peace who had earned the respect of the nation and world. Kennedy acknowledged that Eisenhower would have been a formidable candidate in 1960 had he been able to run again for president. But at the same time, Kennedy hammered the Eisenhower administration for a shameful record and tried to associate its failures with Nixon who as vice president claimed he was a central figure in its deliberations. Throughout August, Kennedy was mostly confined to Washington because of Congress's unusual and ultimately fruitless legislative session but that did not stop him from taking quick trips to test campaign themes. Late that month, in Alexandria, Virginia, he challenged Nixon's claim of vast governmental experience. He conceded Vice President Nixon had considerable experience—but in developing deeply flawed policies. "Never before has this country experienced such arrogant treatment at the hands of its enemies. Never before have we experienced a more critical decline in our prestige, driving our friends to neutralism, and neutrals to outright hostility, never before has the grip of communism sunk so deeply into previously friendly countries. Mr. Nixon is experienced in the policies of weakness, retreat, and defeat."[13]

Speaking a few days later in Detroit to the Veterans of Foreign Wars convention, Kennedy questioned whether the United States had ever been "treated with less respect and with such arrogance by our enemies around the world, and regarded with such doubt by our friends." The grim truth was that American power and leadership were receding and the communist world was rising. "We are the strongest power in the world today. But Communist power has been, and is now, growing faster than our own. And by Communist power I mean military power, economic power, and political power. They are moving faster than we are: on the ground, under the ocean, in the air, and out in space." Twisting the knife, Kennedy declared, "The world's first satellite was called Sputnik, not Vanguard or Explorer. The first vehicle to the moon was named Lunik. The first living creatures to orbit the earth in space and return were named Strelka and Belka, not Rover and Fido."[14] He would later expand the list of American dogs not in space to Nixon's own dog Checkers who was made famous during Nixon's effort to dispute allegations of financial improprieties in a 1952 televised speech that became known as the Checkers Speech.

In early September, Kennedy headed west and told campaign crowds the United States needed to break out of its lethargy. Kennedy vowed the animating theme of his campaign was going to be action—"action here at home to keep pace with the growing needs of an expanding country, and action abroad to meet the challenge of our adversaries." He regretted that for much of the world America was a diminished nation. "The United States looks tired. It looks like our brightest days have been in the past. It looks like the Communists are reaching for the future, and we sit back and talk about the ideals of the American Revolution. The way to put the ideals of the American Revolution into significance is to act on them, not to talk about them." Kennedy said in San Francisco that the world had become increasingly dangerous during Eisenhower's presidency and a new administration was needed to turn things around with bold domestic and foreign policies. "We live in a tumultuous world, a world of change and challenge. This may be the most important election in our lifetime. From Cuba to the Congo, from the Middle East to Formosa Strait, the earth is trembling. Only a party that understands human needs at home can understand the rising hopes of peoples overseas—and to help them peaceably find their way to freedom. Only a party that acts on behalf of the people at home can deserve leadership around the world. Only a party that believes in the future at home can help win the hearts of people who have broken with the past."[15]

Kennedy sharpened his attack on the Eisenhower administration, telling a rally at the Bergen Mall in New Jersey on September 15, "my own feeling is that in the last few years, the influence, the power, and the prestige of the United States in relationship to the Communist world has begun to decline, relatively. We are still moving ahead but we are not moving ahead fast enough. We are still strong, but we are not strong enough. We are still meeting our traditional responsibilities, but we are not doing it with traditional vigor and traditional energy."[16] Kennedy predicted to an audience in Denver the election would turn on the question of whether America had declined or flourished during the Eisenhower years. "I have premised my campaign for the presidency on the single assumption that the American people are uneasy at the present drift in the national course, that they are disturbed by the relative decline in our vitality and prestige, and that they have the will and the strength to start the United States moving again. If I am wrong in this assumption, and if the American people are satisfied with the things as they are, if Americans are undisturbed by approaching dangers, and complacent about our capacity to meet them, then I expect to lose this election. But if I am right, and I firmly believe I am right, then those who have held back the growth of the United States during the last eight years will be rejected in November and America will turn to the leadership of the Democratic Party."[17]

As the election entered its final month, Kennedy tried to exploit apparent fissures in the Republican Party between its liberal, moderate, and conservative factions. He accused Nixon of bouncing between the various groups based on the most recent polls. Kennedy charged Nixon with distancing himself from Eisenhower earlier in the year, but now was frantically seeking help from the president. "During August, he was coming to Governor [Nelson] Rockefeller's defense, and he wasn't mentioning the president, and he was not in September. But now he is attempting to embrace the President. I don't quarrel with the President. The question is the future. The question is not President Eisenhower, but President Nixon."[18]

Addressing a noontime rally outside the courthouse in Peoria, Illinois, in late October, Kennedy described the election as a battle between those who were satisfied and those who believed the nation could do better. "I believe that the 1960s are going to be the most challenging in our history, but I believe they can also be our brightest days. We have been chosen by history to be the great defenders of freedom at a time when freedom is under attack all around the globe. The next ten years may well be decisive, and I don't think any American wants historians to write that these were the years when the tide began to run out for the United States. I believe Americans want to say again that we believe in this country, that our ability to meet our assignments is unlimited, that our brightest days are still ahead, and that we are going to work again."[19]

Kennedy seized on a survey conducted by the United States Information Agency and withheld by the administration which suggested America's prestige in the world was declining. Trying to transform a single survey into definitive evidence of national decline, Kennedy said America's diminished stature in the world had tangible consequences. "But prestige is important. We face a dangerous and powerful enemy. We do not want to face him alone," he said.[20]

In the campaign's final weeks, Kennedy was concerned about Eisenhower's decision to enter the race aggressively on behalf of his vice president.

But Kennedy kept a brave and defiant public face. At a rally in Philadelphia on October 31 at Temple University, Kennedy made light of the coming trip by Nixon and Eisenhower to New York City. "What Mr. Nixon does not understand is President Eisenhower was running only in 1952 and 1956. President Eisenhower is not a candidate. Mr. Nixon is. Mr. Nixon and I are going to face the voters alone next November 8 no matter what the president of the United States may choose to do this week in New York or any place else. It is Nixon versus Kennedy, the Republicans versus the Democrats, and I look to the future with some degree of hope." Pretending to be unconcerned by Ike's forceful entry into the campaign, Kennedy mocked the Nixon campaign's embrace of the president. "President Eisenhower is now leading the rescue squad . . . You have seen the elephants in the circus? Do you know how they travel around the circus? By grabbing the tail of the elephant in front of them. That was all right in 1952 and 1956. Mr. Nixon hung on tight. But now Mr. Nixon meets the people. The choice is not President Eisenhower."[21]

While Kennedy was personally respectful of Eisenhower on the campaign trail, he couldn't resist some jabs. When he arrived late for campaign events Kennedy often apologized by saying he had been busy campaigning, not golfing—an obvious dig at Eisenhower who was an avid golfer. He also sometimes included in his campaign speeches a line from a T. S. Eliot poem: "And the wind shall say: 'These were a decent people, their only monument the asphalt road and a thousand lost golf balls,'" a reference to the thinness of Eisenhower's accomplishments and his love of the links.[22]

IV

The intended recipient of Senator Kennedy's attacks on the Eisenhower administration was not, of course, Dwight Eisenhower, but Vice President Richard Nixon, the Republican candidate for president. Kennedy was determined to blame Nixon for the administration's failures and deprive him of credit for its accomplishments. Nixon's actual role in the administration was complicated. As vice president he attended weekly cabinet, National Security Council, and legislative meetings, and even chaired the sessions in Eisenhower's absence. He served as a liaison with Congress, met with foreign leaders when they visited Washington, traveled extensively as an envoy for the president, and was the administration's top spokesman during political campaigns. Nixon was clearly a central figure in the administration's policy debates, but Eisenhower, as the president himself reminded reporters repeatedly, was the only one who made the final decisions. Kennedy might have painted Eisenhower as a passive president, but in reality, that was hardly the case.

Complicating the campaign was Eisenhower's ambivalence toward Nixon that was palpable—and had been for eight years. Eisenhower never felt comfortable with Nixon; they were from different generations and had starkly different backgrounds, temperaments, and political experiences. When the president discussed with others who should be his successor, Nixon's name was rarely near the top of the list and sometimes seemed to rate only a dutiful mention. As Eisenhower prepared to run for reelection in 1956, he suggested to Nixon that he not run again as vice president but instead take a senior job in the cabinet such as secretary of defense. Ike said this would broaden Nixon's administrative and management skills. Eisenhower proposed this move to Nixon as part of a job rotation practice that was common in the military, not a career-altering demotion. But not surprisingly Nixon had no interest in leaving the vice presidency and Eisenhower ultimately—but not immediately—asked Nixon to run on the ticket with him again in 1956.[23]

Even with Eisenhower's evident coolness toward his vice president, Nixon used his tenure to build strong contacts with Republicans across the country. By late 1959, Nixon was Eisenhower's heir apparent as the Republican nominee for president, especially after New York Governor Nelson Rockefeller announced that he was not going to seek the presidential nomination. Rockefeller was a leading Republican who many in the party believed was best suited for the presidency. His decision not to run effectively cleared the field for Nixon who announced his candidacy through a statement by his press spokesman on January 9, 1960.

Nixon ran in every Republican primary that year and waged a vigorous campaign even though he ran unopposed. He wanted to build a formidable political organization, stay in the news, activate the Republican grass roots, and test themes for the fall. In his travels and on the stump, Nixon repeatedly said he was proud of his role in the Eisenhower administration and was determined to build on its record with new initiatives and not just rest on past accomplishments. However, Nixon's political situation grew more complicated in the spring and summer of 1960 when Rockefeller indicated he was not satisfied with the administration, or Nixon, on a range of domestic and foreign policies, and warned he might not support the Republican ticket enthusiastically in the fall. Given Rockefeller's standing in the party, his opposition or indifference to Nixon's candidacy would be a serious blow. With the Republican National Convention about to begin on July 25 and as the GOP's platform committee hammered together the final version, Rockefeller's displeasure escalated. Fearing a public rift, Nixon sought a meeting and traveled to confer with the New York governor at his Fifth Avenue luxury apartment. After dinner the two men and their aides stayed up all night negotiating a statement—dubbed the Treaty of Fifth Avenue—that Rockefeller released and with which Nixon said he was in "basic agreement." To many, including Eisenhower, Rockefeller's statement was an outrageous and gratuitous attack on the administration in important areas. It cited insufficient spending for defense programs, saying accusingly there should be "no price ceiling for American security." Eisenhower was furious and let Nixon know he was displeased with the Rockefeller-Nixon formulation. Nixon scrambled for acceptable language to submit to the Republican Convention then gathering in Chicago. He cobbled together a compromise that appeased, but did not thrill, either Rockefeller or Eisenhower.[24]

When Nixon addressed the Republican convention in Chicago on July 28 as the party's presidential nominee, he presented himself as a grateful and supportive member of the administration and an admiring fan of the president. Nixon referred to Eisenhower as "one of the great men of our century," adding that "for generations to come Americans, regardless of party, will gratefully remember Dwight Eisenhower as the man who brought peace to America, as the man under whose leadership America enjoyed the greatest progress and prosperity in history, but, above all, who restored honesty, integrity, and dignity to the conduct of government in the highest office of this land." Speaking to a roaring crowd of Republicans, Nixon praised the record of the administration but also indicated that new initiatives were needed. The vice president declared he was proud to be part of the "best eight-year record of any administration in the history of this country," but added he was not content to rest on the administration's accomplishments. A record, he said, "is not something to stand on, but something to build on, and building on the great record of this Administration, we shall build a better America." The next president, he warned, would face challenges even greater than those that confronted Abraham Lincoln when he accepted the Republican presidential nomination in 1860. "The question then was freedom for slaves and the survival of the Nation. The question now is freedom for all mankind and the survival of civilization." It was important to recognize the foreign policy problems of the sixties "will be different and they'll be vastly more difficult than those of the fifties through which we have just passed." Nixon vowed to get America back on the offensive. "It is not enough for us to reply that our aim is to contain communism, to defend the free world against communism, to hold the line against communism. The only answer to a strategy of victory for the Communist world is a strategy of victory for the free world." The vice president assailed Democrats for using their recent convention in Los Angeles to criticize the administration, lament America's decline, and emphasize the problems facing the United States rather than celebrating its preeminence.[25]

After winning the nomination, Nixon selected as his running mate Henry Cabot Lodge, Eisenhower's ambassador to the United Nations and a former senator from Massachusetts. In fact, it was Lodge who Kennedy defeated in 1952 to gain entry into the Senate. Nixon's selection of Lodge further solidified the vice president's identification with the Eisenhower administration. Nixon left Chicago with a clear message for the fall campaign: that he was an active member of the successful Eisenhower team and wanted to build on its record of domestic and international accomplishments. He pledged to travel to all fifty states before Election Day, commending Eisenhower as a strong leader who had produced peace and prosperity. Nixon and Lodge met with Eisenhower after the convention to discuss the battle ahead. The president said he wanted to help the Republican ticket win in November and believed his best contribution would be to continue to do his job as president, explain and defend the administration's record in nonpolitical speeches, and then deliver several political speeches just before the voters went to the polls. According to Nixon, Eisenhower's chief of staff, Wilton Persons, told him he was convinced the president would want to take a more active role in the fall campaign when the race heated up and Democrats stepped up their attacks on his administration.[26]

Like Kennedy, Nixon was also confined to Washington for several weeks in August during the special legislative session in his capacity as president of the Senate. In fact, the two rivals would occasionally see each other in the Senate, with Nixon sitting in the presiding officer's chair at the front of the chamber and with Kennedy chatting easily with his Democratic colleagues in the back row of the Senate. Between the Chicago convention and the August congressional session, Nixon took a quick campaign trip to Hawaii and outlined many of the themes he would use and refine over the coming months. He was "very proud to be a member of the Eisenhower administration" and was convinced Ike "will go down in history as one of the great presidents."[27] While embracing the administration, Nixon also tried to establish some distance from it. In remarks that month in Portland, Maine, Nixon hinted he did not agree with every position taken by the administration but he was evasive about what specific policies he differed with. Nixon said vaguely that he sometimes made policy proposals within the administration that were not accepted. "You argue these points out within an administration. You urge your point of view. And then where your point of view is not adopted, then that is the administration policy." He insisted it would be inappropriate to identify every issue on which he differed with the president but would spell out proposals during the campaign that made these differences evident.[28]

The official launch of Nixon's fall campaign took place at Friendship Airport outside of Baltimore where he and Lodge were joined by Eisenhower and members of the cabinet. Driven indoors by a hard rain, Nixon remained in high spirits and exulted in the presence of the president, whom he addressed with considerable deference. "We are proud of the record that you have made the past seven and a half years, a record that has brought peace to America . . . and that has brought progress to our people. We are proud of that record, and we welcome the opportunity not only to run on it but to build on it and to build on it in the years ahead, as you want the next president and the next vice president to build on it." Then edging toward hero-worship Nixon said, "We thank you for the standards you set in your great campaigns, and we hope that we, in these next eight hard weeks, grueling weeks, can maintain the dignity which you always maintained in your campaigns, that we can take on the great issues, that we can maintain our balance and present always to the people the cause for which we stand in a way that they can understand it, in a way that can have a clear choice between where we stand and where our opponents stand; and if we meet your standards we will have served our party, but more than that, we will have served America, and that will assure the victory toward which we are working."[29]

A day later in Boise, Idaho, Nixon said the main challenge of the next president would be to maintain the peace and prosperity brought about by the current administration. He credited the president with extracting the United States from the Korean War, keeping it out of other conflicts and preserving the peace without surrender. But he also noted there were continuing challenges posed by the nation's communist rivals. "We are in a race and we are confronted with men who, whatever we may think of their system, are determined and fanatical. They are working hard and they are driving their people at an unmerciful pace and they are determined to catch us." Nixon insisted the nation made major advances during Eisenhower's tenure. "America has progressed over the last eight years to unparalleled heights of solid economic accomplishment. But we cannot rest there. To meet the growing needs of an expanding population, and to meet our worldwide responsibilities, we must step up the development of all our national resources."[30]

Speaking on September 24 in Lafayette, Louisiana, Nixon credited the Eisenhower administration with many accomplishments but insisted there was still more to do, and he even offered a few specifics. "We must move forward—better jobs, better living conditions, better security for our old people. We must move forward as well in providing better schools, better hospitals, all the things that spell progress for a people who are as vital and forward-looking as the American people." Nixon recalled that he and Lodge participated in deliberations in the cabinet and the National Security Council and conferred with the president on many issues "which involved maintaining the line between war on the one side and surrender on the other." They had been trained by Eisenhower and they carefully observed him. Nixon was impressed that the president was always measured, remained calm, never answered insults with his own insults, and drew from history to inform his decisions. Eisenhower was a superb role model and Nixon said he hoped to draw on his experiences once he reached the White House.[31]

Nixon frequently ripped into Kennedy for overpromising what he would do as president and for downgrading America. "Senator Kennedy has promised many things in this campaign," Nixon complained in a speech in Charlotte, North Carolina. "These he has promised for a nation which he views darkly as being on the defensive in a world dominated by communism, held in contempt by those who love freedom, its military forces relatively weak and out of date, a tenth of its people verging on starvation, its educational system woefully behind, the entire nation teetering on economic depression—and one of its two great political parties dead set against human welfare, addicted to human misery, against the decent schooling for children, anxious for the elderly to live in poorhouses and unattended when ill—a party truly content only when people are out of work. This strange preoccupation with despair has led Senator Kennedy to urge some very interesting proposals."[32]

In the final week of the campaign Nixon was joined by Eisenhower for events in and around New York City and he basked in the president's star quality and ability to draw massive crowds. On election eve, Nixon spoke about Eisenhower with near reverence. "I do not suggest to you my friends that I have the ability that President Eisenhower has had. Here is one of the wisest men who has ever lived in this nation or on this earth." But he added that he would do all that he could to build on the Eisenhower legacy.[33]

V

Most accounts of the 1960 campaign consider in some detail the four televised debates between Kennedy and Nixon. They have entered into the mythology of the campaign with many contemporary analysts, and later historians, convinced the debates were where Kennedy won and Nixon lost the election. Especially during the first debate with seventy million Americans watching, Kennedy seemed cool, calm, and collected and Nixon looked ill, uneasy, and uncomfortable.

Each candidate largely used the debates to deliver his basic message, reformulating questions so he could return to his familiar talking points.

Kennedy seized on every opportunity to argue that the United States was failing to meet the harsh challenge of its communist adversaries and he posited that America's standing in the world was slipping. The United States, the Democratic challenger declared, had to get moving again and needed a new, vigorous regime to drive the effort. For his part, Nixon praised the accomplishments of the administration, vowed to build on its record of success and rebuked Kennedy for finding so much at fault with America. The vice president said the United States was still the world's preeminent military, economic, diplomatic, and moral leader, and he was eager to build on these strengths while tackling new challenges.

During the first debate in Chicago on September 26, Kennedy quickly seized on an opening to make his central argument. "This is a great country, but I think it could be a greater country, and this is a powerful country, but I think it could be a more powerful country . . . If you feel that everything that is being done now is satisfactory, that the relative power and prestige and strength of the United States is increasing in relation to that of the Communists, that we are gaining more security, that we are achieving everything as a nation that we should achieve, that we are achieving a better life for our citizens and greater strength, then I agree. I think you should vote for Mr. Nixon." But his point was clearly that if voters felt the country needed fresh energy and strong leadership they should vote for him.[34]

Nixon disputed Kennedy's claim of American stagnation, citing economic and foreign policy successes during the previous eight years, and then proclaimed, "Now, this is not standing still, but good as this record is, may I emphasize it isn't enough. A record is never something to stand on, it's something to build on, and in building on this record I believe that we have the secret for progress. We know the way to progress and I think first of all our own record proves that we know the way."[35]

During the second debate in Washington, D.C., on October 7, Nixon sharply disputed Kennedy's assertion that America was losing its global preeminence. Such a claim, he declared, undermined the United States and was particularly unhelpful because the Soviet leader was then in New York attending the United Nations General Assembly. "I don't think he [Kennedy] should say that our prestige is at an all-time low. I think this is very harmful at a time Mr. Khrushchev is here, harmful because it's wrong . . . I think we ought to emphasize America's strength. It isn't necessary to run America down in order to build her up."[36] Kennedy responded that America had slipped during the Eisenhower years but his primary focus was on the future. "President Eisenhower moves from the scene on January 20 and the next four years are critical years. And that's the debate, that's the argument between Mr. Nixon and myself and on that issue the American people have to make their judgment. I think in many ways this election is more important than any since 1932, or certainly, almost any in this century because we disagree very fundamentally on the position of the United States and if his view prevails, then I think that's going to bring an important result to this country in the '60s."[37]

For the third debate on October 13, Kennedy was in New York and Nixon in Los Angeles. Despite being separated by a continent the two candidates remained on attack and on message. Kennedy said the United States should go on the offensive. "If we are on the mount, if we are rising, if our influence is spreading, if our prestige is spreading, then those who stand now on the razor edge of decision between us or between the Communist system . . . they will be persuaded to follow our example."[38] Nixon repeated that he was proud of the administration's record but pledged to do even more. "America has not been standing still. Let's get it straight. Anybody who says America has been standing still for the last seven and a half years hasn't been traveling around America. He's been traveling in some other country. We have been moving. We have been moving much faster than we did in the Truman years, but we can and must move faster."[39]

During the final debate on October 21 in New York, Nixon reiterated that the administration had accomplished a great deal and he would do even more. "And so I say that the record shows that we know how to keep the peace, to keep it without surrender. Let us move now to the future. It is not enough to stand on this record because we are dealing with the most ruthless, fanatical leaders that the world has ever seen. That is why I say that in this period of the sixties America must move forward in every area." Nixon chided Kennedy for reflexively criticizing the United States. "America's prestige abroad will be just as high as the spokesmen for America allow it to be."[40] Kennedy said the rivalry between the United States and the communist world might be decided in the coming decade, and that America needed to do more. "I believe the world is changing fast . . . I think we're going to have to do better. Mr. Nixon talks about our being the strongest country in the world. I think we are today, but we were far stronger relative to the Communists five years ago. And what is of great concern is that the balance of power is in danger of moving with them . . . I'm not as confident as he is that we will be the strongest military power by 1963." But Kennedy also offered a hopeful vision for the future. "I want people all over the world to look to the United States again, to feel that we're on the move, to feel that our high noon is in the future . . . I don't believe there is anything this country cannot do. I don't believe there's any burden or any responsibility that any American would not assume to protect his country, protect our security, to advance the cause of freedom."[41] While the 1960 presidential debates were not the one-sided trouncing of Nixon by Kennedy that many now assume, they constituted a watershed event in which many millions of Americans decided they could envision the much less known Kennedy as president.

VI

Dwight Eisenhower was not eager to relinquish the presidency, certainly not to John Kennedy, and not even to his long-serving vice president for whom he had both grudging respect and substantial reservations. Eisenhower almost dropped Nixon from the GOP ticket in 1952 over a campaign finance controversy that Nixon defused with his Checkers speech in which he insisted he had done nothing wrong and was not going to return various gifts, especially the family dog. By 1960, Eisenhower regarded Nixon as a loyal and diligent member of his administration. But he was slow to endorse him as the Republican presidential nominee even as he ran unopposed. Eisenhower frequently offered muted praise for Nixon and occasionally derided him to his friends and aides in private. He told one aide, Len Hall, that Nixon "looks like a loser to me."[42] Several times throughout the first weeks of 1960 Eisenhower pointedly declined to endorse his vice president to become the Republican nominee. During a press conference on February 3 the president was asked if he supported Nixon as the Republican candidate for president. His answer was almost painfully evasive. "I maintain that there are a number of Republicans, eminent men, big men, that could fill the requirements of the position. And until the nominations are a matter of history, why, I think I should not talk too much about an individual."[43] Finally, speaking at the Gridiron Club gala in early March, Eisenhower indirectly endorsed Nixon. When he was pressed by reporters to go on the record with his endorsement at a March 16 press conference he finally did, but he did not bring up the subject and only confirmed it when a reporter mentioned Nixon by name.[44]

If Eisenhower was reluctant to endorse Nixon—or anybody else—for president, he was eager to recite the accomplishments of his administration. Throughout 1960 Eisenhower looked for opportunities to explain what his administration had done since assuming power in 1953. He used speeches to explain and defend his record and make the case for the election of a Republican successor. Eisenhower was angry and frustrated by frequent Democratic attacks on his record, especially those unleashed by the leading Democratic presidential candidates: John Kennedy, Lyndon Johnson, Stuart Symington, and Hubert Humphrey. Eisenhower responded forcefully to Democratic criticisms but rarely mentioned the names of his critics. He vowed to avoid personalities and believed that addressing specific critics only served to elevate them.

In his State of the Union address to Congress on January 7, 1960, Eisenhower said there had been considerable progress in the past seven years and he felt certain that 1960 would be the most prosperous year in American history.[45] Later that month, Eisenhower traveled to Los Angeles and addressed, via closed circuit TV, party rallies across the country. "Republicans," he declared, "have faith in America, her strength, her destiny. Yet, in late years, the tendency to disparage the unmatched power and prestige of our country has become an obsession with noisy extremists. Time and again we hear spurious assertions that America's defenses are weak, that her economic expansive force can be sustained only by federal spending, that her educational and health efforts are deficient."[46]

During the early weeks of 1960, Ike grew testy when reporters suggested that Nixon was trying to distance himself from various administration policies, but declined to spell out what those differences were. On February 11, Eisenhower told a press conference that he had worked with Nixon for more than seven years and did not know of any major issue on which they differed. The following month Eisenhower repeated this contention saying, "So far as I know, there has never been a specific difference in our points of view on any important problem in seven years."[47] At another press conference in March, the president acknowledged that Nixon needed to show that he would do more as president than rest on the record of the Eisenhower administration. "Now I should think he would be absolutely stupid if he said that you were going as far as the record of this administration would carry you and then stop. This world moves. . . . If he doesn't say that he is going to build on what has been so far accomplished, I think he would be very foolish."[48]

The high point of Eisenhower's defense of his own record occurred when he addressed the Republican National Convention in Chicago on July 26. After a raucous welcome by the convention, the president had much to say about his accomplishments, notably on the economy, medical research, science and technology, and foreign policy, but nothing to say about his vice president who was poised to claim the Republican presidential nomination. In fact, in his prepared speech, Eisenhower did not even mention Nixon's name. He was more intent on explaining his record and answering Democratic attacks than in advancing Nixon's candidacy. "I glory in the moral, economic, and military strength of this nation, in the ideals that she upholds before the world," he intoned. "So to this convention I bring no words of despair or doubt about my country—no doleful prediction of impending disaster. In this election campaign of 1960, I pray that Republicans will always remember the greatness of our nation and will talk only the truth about her—because, my friends, in spreading the truth we are not only being true to our national ideals but we are planting the fertile seeds of political victory." Eisenhower said Republicans should use the coming presidential campaign as an educational endeavor in which they presented their record to the American people. "The irrefutable truths are that the United States is enjoying an unprecedented prosperity; that it has, in cooperation with its friends and allies, the strongest security system in the world, and that it is working ceaselessly and effectively for peace and justice, in freedom." The United States was a stronger force in the world, according to the president, because of his administration and he rebuked the "cult of professional pessimists who, taking counsel of their fears, continually mouth the allegation that America has become a second-rate military power. This extraordinary assertion amazes our friends in the world who know better; it even bewilders many of our own people who have examined our seven and a half year record of military expansion and who are not used to hearing their gigantic defense efforts so belittled . . . In this Administration we have employed the whole might of our military, economic, political, and moral strength to prevent war and to build a solid structure of peace."[49]

At an August 10 press conference, Eisenhower reiterated that he strongly supported the new Republican ticket and was eager to do all that he could to help secure its victory in November. He said he could best promote the Republican ticket by continuing his work as president and allowing Nixon and Lodge to fend for themselves on the campaign trail.[50] On August 24, the president repeated that he wanted to help the new ticket, adding he expected to deliver two or three political speeches on behalf of the GOP candidates for president and vice president. It was at this press conference that Eisenhower made a comment that did Nixon considerable political damage. Asked several times about Nixon's role in his administration, Eisenhower said he had participated in critical meetings and delibera-tions but he—the president—naturally made all decisions. When pressed again by Charles Mohr of *Time* to provide an example of a major decision that Nixon helped make, Ike quipped, "If you give me a week, I might think of one. I don't remember."[51] Eisenhower later told Nixon he was being facetious but this comment was seized on and frequently cited by Democrats throughout the fall. It appeared to undermine one of Nixon's central claims—that he had been an active and influential participant in the Eisenhower administration.

As noted earlier, the president attended the Nixon-Lodge campaign launch at Friendship Airport near Baltimore on September 12 and lavished praise on the new Republican ticket. "They are going out as messengers—messengers to carry to every nook and corner of this country the story of the record that has been established by Republican leadership in the House, the Senate, and in the executive department over the past eight years. They are going out with a promise to build upon that record, respectful of its past accomplishments, but never satisfied that the answers have yet been reached to America's problems."[52]

At a 1960 Victory Fund Rally in Chicago in late September Eisen-hower touted Nixon's role in his administration, citing his experience in both domestic and foreign policy. "For eight years I have worked closely with him. During these years Dick Nixon has participated with me, and high officials of your government, in hundreds of important deliberative proceedings of the Cabinet, the National Security Council, and other agencies . . . His counsel has been invaluable." Eisenhower then took some clear swipes at Kennedy. "Leadership is not proved by a mere whirling across the public stage in a burst of glib oratory . . . We want presidential leadership that rejects both irresponsible promises and deceptively simple solutions to national problems. We are against leadership that seeks to center all government in Washington. We want leadership that sees government as the willing partner, not the controller of human progress and achievement." Eisenhower also rebuked Kennedy—without mentioning his name—for running a campaign that focused on America's problems. "We do not want leadership that sees only dark continents of despair in American life—leadership that has a stultifying preoccupation with our faults. We do want leadership that gauges our problems with definitive care, and then produces a solution patterned carefully to the problem, regardless of the carping of the irresponsible." The president urged Americans to vote in November for "a trained team, unmatched in experience in the affairs of modern diplomacy."[53]

As the campaign entered its final month, Eisenhower received pessimistic assessments from Republican officials about the Nixon-Lodge ticket. He suggested to Nixon that his campaign needed more "zip." The president grew increasingly angry as Kennedy and other Democrats charged the nation had lost its energy and purpose. In a speech at Rice University on October 24, Eisenhower derided the "false fears and empty promises" coming from some quarters. He also hit the glamour and glitz of Kennedy at the expense of less celebrated virtues. "Steadiness, solvency, and balance. These may seem prosaic and uninteresting to talk about in times when people are being promised, without cost, the good life for all," he said.[54]

After the four presidential debates bolstered Kennedy's candidacy and weakened Nixon's, Eisenhower decided to take a more active role in defending his record, attacking the Democrats and advocating for the Nixon-Lodge ticket. He had been waiting anxiously for Nixon to ask him to aggressively join the campaign. Other Republican leaders pleaded with Eisenhower to step forward and promote the ticket. Eisenhower addressed a Republican rally in Philadelphia on October 28, successfully energizing the crowd with his forceful remarks. He rebuked the "glib political oratory" of the Democrats and said a leader needed character, ability, responsibility, and experience. He must, the president intoned, be "free of rashness, of arrogance, of headlong action, of the inclination to easy compromise." Eisenhower seized on Kennedy's remark that he would make swift and strong decisions. "My friends, America needs a man who will think first, and then act wisely." He then blamed Kennedy—again without directly mentioning his name—for bashing America. "Whatever was America's image abroad at the beginning of this political campaign, it tends to become blurred today. This is because of unwarranted disparagement of our own moral, military, and economic power . . . Anyone who seeks to grasp the reins of world leadership should not spend all of his time wringing his hands." He also disputed Kennedy's claim the nation had grown stagnant. "Of course 'America must move.' But forward—not backward. Not back to inflation—not back to bureaucratic controls—not back to deficit spending—not back to higher taxes, and bigger government. We found all of these in 1952. America must continue to go forward—with maturity, with judgment, with balance. I see no good in America galloping in reverse to what has been called a New Frontier." The president endorsed the Nixon-Lodge ticket as a "superlative team, prepared in every respect to lead our country responsibly and well."[55]

In the final week of the campaign, Eisenhower joined Nixon and Lodge for events in the New York City area, including a remarkable ticker tape parade down Broadway past several hundred thousand people. Speaking at the Westchester County Airport, the president defended his administration and the Republican ticket. "The last eight years have been the most remarkable in the growth of the United States than in any other peacetime period in its history." He challenged the central premise of Kennedy's campaign. "Now I've heard complaints about the country not moving. My contention is that isn't good enough. Of course you can move easily—you can move back on inflation, you can move back to deficit spending, you can move back to the military weakness that allowed the Korean War to occur, you can move back to a lot of things—no trouble at all."[56] Later that day at a rally at the New York Coliseum, the president continued to defend his record. "At home our economy has become immeasurably stronger. In every index by which we measure strength and development, the last eight years have been the brightest of our history."[57]

Two days later in Cleveland, Eisenhower accused the Democrats of trying to impose big government solutions on the nation and ridiculed Kennedy's foreign policy credentials. "Now where did this young genius acquire the knowledge, experience, and the wisdom through which he will make such vast improvements over the work of the Joint Chiefs of Staff, and the dedicated civilian and service men who have given their lives to this work?"[58] Speaking later that day, Eisenhower responded to Kennedy's taunt that Nixon had begged the president to lead a Republican rescue squad to save his faltering presidential bid. "This morning my headlines in the Washington papers said I was a member of a rescue squad. I said this is right. In 1952 I joined with a good many million Americas to rescue us from a lot . . . So I am very proud to be in this rescue squad, because I think that the millions with whom I joined at that time have done a very splendid job."[59] Eisenhower continued to hammer Kennedy in a speech in Pittsburgh, ridiculing "the juggling of promises by the inexperienced, the appeal to immediate gain and selfishness, the distortion of fact, the quick changes from fantastic charge to covert retreat—all these are intended to confuse the voter; not to enlighten him." He accused Kennedy of planning to throw money at problems without regard to cost. "These wizards in fiscal shell games try to prove that all problems can be solved by bigger government, bigger spending, bigger promises. They are idolatrous worshippers of bigness—especially government." The president also praised Nixon and Lodge as leaders he had groomed, saying they were "tried and trained, tested and proved worthy." And he warned the world would be more dangerous, and America more imperiled with Kennedy in the Oval Office. "When the push of a button may mean obliteration of countless humans, the President of the United States must be forever on guard against any inclination on his part to impetuosity, to arrogance, to headlong action, to expediency, to facile maneuvers, even to the popularity of an action as opposed to the rightness of an action."[60]

On election eve, Eisenhower addressed the nation on radio and television. He challenged Kennedy's claim of American decline and praised Americans for the strong progress they had achieved over the past eight years. "You made the United States the most powerful nation on earth—militarily, economically and spiritually . . . Far from standing still, you have advanced dramatically." He pleaded with voters to think very hard about their coming decision. "My friends, I have one all-consuming desire: I want our country to continue along the paths of peace and progress that she has trod so confidently for eight years. I want America to have the most experienced, the most responsible leadership that we can produce."[61]

However, on Election Day 1960 Americans narrowly decided to make Kennedy their next president. This was a devastating blow for Eisenhower that seemed to repudiate his work over the previous eight years and rejected his passionate warnings on the campaign trail. He was disappointed, angry, and hurt by the outcome. All these feelings would continue throughout the next ten weeks, but he was committed to presiding over a transfer of power that would serve America well.

As the campaign ended and the transition began, Eisenhower and Kennedy didn't really know each other. They had met several times in group meetings and had exchanged routine correspondence. Needless to say, the 1960 presidential campaign did not bring them closer together. While Kennedy had carefully avoided direct attacks on Eisenhower, he had ridiculed his administration and derided and ultimately defeated his vice president. While Eisenhower had barely uttered Kennedy's name during the campaign, he had alluded to him as a "young genius" and a "wizard of shell games." His contempt for him was unmistakable. To aides, he was both more colorful and withering in his assessment of the young senator who he referred to as "Kennedy," as if he were still a junior officer during the war—which is how he seemed to view him.

But now the two men had to put this all aside and organize a transfer of power in ten weeks. Eisenhower confronted the challenge and sadness of shutting down an administration, closing out a long and distinguished career of public service, and saying farewell to the American people. Kennedy faced the challenge of confirming his electoral win, closing down his Senate career, staffing a new administration, developing a policy agenda, and preparing an inaugural address that would unite the nation that was so evenly divided, as the election results showed. There was a lot to do in ten weeks and the country and the world were watching. To better understand this transition, it is important to better understand the two men who presided over it: Dwight Eisenhower and John Kennedy.

FOUR

THE AGE OF EISENHOWER

I

At the end of his first full day as president of the United States on January 21, 1953, Dwight Eisenhower took a few minutes to gather his thoughts and jot down a diary entry. The new president could have been forgiven for feeling triumphant, or awed, or overwhelmed by his new responsibilities. Instead he was resolved. "My first day at the President's desk," he wrote. "Plenty of worry and difficult problems. But such has been my portion for a long time—the result is that this just seems like a continuation of all I've been doing since July '41—even before." Later he was to recall his first visit to the Oval Office as president in more grandiose terms. "There had been dramatic events in my life before but none surpassed, emotionally crossing the threshold to an office of such awesome responsibility. Remembering my beginnings I had to smile."[1]

Eisenhower's journey to the White House was remarkable, forged by a buoyant personality, loving family, iron discipline, remarkable mentors, considerable good fortune, and unwavering self-confidence. His was a Norman Rockwell–like life story.

Eisenhower was born in Dennison, Texas, on October 14, 1890, the third of seven sons of Ida and David Eisenhower. He spent his childhood years in Abilene, Kansas, where his mother was the family's all-purpose problem-solver and his father the breadwinner who worked at the local creamery. Ida was warm and vibrant; David was stern and imposing. "Father had quick judicial instincts. Mother had, like a psychologist, insight into the fact that each son was a unique personality and she adapted her methods," Ike later recalled.[2]

Eisenhower fondly described his "cheerful and vital" family in which everyone worked together, the children respected their parents, and the boys were encouraged to be confident and ambitious but not arrogant or cocky. Eisenhower was an affable boy with solid work habits, a love of history and sports, and a fierce temper. He once punched a tree with his hand in frustration and his mother admonished him by quoting from scripture that the person who conquers his own soul is greater than the one who would capture a city. "I have always looked back on that conversation as one of the most valuable moments of my life," he said.[3]

Young Ike got into various scrapes with local boys and drew from them several lessons. "I quickly learned never to negotiate with an adversary except from a position of strength," he said. Ike also learned that the "pounding from an opponent is not to be dreaded as much as constantly living in fear of another." Still another lesson was the importance of a little help from his brothers to get out of a jam. Once cornered by two local toughs, Ike braced for their attack. But to his astonishment and delight his brother Edgar unexpectedly arrived on the scene to save the day. "I cannot recall any time, even in World War II, when unexpected reinforcements were more gladly received," he said years later.[4]

With modest family resources, Ike worked in a creamery after graduating from high school before taking entrance exams for both the Naval Academy and West Point. He said he was initially less enamored with a military career than attending a military academy for an expense-free college education. He passed regional exams for both. But he was then too old to enter Annapolis, and so Ike, despite his mother's strong misgivings, left home and entered the U.S. Military Academy at West Point in 1911. He was part of the fabled class of 1915, which produced sixty generals. Ike was an average student, finishing 61 out of 164. He displayed an affinity for football, a penchant for mischief, flashes of excellence, and unmistakable leadership skills.

After graduation he was commissioned a second lieutenant and sent to a post in San Antonio where, among other things, he met his future wife, Mamie Geneva Doud, who was the daughter of a successful Denver businessman. They were married in 1916, had one son in 1917 who died as an infant from scarlet fever, and a second son, John, who was born in 1922. During World War I, Eisenhower commanded a tank training center. But much to his disappointment the war ended before he was sent overseas. He felt certain this would damage his career. "I suppose we'll spend the rest of our lives explaining why we didn't get into this war," Ike lamented.[5]

In 1919 he joined the Army's Transcontinental Motor Convoy, involving more than eighty vehicles and nearly three hundred men on a trip across the United States to study the nation's roads. The cavalcade stretched more than two miles and included cars, trucks, ambulances, and motorcycles. Beginning near the White House in Washington and ending in San Francisco, the 3,250-mile trip was, according to one historian, "an adventure, a circus, a public relations coup, and a war game all rolled into one."[6] Ike was a hard-working part of the team who was also renowned as a skilled prankster. He said he participated in the trip "partly as a lark, partly to learn." He saw a slice of the United States, experienced the nation's woeful roads, and was part of a team which he relished. "We were like a troupe of traveling clowns," he recalled.[7]

While serving with the army in the Panama Canal Zone from 1922 to 1924 Eisenhower came under the tutelage of General Fox Conner. A modest Mississippian, Conner encouraged Ike to read widely, think seriously, and aspire for excellence. Conner took Eisenhower under his wing and inspired him to study military history and the classics, and ultimately redirected his career. Ike later said Conner was "the ablest man I ever knew" and one whom he owed an "incalculable debt."[8] Conner helped Eisenhower secure a coveted spot in the army's command and general staff school at

Fort Leavenworth, Kansas. The once average student finished first in his class and graduated from the Army War College two years later. He took pride in his profession and was determined to excel. "My ambition in the army was to make everybody I worked for regretful when I was ordered to other duty," he later said.[9]

General John Pershing was another important mentor to Eisenhower. In 1927 Ike worked for Pershing on the Battle Monuments Commission, which was charged to chronicle America's World War I effort and prepare a battlefield guide. For this assignment Ike visited Europe for the first time, traveling extensively in France. Though charmed by France, where he shared lunches with farmers in the countryside, Eisenhower found Pershing cool and remote. While helping Pershing with his memoirs, Ike met another soldier who was to become critical to his career, George Marshall. Eisenhower and Marshall disagreed on how Pershing should organize his writings but the encounter created respect, not acrimony, between the two young men.

General Douglas MacArthur was Eisenhower's most challenging and difficult boss. Eisenhower worked for MacArthur, then the Army Chief of Staff, in Washington in 1930, and their association continued until 1939 when they helped the Philippines reorganize its army. Ike found MacArthur brilliant, demanding, and mostly indifferent to the line between civilian and military affairs. If MacArthur "ever recognized the existence of that line, he usually chose to ignore it," Ike observed.[10] Reflecting his volatile nature, MacArthur lavished praise on Eisenhower as the best staff officer he ever met and later ridiculed him as the "best clerk I ever had."

George Marshall was the final critical mentor in Eisenhower's life, although they were near contemporaries. While they had met briefly during Eisenhower's work for Pershing, Ike caught Marshall's eye during war games in Washington State in 1940 and Louisiana in 1941 in which Ike skillfully orchestrated the movements of hundreds of thousands of soldiers. Marshall was the Army Chief of Staff when the Japanese invaded Pearl Harbor in 1941, about fifteen years after Marshall first focused on the promise of Ike. He immediately summoned Eisenhower, then a Lieutenant Colonel, to Washington and asked for his advice on American strategy in the Pacific. Eisenhower retired to a private office and in the course of several hours conceived of a plan that he typed on three pages and presented to Marshall in an oral briefing. It became the basis of the American strategy.

Marshall assigned Eisenhower jobs of steadily escalating responsibility, first in his war planning office in Washington and then in London as head of the European theater. Eisenhower rose steadily up the ranks, commanding Operation Torch that captured North Africa from the Nazis, directing the Sicily invasion that led to the conquest of Italy, and ultimately commanding Operation Overlord and the historic D-Day invasion on June 6, 1944. When American involvement in World War II began on December 7, 1941, Eisenhower was a well-regarded but obscure military man. By the time of Germany's surrender and Hitler's suicide in the summer of 1945 he was a global superstar. Marshall, famously reluctant to give compliments, sent Eisenhower a letter for the ages after the German surrender. "You have completed your mission with the greatest victory in the history of warfare . . . Since the day of your arrival in England three years ago, you have been selfless in your actions, always sound and tolerant in your judgments, and altogether admirable in the courage and wisdom of your military decisions. You have made history, great history, for the good of mankind, and you have stood for all we hope for and admire in an officer of the United States Army. These are my tributes and personal thanks."[11]

General Eisenhower returned to the United States in 1945 as a conquering hero and participated in rapturous celebrations and victory parades in Washington, New York, and, most poignantly, Abilene, where he was greeted by more than 20,000 people from the entire area and reunited with all the living members of his family. "This was a rich moment," he recalled. "We had been separated through trying years."[12]

Eisenhower served as Army Chief of Staff from 1945 to 1948 and then decided to leave the military and took on a new challenge when he served as the president of Columbia University in New York City. Eisenhower was a dutiful if somewhat distracted university president. He attended football games, presided over special events, regaled alumni, and raised money for the university. From his post in academia, he informally advised the secretary of defense and was involved in various projects in Washington. In late 1950 he was asked by President Harry Truman serve as the first supreme commander of the newly established North Atlantic Treaty Organization. He served as NATO's chief in Paris until he announced in April of 1952 that he was stepping down in June to pursue other challenges—those of a decidedly political nature.

II

According to Eisenhower, in 1943 journalist Virgil Pinkley was the first to mention him as a future president but it is unclear if Ike had entertained that possibility privately before then. Two years later, in the wake of Eisenhower's stunning military accomplishments, leaders from both political parties had little trouble imagining Eisenhower as their standard-bearer. Eisenhower said President Truman indicated to him several times that he would step aside in 1948 if Eisenhower wanted to run for president as a Democrat.[13]

Ike resisted, and Truman won a stunning upset that year over Republican Thomas Dewey. However, Eisenhower grew disgruntled over continuing Democratic governance and by the ineffectual and splintered Republican opposition. Ike insisted he was prepared to take himself out of national politics if Senator Robert Taft, the presumed Republican nominee in 1952, would commit to an internationalist foreign policy and support collective security in Europe. Eisenhower and Taft met in the Pentagon for a private conversation and Taft's noncommittal responses troubled Eisenhower, and he left the door open for his own presidential campaign.

Ensconced in Paris in 1951 as the supreme allied commander in Europe, Eisenhower oversaw NATO and also received a steady stream of Republican visitors encouraging him to return to the United States and run for president. Senator Henry Cabot Lodge Jr., a Massachusetts Republican, was vocal, aggressive, and insistent. He later told officials in New Hampshire, the site of the first 1952 Republican primary, that he could confirm that Eisenhower was indeed a Republican and deserved their support over Taft. Eisenhower, still in Paris, easily won the New Hampshire primary, though Taft continued to enjoy strong support from party regulars.

Herbert Brownell, a respected Republican operative from New York, spent a March day in Paris talking to Eisenhower about presidential politics. He found Eisenhower amiable, focused, and uninterested in small talk. Brownell told Eisenhower he could win the GOP nomination for president in 1952 but he would have to come back to the United States to do so. It would not be given to Ike without an effort and a campaign.[14] Eisenhower's brother Milton depicted Ike as both tortured and reluctant at this time. "He wanted desperately to stay out of politics, but his growing concern over foreign affairs and his high sense of duty made him somewhat vulnerable to the appeals and pressures of men and women he respected who truly believed the welfare of the nation depended on him," Milton later wrote, with more than a touch of melodrama.[15]

Eisenhower informed Truman in April 1952 that he intended to resign as the supreme allied commander in Europe. He returned home in June to run for the Republican nomination for president. However, his candidacy began inauspiciously. Eisenhower's campaign announcement on the fourth of June in his hometown of Abilene was disrupted by a heavy downpour, and Ike replicated the day's bleakness with a dreary, listless, and uninspiring speech. But he quickly steadied his campaign, brought in political professionals, sharpened his message, and launched an aggressive bid for the Republican nomination. The battle between Eisenhower and Taft was fierce and ideological, with Ike imploring Republicans to support conservative domestic policies while also accepting the reality that New Deal–era programs should be restrained but not eliminated. He also strongly believed the United States should be an active member of the international community and lead in the defense of the West. Taft was a more doctrinaire conservative on domestic issues, and strongly opposed the United States taking an active role internationally.

In July, on the eve of the Republican National Convention in Chicago, the Associated Press reported that of the 604 delegates needed to secure the Republican nomination, Taft had 530 to Ike's 427. Earl Warren of California, Harold Stassen of Minnesota, and General Douglas MacArthur, who were all also making bids for the GOP nomination, trailed well behind Taft and Eisenhower. His competitive juices now in full flow, Ike was willing to play hardball to win the nomination. Brownell, now his campaign manager, spent a week at the New York Public Library poring over the records of the deadlocked 1912 Republican convention and drew from this history a clever strategy to challenge the credentials of disputed delegates from Texas, Louisiana, and Georgia.[16] Under the auspices of Brownell's "Fair Play Amendment," Eisenhower won several important procedural battles at the convention, prevailed in getting his delegates seated, and went on to win the Republican presidential nomination. He left his hotel that night after winning the nomination to pay a courtesy visit to his defeated opponent, Taft, and to try to smooth over the deep divisions in the Republican Party. Eisenhower chose California's hardline thirty-nine-year-old senator Richard Nixon to be his vice president to help bridge the party's moderate and far right factions.

In the autumn campaign Ike faced the Democratic nominee, Governor Adlai Stevenson of Illinois, who stepped to the fore when Truman decided not to run for reelection. Eisenhower's campaign offered both an uplifting message and vitriolic attacks. He pledged to bring fiscal responsibility and clean government to Washington and lead a vibrant American foreign policy based on collective security and international cooperation. He hammered Democrats for tired and incompetent governance—for the "mess" in Washington—and blamed Truman and other Democrats for the stalemated Korean War and the rise of the communist threat both externally and internally.

Eisenhower traveled over 50,000 miles that fall, visiting more than 230 cities and towns to make the case for his candidacy and to excoriate Democrats. In a Peoria, Illinois, campaign speech Ike fully embraced fiscal discipline and set an agenda that would guide his policies for the next eight years. "My goal, assuming that the Cold War gets no worse, is to cut federal spending to something like $60 billion within four years. Such a cut would eliminate the deficit in the budget and would make way for a substantial tax reduction."[17]

In addition to retail politicking, Ike taped a slew of skillful and polished twenty-second ads created by Madison Avenue to tell his story and to hammer Democrats. This was a watershed moment in American presidential campaigns, ushering in a new technique in political communications. Eisenhower lamented the superficiality of this technique. "To think an old solider should come to this," he said.[18] But he knew the ads were effective so he made them, and his campaign paid for their wide distribution. His campaign also distributed more than thirty million "I Like Ike" buttons, and Irving Berlin even had the slogan immortalized in a popular song. Arguably the decisive moment in the campaign came when Eisenhower declared on October 16 in Detroit that he would personally find a way to break the stalemate in Korea. "I shall go to Korea," he intoned to wide-spread approval.

Eisenhower soundly defeated Stevenson on November 4. He captured 55% of the popular vote and 442 votes in the Electoral College. For jubilant Republicans, two decades in the political wilderness were ending. It was, proclaimed actor George Murphy, a staunch Republican and an Eisenhower campaign aide, like "walking into bright sunshine after being in darkness for a long time."[19]

III

Who was this man who confidently strode into the White House on January 20, 1953, poised to dominate American politics for nearly a decade?

President Eisenhower radiated health, vitality, and optimism. He was 5 feet 10 inches tall and weighed about 175 pounds, roughly the same weight as when he attended West Point forty years earlier. He had large, slightly gnarled hands and a dignified, upright posture. Exuding confidence and command, most thought of him as physically larger than he was. "Upon first encounter, the man instantly conveyed one quality—strength," said Emmet John Hughes, an aide. Eisenhower dominated a room.[20] "He has the power of drawing the hearts of men towards him as a magnet attracts the bits of metal," observed British general Bernard Montgomery, who had a sometimes contentious relationship with Eisenhower.[21]

Ike's public persona was genial and approachable. But up close, Eisenhower possessed what William Ewald, another aide, called, "extraordinary personal force." He had a vibrant, decisive, extroverted personality that included an explosive temper that erupted suddenly and calmed down quickly.[22] Bryce Harlow, a key political adviser, likened an Eisenhower temper eruption to looking into a Bessemer furnace, and said it showed "the enormous vital force in him." Wilton Persons, Eisenhower's legislative strategist and later chief of staff and transition coordinator, likened Ike's temper to a skyrocket: there would be a huge explosion and then everything would fade away. Eisenhower had an energetic, even restless, temperament. He was a man of "pronounced and changing moods," said journalist Robert Donovan.[23]

Eisenhower's most distinctive trait was his eyes, which Donovan called "luminously blue and intensely expressive." Hughes said Ike's eyes were "expressive, almost articulate." They could be "icy with anger, warm with satisfaction, sharp with concern, or glazed with boredom." The president also had "a leaping and effortless smile," according to Donovan. His face could go from midwestern genial to five-star-general formidable in an instant.

Although affable and sometimes chatty, Eisenhower usually got right to the point. When conducting business he was not a man for lengthy pleasantries. Seemingly straightforward, Ike was, according to Richard Nixon, a "far more complex and devious man than most realized, in the best sense of those words." Nixon also said Ike was the "most unemotional and analytical man in the world."[24]

As president, Eisenhower was polite to his staff and engendered tremendous respect, loyalty, and even reverence. He rarely praised staff to their faces, although he sometimes did to others. He enjoyed seeing old friends from Abilene—briefly; he told his secretary that ten minutes was usually enough. He didn't like people to touch him or people who were intimidated by him. He liked charts and careful presentations. He did not like generalizations or abstractions. Tackling practical problems, he said, "have always been my equivalent of crossword puzzles."[25]

The president liked to have familiar faces around him. Many who joined him when he entered the White House in 1953 would remain with him until he left Washington in 1961 and several worked with him during his retirement.

Sitting near the president every day was Ann Whitman, his dependable, and formidable, confidential secretary. She understood Eisenhower's habits, moods, and preferences better than anyone and was at the center of White House operations. She had been his personal secretary since the 1952 election, was totally devoted to the president, and committed to stay with him beyond the end of this presidency and into the early part of his retirement. She spoke to him respectfully but also directly, and was undaunted by his temper. Whitman's devotion to the president, says her biographer, was "so deep as to be all but indistinguishable from love."[26] Perhaps this was one reason that she was not a favorite of Mamie, who was aware of rumors of her husband's alleged World War II romance with Kay Summersby.

The president's son John, who joined the White House staff in 1958, and his brother Milton, the president of Johns Hopkins University, were enmeshed in the president's regular routine. John saw his father every day at work and sometimes visited with his parents in the evenings. Eisenhower was a demanding boss and often a remote and difficult father. John often found himself in the position of delivering unpleasant news to his father, a task he did not enjoy. The president's relationship with Milton, his younger and favorite brother, was easier. Eisenhower regarded Milton as able, astute, and totally loyal—a near peer. He called on Milton to help with special projects and important speeches, used him as sounding board, and trusted him completely. He often said Milton would have made a superb American president, a compliment he did not bestow on many.

Sherman Adams, Eisenhower's first chief of staff, was tough-minded and terse even to the president. He was all business and had little time for pleasantries or even politeness. Wilton Persons, Eisenhower's savvy and soft-spoken legislative strategist, and Adams's successor as chief of staff, was a warmer, more avuncular, and less rigid man. Eisenhower had known Persons for nearly three decades; they met in 1931 when both were in the army. Eisenhower trusted Persons to be discreet, honest, and effective. Persons, a lieutenant general, understood Eisenhower's military lexicon, work habits, view of the world, and his insistence on order, albeit of an informal variety. He knew that Eisenhower liked verbal updates on matters and did not want to be swamped with unimportant details. "Why is this something I need to know?" he sometimes asked Persons.[27]

Thomas Stephens, the president's scheduler and the office wit, was a mischievous Irishman who everyone loved. He was Eisenhower's gatekeeper who often brought an end to the president's meetings by entering the Oval Office and pointing to his watch. Andrew Goodpaster was the White House staff secretary and the president's liaison to military and intelligence agencies. Not only did Eisenhower respect Goodpaster, he adored him like a son. The president's press secretary, James Hagerty, was smart, terse, and deadpan. Malcolm Moos, a scholarly looking professor from Johns Hopkins University, drafted the president's speeches. Bryce Harlow was his top legislative assistant and Gerald Morgan his respected legal counsel.

Eisenhower also relied on other staffers such as Gordon Gray, his National Security Council assistant; David Kendall, another legal counsel;

Bob Merriam, who headed up intergovernmental relations; Robert Gray, secretary of his cabinet; and William Hopkins, the executive clerk who ensured the White House operated effectively and that letters were responded to, the phones were answered, and the files kept in order.

The president had several military aides who served as personal assistants: Sergeant John Moaney, who Eisenhower called his orderly; Colonel Bob Schulz, who the president referred to as his army aide-de-camp; Peter Aurand, his naval aide; and Colonel William Draper, the president's personal pilot for more than a decade.

Eisenhower's cabinet met weekly and each member was expected to contribute to policy debates that concerned all government issues, not just developments in his or her department. Ezra Benson, the secretary of agriculture, and Arthur Summerfield, the postmaster general, stayed in their jobs during all eight years of the Eisenhower presidency, and a number of others were part of the administration for most of its two terms and rose through the ranks. This included Attorney General William Rogers, Secretary of Labor James Mitchell, Secretary of State Christian Herter, Defense Secretary Thomas Gates, and Treasury Secretary Robert Anderson.

The Eisenhower team was calm, experienced, and professional, reflecting their president. According to staffer Ralph Williams, "There was this glacial calm; nobody was flustered, nobody was upset." He added, "You got the idea that these people were there to take care of things and here was one more damned problem that came with the territory and they were going to get it subdued somehow or another—and they did."[28] Most were eager to return to the private sector after their time in government service. They were devoted to Ike but found him demanding. "To be blunt, I think he took advantage of people on his personal staff," Schulz later recalled.[29] Ike's own son John said his dad was "not inclined to be generous," but added that working for his father was "pretty heady stuff."[30] Many of his staff were committed to stay with him and serve their revered president until the final hour of the final day of his tenure, helping him pass the baton of power with dignity.

While he was fully in charge of his administration and had subordinates, not equals or partners, he spoke about governance in modest terms. He referred to *the* administration and *the* cabinet not *my* administration or *my* cabinet. Often depicted as plodding and stodgy, he actually had what one aide called a "wonderfully facile" mind. Nixon said Ike could be "bold, imaginative, and uninhibited" as he thought through problems.

For a man of such enormous accomplishment and global stature, Eisenhower was sensitive to criticism. He urged his staff to vigorously debate and even challenge the ideas of others but to never question their motives. This would forestall future cooperation. He disliked leaders who abused underlings. "I have always deplored and deprecated table pounding and name calling," he said.[31] Even upon entering the Oval Office, he retained a military man's skepticism of politics—and politicians. "Politics has become far too important to entrust to politicians," he told a business group. He enjoyed businessmen and stocked his cabinet and advisory panels with them. Eisenhower's manner was captured by a black paperweight given to him by his aide Gabriel Hauge, with a Latin inscription that translated to "Gently in manner, strongly in deed."

Eisenhower was a direct man and forthright. "He had this thing about honesty," said Douglas Dillon, a senior official in Eisenhower's State Department and later treasury secretary under President Kennedy. Tightly controlled, Eisenhower could usually hold his emotions in check, although there were still those flares of temper. As president he refused to go to the annual Army-Navy football game because, according to a biographer, he felt "physically incapable of displaying needed impartiality."[32]

A man of habit, Ike usually got up by 6:00 A.M. and had breakfast alone, browsed a half dozen newspapers, and was at his White House desk by 7:30 A.M. He worked steadily through the day, preferring face-to-face meetings to phone calls. While insistent on an orderly flow of paper, he preferred oral briefings and well-structured conversations to lengthy reports. Eisenhower advocated planning as a discipline and as a tool of team building. He often said that plans were worthless but the discipline of planning was essential.

He worked steadily until 6:00 P.M., except for an hour lunch break in the residence. He often set aside an hour at the end of the day for informal conversations with either his secretary of state, John Foster Dulles, or one of his friends. He and Mamie routinely ate dinner in front of the TV and enjoyed quiet evenings. The president was usually in bed by 10:00 P.M. but she was up much later. He organized periodic stag dinners in which he invited between eighteen and twenty-four successful men from various walks of life to discuss the events of the day. The dinners began with cocktails in his White House residence and then dinner followed by a roundtable discussion. The conversation was brisk and wide-ranging. Guests received mementos of their White House dinners: a black jackknife and a lucky penny. Eisenhower instituted these dinners to gain the views from a wide range of people, most of whom were not members of his administration.

While the ebb and flow of events and crises influenced his schedule, Eisenhower maintained a weekly routine. He typically met with legislative leaders on Tuesday, held press conferences on Wednesday, attended National Security Council meetings on Thursday, and presided over cabinet meetings on Friday.

Eisenhower insisted on systematic record keeping and precise adherence to the organizational procedures he created. He demanded careful work from the cabinet and White House staff secretaries. "Never bring me a sealed envelope," he said. He was appalled by the loose management styles of his two Democratic predecessors, Franklin Roosevelt and Harry Truman. "With my training in problems involving organization it was inconceivable to me that the work of the White House could not be better systematized than had been the case during the years I observed," he wrote in his presidential memoir.[33]

Eisenhower was the quintessential problem solver. He relished breaking a problem down to its essentials, considering its long-term implications, and then determining the best short-term response. He was a keen and critical listener, and an active debater. He told his staff that if they had something to say they should say it in meetings and not withhold their opinions or defer them to private conversations with the president. He was willing to do a deep dive on issues he felt he needed to understand and master. He once spent four hours reviewing a ballistic missile system and set aside part of his New Year's Day to review the administration's budget. He was an inveterate and skilled editor of letters, speeches, and policy papers, and did not like to be interrupted while doing so. Eisenhower's razor sharp writing and editing was in striking contrast to his public speaking style, in which, according to one reporter, "his numbers and genders collide, participles hang helplessly, and syntax is lost forever."[34]

Eisenhower was extremely disciplined in all aspects of his life. He was a heavy smoker until 1949 then he stopped cold turkey. "I simply gave myself an order," he recalled. This discipline also extended to his work habits and his demand for order. "Organization cannot make a genius out of an incompetent; even less can it, of itself, make the decisions which are required to trigger necessary action. On the other hand, disorganization can scarcely fail to result in inefficiency and can easily lead to disaster," he wrote. "Organization makes more efficient the gathering and analysis of facts and the arranging of the findings of experts in logical fashion. Therefore, organization helps the responsible individual make the necessary decision and helps assure that it is satisfactorily carried out." The purpose of careful organization, he said, is to "simplify, clarify, expedite, coordinate."[35]

Ike was a clean desk man. He had four pens and two phones on his desk. His office displayed color photos of his mother and his wife and prints of Benjamin Franklin, Abraham Lincoln, George Washington, and Robert E. Lee. His bookshelves included a collection of Abraham Lincoln's speeches and writings. He had a careful system of organizing his personal library with sections for encyclopedias and reference books, military books, histories, biographies, technical books on painting, classical literature, and modern fiction. By most accounts he was not a voracious reader, preferring Western paperbacks for evening pleasure, but he did read extensively on the Civil War.

Eisenhower relaxed by playing bridge, golfing, painting, and cooking. He recalled that he cooked vegetable soup after learning about Japan's attack on Pearl Harbor. He loved to grill steaks and did so in Paris for the U.S. embassy staff just after a key summit unraveled in the summer of 1960. Cooking allowed him to unwind and sort out his thoughts. His enjoyment of golf became part of American popular culture. According to one historian Eisenhower golfed over eight hundred rounds during his presidency, including more than two hundred rounds at Augusta National, where he had a cottage near the 10th tee.[36] The U.S. Golf Association installed a putting green on the South Lawn of the White House where staffers often saw the president practicing iron shots while an aide retrieved the balls and put them in a yellow bag.

Ike brought to the White House a philosophy of governing that he adhered to over his eight years in office. Summarizing Lincoln, Eisenhower believed government should do those things that individuals could not do well for themselves. He was convinced the federal government had grown too large and intrusive during the previous twenty years of Democratic administrations, and its growth needed to be controlled and its tentacles pruned. But he opposed trying to repeal the New Deal, telling one of his brothers that any political party that attempted to do so would render itself irrelevant. Eisenhower had no interest in trying to dismantle the federal government, but wanted to limit its growth and cut unnecessary spending.

Eisenhower believed America's security in the Cold War depended on a strong defense and an expanding economy with limited regulations and firm controls on spending, including the military budget. "We need an adequate defense, but every dollar we spend above adequacy has a long-term weakening effect upon the nation and its security," he said. On another occasion he warned, "This country could choke itself to death on piling up military expenditures just as surely as it can defeat itself by not spending for protection."[37]

He was convinced there was no such thing as total security, that nuclear supremacy was an illusion, and the nation needed to position itself for the long haul because the Cold War could continue indefinitely. Eisenhower was adamant that there would be no victor in a global war. There was a fatalistic, or at least a very practical, dimension to Ike: he often said his administration must focus on playing the cards it was dealt.

Ike frequently called for balance between government and the private economy, between domestic and military programs. He described himself as conservative when it came to the economy and liberal when it came to people. He frequently touted what he called "the Middle Way." He was reluctant to commit force but believed that when force was deployed it should be used decisively. "In my career I have learned that if you have to use force, use overwhelming force and save lives thereby," he told Brownell.[38] Eisenhower later said that when a nation went to war it should do so "prayerfully."

With Democratic majorities in Congress for six of his eight years, Eisenhower was a proponent of reasonable compromises. He often found it easier to deal with Democratic leaders such as House Speaker Sam Rayburn and Senate Majority Leader Lyndon Johnson than conservative, hardline Republicans such as Senate Republican leader William Knowland and Ohio senator John Bricker. He toyed with starting up a progressive Republican party in 1954 and 1955. He dropped the idea but never his commitment to negotiations and incremental progress. "You can't drastically reform everything at once . . . If you strive to gain everything at once, without compromise, you end up with nothing," he said.[39]

He used his cabinet to debate policy issues and urged his secretaries to be informed on all matters and express informed opinions. He created a rigorous National Security Council with both planning and operating units. He was an institutional innovator, creating a White House chief of staff, a National Security Council director, a legislative liaison office, and a secretariat for both his White House staff and cabinet.

The president had the temperament and inclination of a judge who carefully assembled and then honestly pondered the evidence. He liked complex issues presented to him through well-organized oral briefings and then had the key relevant parties debate the issues vigorously in front of him. "Clearly, there are different ways to try to be a leader," he said in a letter. "In my view, a fair, decent, and reasonable dealing with men, a reasonable recognition that views may diverge, a constant seeking for a high and strong ground on which to work together is the best way to lead our country in the difficult times ahead of us."[40]

Eisenhower, Brownell said, "ingeniously embraced a style of leadership that made him appear to be a benign figurehead. Yet underneath the benevolent demeanor was a knowledgeable and astute political mind that worked behind the scenes to achieve his political goals and that usually ended up attaining them." Brownell added that Ike keenly understood his differing roles as chief of state and as head of government. "Few recent presidents have understood, much less reconciled, these different aspects of the presidency, but Eisenhower did."[41]

Eisenhower had layers of staff who tended to his needs and desires. Despite the simplicity of his Midwestern upbringing, during the later stages of his professional life Eisenhower expected to be attended to by servants, cooks, staffers, valets, butlers, and caddies.

Eisenhower's people hovered around him, largely in concentric circles that did not overlap. First, there was his personal staff: John Moaney, his orderly who literally helped dress him in the morning; Bob Schulz, who took care of his personal affairs; Leonard Dry, his chauffeur; and Deeter Flohr, his personal bodyguard. They were like his extended family. His top policy advisers including chief of staff Sherman Adams and his successor,

Wilton Persons; his morning briefer and foreign policy aide, Andrew Goodpaster; additional foreign policy aides, Robert Cutler and Gordon Gray; schedulers Tom Stephens and Bernard Shanley; his indispensable private secretary Ann Whitman; his son John; and his younger brother Milton, a college president and valuable sounding board and troubleshooter for the president.

He relied on his cabinet to run their departments and to advise him more broadly. The standouts included Secretary of State John Foster Dulles, Attorney General Herbert Brownell, and his two Treasury Secretaries, first George Humphrey followed by Robert Anderson. There was an assortment of personal friends, many of whom were wealthy businessmen, who joined Ike in Washington, Augusta, and elsewhere to golf, play bridge, and chat. These included Al Gruenther, president of the American Red Cross; Bobby Jones, a former professional golfer and an Atlanta attorney; W. Alton Jones, president of Cities Service Oil Company; Ellis Slater, president of Frankfort Distilleries; Doug Black, president of Doubleday; Bill Robinson, business manager of the *New York Herald Tribune*; Aksel Nielsen, president of Title Guaranty Company of Denver; Cliff Roberts, an investment banker and chairman of the Augusta National Golf Club; and Lucius Clay, president of Continental Can. They were often summoned by Whitman to stop by the White House for an evening visit or meet the president for a golf weekend in Georgia. Accomplished businessmen, they were still clearly in awe of Ike. "What excitement his world stature had added to our lives. To have known him as a close friend somehow made me feel a little more worthy," Slater wrote in his diary years after Ike died.[42]

IV

During his presidency, Eisenhower's domestic agenda focused on consolidating the New Deal, not killing it. Ike supported measures to expand Social Security, retain the Taft-Hartley labor law, construct the Saint Lawrence Seaway, build the Interstate Highway System, substantially expand the space program and ultimately create NASA, and give statehood to Alaska and Hawaii. He balanced the budget during three of his eight years in office and supported modest tax cuts. He was not an ideologue when it came to downsizing the federal government. Early in his presidency, he proposed creating the Department of Health, Education, and Welfare to address the needs of a rapidly growing American population. Congress supported his request. "Our goal was a progressive America," he said, an assertion that not all of his fellow Republicans agreed with. Many wanted to create a conservative America.

Eisenhower believed in the executive branch as one of three coordinate branches of the federal government. He respected the Congress's Article I legislative role in the federal scheme of government but tended to have much less respect for individual lawmakers. "Ike's natural home was Article II, the Executive," said Stephen Hess, an aide and later a presidential scholar. "It was the type of leadership he had successfully practiced in the army and the university, and he was most comfortable with and most admired other successful executives."[43]

Arguably Eisenhower's most important domestic policy decision was appointing Earl Warren to the Supreme Court as chief justice. Warren was the lead author of the historic *Brown v. Board of Education* ruling that declared school segregation was illegal. Eisenhower also quietly desegregated army post schools, civilian navy yards, Washington, D.C., restaurants, and introduced legislation that became the basis of the 1957 Civil Rights Act. That same year he also dispatched federal troops to Little Rock when Arkansas Governor Orval Faubus resisted a federal court order to allow several black students to enroll in Little Rock's Central High School.

On the foreign policy front, Eisenhower was an unabashed internationalist and a strong champion of collective security, especially in Europe. He was a staunch supporter of NATO. He frequently said one of the chief goals of his presidency was to bring about peace. "I think the people want peace so much that one of these days governments had better get out of the way and let them have it," he declared.[44] But he also backed aggressive covert operations by the Central Intelligence Agency that deposed leaders in Iran, Guatemala, and the Congo and he tried to remove leaders in Indonesia and Cuba. These operations caused deep unrest in the affected nations with destabilizing consequences that continued for decades.

Arguably the most consequential foreign policy decision of Eisenhower's presidency was securing a peace agreement in Korea during his first year in office. After inspecting the Korean battlefront the month after the 1952 election and meeting with the South Korean President Syngman Rhee and American military officials, Eisenhower concluded the U.S. needed to either agree to a truce or dramatically expand the war into China, possibly using nuclear weapons. "My conclusion as I left Korea was that we could not stand forever on a static front and continue to accept casualties without any visible results. Small attacks on small hills would not end this war," he wrote.[45] He preferred a truce to a dramatic military escalation and the armistice was signed on July 27, 1953.

With the death of Joseph Stalin just months after Eisenhower entered the White House, the new American president decided to make overtures to the Soviet Union and the communist world, first in April with his "Chance for Peace" speech, and then in December with his "Atoms for Peace" speech in the United Nations. In the first, Eisenhower decried the lunacy of massive military expenditures, and he followed up in the second by proposing to pool atomic information and materials under the auspices of an international agency that several years later became the International Atomic Energy Agency.

Eisenhower declined a French plea in 1954 to send American ground troops to Indochina to help France prevail over an insurgency. Ike set conditions for U.S. involvement that were unappealing to France and probably designed to ensure they would never be met. Before he would send American troops, Ike said France would have to grant independence to Vietnam, Laos, and Cambodia; the U.S. troops must be joined by troops from other nations such as Great Britain, New Zealand, and Australia; and U.S. troops would not serve under French command. France declined the offer and with no American help forthcoming the French fortress at Dien Bien Phu was overwhelmed in May of 1954. A few months later, the Geneva Conference divided Vietnam at the 17th parallel and set up an election in 1956 that never took place. While the Eisenhower administration avoided deploying U.S. ground troops to Indochina it substantially ramped up assistance to President Diem in South Vietnam, including sending more than five hundred advisers, some of who became the first American casualties of the Vietnam War. Eisenhower deepened America's commitment to Diem, something that would have profound consequences in the decade to come.

Eisenhower attended another Geneva summit the following year, conferring with the leaders of Great Britain, the Soviet Union, and France to ease the strains of the Cold War. His "Open Skies" proposal called on the United States and the Soviet Union to permit continuous air inspection of their military installations as a way of increasing transparency and building trust. The Soviet Union declined the offer but the possibility grew for constructive negotiations. The Spirit of Geneva in 1955 calmed the world for a time.

Months before Eisenhower's 1956 reelection, Egypt seized control of the Suez Canal. Great Britain, France, and Israel then attacked Egypt, gaining control of the canal and other territory. Breaking with his allies, Eisenhower said the principle of unprovoked force must be opposed even when perpetrated by America's friends, whom he rebuked for "old fashioned gunboat diplomacy." Eisenhower's actions won wide praise across the world. However, Eisenhower adopted a tough unilateral stance in 1957 with the Eisenhower Doctrine, a pledge to send U.S. armed forces to aid Middle Eastern nations seeking help from communist aggression.

The administration, and all Americans, were jolted in October 1957 by Russia's successful launch of Sputnik, the first artificial Earth satellite. Sputnik and other Soviet military advances challenged the presumption of American scientific and strategic preeminence. A later report by the Gaither Committee, convened by Ike, also raised questions and doubts about America's military strength in the world compared to its communist adversaries.

The Cold War appeared to thaw slightly in 1959 when Nikita Khrushchev hosted Richard Nixon in Moscow, then visited the United States and had productive meetings with Eisenhower at Camp David. Many believed this new environment would flourish in May of 1960 with a summit of world leaders in Paris. However, the eagerly awaited summit unraveled when the Soviet Union shot down an American U-2 spy plane and U.S. officials provided false explanations about it. The summit collapsed in acrimony, and with it, hopes of a peaceful resolution to the Cold War. The disappointment in the United States and around the world following the collapse of the Paris summit provided a grim backdrop to Eisenhower's last six months as president and challenged his claim that his administration had brought the nation closer to peace with its chief rival.

V

Perhaps the quintessential Eisenhower foreign policy moment occurred shortly after he assumed the presidency in 1953. Determined to chart a new security path for his administration and the country, Eisenhower rigorously reviewed his foreign policy options after the death of Stalin in March. Eisenhower inherited Truman's muscular and expensive containment strategy that assumed a long and costly struggle with the Soviet Union. Eisenhower wanted to put United States foreign policy on a more sustainable trajectory.

On the evening of May 8, 1953, Eisenhower had a spirited foreign policy discussion in the White House solarium with Secretary of State John Foster Dulles, CIA Director Allen Dulles, Undersecretary of State Bedell Smith, NSC Director Robert Cutler, and several others. As a result of the vigorous exchange, Eisenhower realized he needed a fundamental reassessment of American foreign policy. He decided to set up teams of "bright young fellows" to develop and defend several distinct foreign policy strategies and present them to Eisenhower and his senior national security team.[46]

Eisenhower conceived of what became called Project Solarium as an opportunity to think clearly about foreign policy alternatives, explore them deeply, educate his national security team about the challenges ahead, foster teamwork, and then forge a strategy that his administration would fully understand and aggressively implement.

Eisenhower charged his foreign policy staff to assemble three task forces and give them detailed guidelines to use as they drafted their strategies. Task Force A was to describe and defend the current containment strategy. Task Force B would articulate a deterrence strategy that would clearly define America's overseas interests, which it would defend with force if necessary. Task Force C would develop an approach that would, short of war, roll back the communist world's recent advances. Each task force was instructed to assemble its plan like an advocate would in a court proceeding, but also to be open about the weaknesses of its approach.

The president took an active role in Project Solarium and reinforced its urgency with his cabinet. He insisted it be conducted rigorously, and secretly, at the National War College. He proposed members for the task forces and diligently worked out the mechanics of the presentations.

Eisenhower set aside a full day for his national security team to review the work of the task forces. He wanted the sessions to begin at 8:30 A.M. to allow each task force two hours for its briefing, a short break between presentations, and a lunch break. A veteran of thousands of military briefings over the years, Eisenhower wanted all questions reserved until the conclusion of the three presentations. When Cutler suggested they hold the sessions in the theater of the basement of the White House, Ike said it was important the room was air conditioned and had a platform. He also inquired whether the task forces would want to use slides.

The task forces began work secretly at the War College in early June 1953. Cutler arranged for a practice session for the three task forces on June 26 and then a full-scale briefing on July 16 at the White House for Eisenhower, the National Security Council, senior members of the cabinet, and others. The president and his team took the exercise very seriously. Eisenhower listened carefully, asked probing questions, and gave a masterful summary.

He said there was some common ground in the three approaches that were more important than the differences between them and that the only thing worse than losing a global war was winning one because it would end individual freedom. The president warned that if American leaders demanded more from their citizens over time than they wanted to give, substantial controls would be required thus creating a garrison state.

Eisenhower argued that the American people didn't want to occupy territory after a war. "What would we do with Russia, if we should win a global war?" He said the United States had to persuade her allies to go along with it because America's forward bases were in the territories of its allies. He believed there was a need for a vigorous campaign to educate the American people and their leaders.

The president indicated that there was still more for the three task forces to do. He wanted to see if they could agree on the framework of a unified policy. He contemplated a presentation to congressional leaders and for the project to be the basis of a new strategic plan.

George Kennan, already a legendary American diplomat, chaired one of the task forces and said Eisenhower's participation showed his "intellectual ascendancy" over the entire group. "He spoke, I must say, with a mastery of the subject matter and a thoughtfulness and penetration that I found remarkable," Kennan recalled. Goodpaster, another task force member, called Ike's performance a "tour de force."[47]

When task force members said they saw no use in additional meetings, Eisenhower called on Cutler to find a way to bring the project to a conclusion. Cutler wrote a summary draft of the task force findings that was sent to the president and the NSC. This draft triggered intense staff and NSC work from August through October 1953 when a new national security strategy was agreed to that drew from each of the task forces.

After intense analysis and careful debate within the administration, Eisenhower released a new national security strategy in 1954, dubbed the New Look, which drew from Project Solarium and several other studies. The new strategy envisioned a smaller conventional force, a more robust nuclear force, and restrained defense expenditures. This became the basis for the national security strategy that guided American foreign policy from 1953 to the end of the Cold War in 1991.

VI

Project Solarium showed Eisenhower at his creative, purposeful, and analytical best. These qualities wore well with the American people. Eisenhower entered the final year of his two-term presidency popular and respected. Ike was revered as a steady, competent, calm, and calming leader—a war hero who transformed himself into a capable civilian leader. More than a few likened him to George Washington, one of his heroes. His average approval was more than 60% during his presidency, dipping below 50% only once.[48]

Even his decidedly middlebrow interests—bridge, golf, fishing, camping, reading Westerns, eating dinner in front of the TV with Mamie—were viewed as familiar and even reassuring. He was confident and capable, but not pretentious or arrogant. He was religious, but not overly so. He supported placing "One Nation Under God" in the Pledge of Allegiance in 1954 and "In God We Trust" on the currency in 1955, but did not join a church until he entered the White House.

New York Times columnist James Reston wrote that Eisenhower's popularity with the American people was a "national phenomenon like baseball."

Ike, Reston argued, was the object of a "national love affair, which cannot be analyzed satisfactorily by political scientists and will probably have to be turned out to the head shrinkers." Reston believed Ike was popular because he was "in tune with the worldwide spirit of the age." But he also argued that Eisenhower failed to convert his popularity into "vote getting appeal for his party and its principles."[49] Ike's appeal did not extend to his party or his fellow Republicans.

As his presidency was winding down, John Cogley wrote in *Commonweal* that it was "hard to imagine any other public figure in either party playing the role Eisenhower played during the last eight years." Richard Rovere, in a series of essays for *Harper's Magazine* in May and June of 1960, stipulated that Ike dominated the political landscape. "Politically, the Eisenhower Administration has been little less than triumphant. The people have liked it and trusted it," he wrote. Eisenhower was "inimitable in the sense that he is a hero-statesman and the only one about." Rovere added that Ike "has projected an image of an American President which no other man can come close to duplicating. He has drawn not on the soundness of his policies, not on the prestige of the office, not on the morale of the nation but on the touching coincidence of the masses who believe that Eisenhower knows best because—well, because he is Eisenhower."[50]

Still the dominant force in American politics in 1960, he had nevertheless been worn down by eight hard years of Cold War struggle, a deeply divided Republican Party, tough Democratic adversaries such as Lyndon Johnson and Sam Rayburn, and three major illnesses. He had a serious heart attack in 1955, an attack of ileitis in 1956, and a miled stroke in 1957. He also became the first American president ever to reach the age of seventy while in office. His secretary, Ann Whitman, said he was grumpy and unhappy for most of 1960, his last year in office. Running again was not an option. Ike was the first president to be limited to two terms by the 22nd Amendment.

As Eisenhower entered the last year of his presidency, he was restless and determined to end his second term with a flourish and a push for global understanding. He said he had "no interest in marking time." He was furious at Senator Kennedy's frequent use of the missile gap charge on the campaign trail and his assertion that the Eisenhower administration was ponderous, tired, and impassive. His brother Milton said Ike and the

White House were angry at the "blatant misrepresentations" by Kennedy and his campaign.

Eisenhower was not eager to hand the keys to the White House either to Nixon, for whom he had mixed feelings and modest regard for his leadership skills, or especially to Kennedy, whom he saw as untested, impertinent, and lacking in presidential stature. He told an associate he would do almost anything to avoid turning the country over to Kennedy. But that choice would not be made by Eisenhower, but by the American people.

FIVE

THE JUNIOR SENATOR FROM MASSACHUSETTS

I

John F. Kennedy was sworn in as the junior U.S. senator from Massachusetts on January 3, 1953. He was young, famous, and wealthy. The son of a prominent father, Kennedy was a war hero in his own right, a three-term congressman, the victor of the previous year's marquee Senate race against Republican incumbent Henry Cabot Lodge, and a dashing bachelor. Kennedy had unmistakable star quality.

But seen up close he was tightly wound, driven, and sometimes disheveled. As a new senator, Kennedy was assigned to move into Room 362 in the Senate Office Building. However when the new Congress convened the office had not yet been vacated by Senator Robert Kerr of Oklahoma, who was moving to a larger suite. Kennedy and his staff spent the first days of his Senate term working out of a room in his old House of Representatives office. His staff gathered there on the morning of January 3 and strolled together to the Senate visitors gallery to watch their boss be sworn in as a U.S. senator. "He seemed so ill at ease, so nervous," recalled his secretary Evelyn Lincoln. "And his necktie, the short end was clear up by the collar and the long end down below his belly. And he was forever trying to stuff his necktie into his pants . . . He was standing out in front trying to push his necktie down. It was way out of proportion."[1]

Kennedy managed to gather himself and was escorted down the main aisle of the Senate chamber by the senior senator from Massachusetts, Republican Leverett Saltonstall. Kennedy took the oath of office and was ready to begin work.

In his first days as a senator, Kennedy was, according to Lincoln, pre-occupied with the accumulating mail. When his suite was finally available, Kennedy declined the ritual of repainting the office and ordered his staff to move in immediately and begin sorting the mail. Kennedy would leave his private office, step into the main room, read some of the correspondence, and then impatiently ask his staff when responses would be prepared for him to sign. His staff worked late into the night. They researched and drafted responses and placed stacks of letters on his desk for his review and signature. He read the draft responses carefully, found occasional errors, and chastised his staff. "He'd catch errors, and call you in, be real exasperated, if you didn't get it right," Lincoln recalled. He personally signed all the letters.

Kennedy continued to leave the main door to his office suite open as he had during his time in the House of Representatives, an unusual practice at the time. Visitors to the Capitol complex would drop by his office without invitations or appointments, sometimes to Kennedy's consternation. But he still insisted the door be kept open.

Kennedy generated more interest than the average freshman senator. He had been one of the stars of the 1952 campaign and one of the few bright spots for Democrats in a dark political year. "His coverage was immense for a freshman senator," Lincoln said. And it would only grow. Within months he would be on national magazine covers. In Kennedy's first spring as a senator the popular *Saturday Evening Post* ran a cover story about him called "The Gay Young Senator," depicting Kennedy as a dashing bachelor with an active and exciting social life. A few months later *Life* ran a cover story titled, "Senator Kennedy Goes a Courting," which showed the young senator on a sailboat with a striking young woman, Jacqueline Bouvier, who would become his wife later that year. Just months into his Senate career, John Kennedy was already a celebrity-politician.

II

John Fitzgerald Kennedy was born on May 29, 1917, the second of what became a family of nine children. His mother, Rose, was a devout, prim, tightly coiled daughter of a popular Boston political figure, John Fitzgerald. Also known as "Honey Fitz," Fitzgerald was former mayor of Boston and had served in the U.S. House of Representatives. Rose was a remote and distant mother to her son John, who was usually known as Jack. She responded to her growing family and her domineering and philandering husband by withdrawing, frequently taking long vacations with friends or by herself. Once, when she was getting ready to depart on another trip away from the family, her then seven-year-old son Jack challenged her. "Gee, you're a great mother to go away and leave your children all alone," he groused. She vividly recalled her son's comments years later but they did not dissuade her from taking the trip, leaving her children in the care of their nannies.[2]

Rose's husband, Joseph Kennedy, was the son of P. J. Kennedy, a wealthy Boston businessman. Joe was an assertive, hard-driving man who was the dominant force in Jack's life. He was tough, combative, even ruthless, and succeeded at almost everything he tried. By the age of twenty-five he was the president of a Boston bank and then went on to successful careers as a shipping company executive, investment broker, studio executive, liquor importer, chairman of the Securities and Exchange Commission and head of the Federal Maritime Commission. According to a biographer, Joe had one indisputable skill. "When it came to making money, in up markets and down markets, good times and bad, Joseph P. Kennedy was in a league by himself."[3] He was also a devoted father who demanded excellence from his children and offered them love and support, especially when they succeeded. "We don't want any losers around here. In this family we want winners," he proclaimed. His youngest son, Edward, recalled receiving a stern lecture from his father when he was a teenager and had been involved in some mischief. "You can have a serious life or unserious life, Teddy," Joe said. "I'll still love you whichever choice you make, but if you decide to have a nonserious life, I won't have much time for you. You make up your mind. There are too many children here who are doing things that are interesting for me to do much with you."[4]

Rose and Joe Kennedy's oldest son Joe Jr. most resembled his father. He was confident, outgoing, and combative. Jack was different. He was an irreverent and rebellious underachiever who battled endless illnesses including whooping cough, scarlet fever, measles, chicken pox, colds, fevers, and stomach problems. "When we were growing together we used to laugh about the great risk a mosquito took in biting Jack Kennedy—with some of his blood, the mosquito was almost sure to die," recalled his brother Robert. More poignantly, Robert said that at least half of the days Jack "spent on this earth were days of intense physical pain."[5]

Jack was a mediocre student who underachieved his way through public schools in Brookline, Massachusetts, and suburban New York City as well as two private schools, Canterbury and Choate. He loved to read, had a creative streak, excelled at subjects that interested him, and disregarded everything else. His father was frustrated by his careless approach to school, to money, to clothes, and to his own health. Joe sent a letter of concern about Jack to Choate headmaster, George St. John, who sent a perceptive response. "Jack has a clever, individualist mind. It is a harder mind to harness than Joe's [his older brother]—harder for Jack himself to harness." His father tried to understand Jack but often found it difficult. "Don't let me lose confidence in you again, because it will be pretty nearly an impossible task to restore it . . . You have the goods why not try to show it?" he wrote to him.[6]

Jack's first years at Harvard in the late 1930s were also subpar. "Jack has a brilliant mind for the things in which he is interested, but is careless and lacks application in those in which he is not interested. That is, of course, a bad fault," Joe told the Harvard dean of freshmen.[7] But then his son blossomed, stirred by the turmoil of current events as the world careened toward World War II, and also stimulated by his front row seat to history while his father served as the highly controversial U.S. ambassador to the

United Kingdom from 1938 through 1940. Jack's senior thesis at Harvard focused on the British policy of appeasement toward Germany during the 1930s, and later was published as a book, *Why England Slept*, which generated solid sales and mostly positive reviews, especially given that the author was still a young man in his early twenties. In his book, Kennedy argued that Britain's failure to swiftly rearm in the face of Nazi aggression was the fault of the entire society and not just a few politicians.

Following a restless year after his Harvard graduation that included a brief stint at Stanford Graduate School of Business and an extensive trip to Latin America, Kennedy enlisted in the navy on October 1, 1941, just months before the United States entered World War II after Japan's attack on Pearl Harbor. He began in Navy Intelligence and secured an assignment on patrol torpedo boats, known as PT boats, in the South Pacific. The boat that Kennedy commanded, the PT-109, was patrolling near the Solomon Islands when it was shattered by a Japanese destroyer on the night of August 2, 1943. Kennedy helped save ten of his crew and they were eventually rescued after a harrowing week in which all were assumed dead. While Jack's acumen as a PT skipper is subject to debate, his bravery was evident. His exploits won considerable praise, several medals, headlines in the *New York Times* and the *Boston Globe*, and later a laudatory profile in the *New Yorker* by John Hersey. For Jack's older brother Joe, participation in the war ended far more tragically; he was killed in August of 1944 taking part in a dangerous bombing mission. Joe's death devastated his father, who was devoted to his eldest son and envisioned him as successful politician. "You more than anyone else know how much I had tied up my whole life to his from here on. You know what great things I saw in the future for him and now it's all over," Joe Sr. wrote to a cousin.[8]

III

Jack's strenuous service in the South Pacific further undermined his fragile health. When he completed his naval service on March 1, 1945, he was a sick young man with a damaged back, malaria, and a razor-thin frame. After convalescence, Jack tried journalism, writing for the *Chicago Herald American* and the International News Service. He covered the founding conference of the United Nations in San Francisco, the Potsdam Conference in Germany, and the British election in which Winston Churchill was defeated. But journalism did not fully engage Kennedy and when a vacancy came up in the Massachusetts 11th Congressional District he decided to run for office. It's unclear if Joseph Kennedy provided inducements to Congressman Michael Curley not to seek reelection in 1946 but instead run again to be the mayor of Boston, thus opening a congressional seat for his son to seek. Jack had never actually lived in the district that encompassed Cambridge, Charlestown, the North, South, and West Ends of Boston, and parts of Brighton and Somerville. Jack later said he felt pressure to enter politics by his father. "It was like being drafted . . . He wanted it. He demanded it."[9]

Jack Kennedy moved into the Bellevue Hotel, thus becoming a resident of the 11th district. He later rented an apartment at 122 Bowdoin Street that became his legal address. Kennedy was, by his later admission, an outsider to the district. He was not a natural politician. Jack was a reserved, even reticent, man. But he plunged into his first political campaign with an intensity that surprised, even stunned, his father and the rest of his family. He forced himself to reach out to voters, going door-to-door, visiting factory gates and wharfs, attending church receptions and community events. He ran as a proud veteran and the representative of a new era. "The New Generation Offers a Leader" proclaimed his campaign literature.

Kennedy was not the only person interested in this congressional seat. He entered a ten-person Democratic primary and ultimately prevailed due to his hard work, prominent name, and the ample resources of his father, who spent more than $250,000 in the race, which was a very large sum for that time and more than all of his opponents spent combined. Kennedy's opponents did not think he waged a fair fight. One came up with a sarcastic ad: "Congress seat for sale—No experience necessary—Applicant must live in New York or Florida—Only millionaires need apply." There were allegations of dubious tactics. One of Kennedy's most formidable rivals was a popular undertaker in the district, Joe Russo. He was soon joined in the race by another man named Joe Russo, a plumber who had less standing in the community but the same name. The second Mr. Russo's candidacy was attributed by a Kennedy aide to Joe Kennedy and was cited as an example of his win-at-all-costs mentality.[10]

Jack won the Democratic primary on June 18, 1946, with slightly more than 40% of the vote, which was tantamount to winning the seat in the heavily Democratic district. He easily won the general election that November, defeating his Republican opponent, Lester Brown, by 69,093 votes to 26,007. His first political race became the prototype for future campaigns: a hard-working candidate, active family support, an effective organization, and substantial funds from his father. Jack later said this race taught him that to succeed in electoral politics, "the most important ingredient is to submit to long, long, long labor."[11]

Kennedy entered the U.S. House of Representatives as a youthful-looking twenty-nine-year-old who was sometimes confused with a congressional page or a young staffer. He served for six years in the House, a tenure that was neither lengthy nor distinguished. Kennedy enjoyed a pampered Washington life, residing in an upscale home in Georgetown with a valet, George Thomas, and housekeeper, Margaret Ambrose. He dated beautiful, sometimes glamorous, women and had no financial concerns. He sent his bills to his father's office in New York and they were taken care of.

Kennedy displayed a modest interest in domestic policy, adhering to a traditional Democratic stance on housing, veterans' issues, labor, health, the minimum wage, and Social Security. He served on the House Education and Labor Committee as well as on the District of Columbia Committee. He was far more interested in foreign policy and developed a reputation as a tough critic of the Truman administration, blasting it for the stalemate in Korea and for the communist victory in China. "This is a tragic story of China whose freedom we once fought to preserve. What our young men had saved, our diplomats and president have frittered away," Kennedy charged in January of 1949.[12]

The young congressman took several overseas trips, often using private funds since he did not sit on committees whose main jurisdiction was foreign affairs. He took two extensive excursions in 1951—a five-week trip to Europe in the spring and a seven-week journey to the Middle East and Asia in the fall. He met top political, military, and cultural leaders as well as journalists. After the European trip, Kennedy outlined his impressions in a nationwide radio address paid for by his father. He also secured an invitation to testify before a joint meeting of the Senate Foreign Relations Committee and the Senate Armed Services Committee about a pending resolution prohibiting the president from sending American troops to Europe. Kennedy had the least experience of the thirty-seven witnesses. But the opportunity to testify before two distinguished Senate panels was an honor, and Kennedy had ten thousand copies of his testimony printed and distributed to his constituents and others.

Nonetheless, Kennedy's House years were difficult. He was persistently ill. He was diagnosed with Addison's disease in 1947 and suffered from a chronically bad back. And he was bored with the House. "We were just worms. Nobody pays attention to us," he grumbled. House members, as he saw it, were at the bottom of Washington's policy-making food chain. "You are one of 435 members. You have to be there many, many years before you get to the hub of influence, or have an opportunity to play any role on substantive matters," he later said.[13]

Kennedy had a cool relationship with House Democratic leaders, especially John McCormack, a senior congressman from Kennedy's home state and the second-ranking House Democrat. McCormack did not think Kennedy was sufficiently loyal to the Democratic agenda or attentive to his House duties. Kennedy was generally liked by his colleagues but many were underwhelmed by him. "He was pleasant and attractive. He just wasn't much of a House member," said Congressman Richard Bolling of Missouri, adding that during his House years Kennedy was a "frail, sick, hollow man." Another Democratic congressman, George Smathers of Florida, who became a close friend of Kennedy, said few detected star quality in Kennedy during his House years. "In those days, he was a rather sickly fellow. In addition to his bad back he was constantly plagued with colds and one thing after another—constantly laid up. If you had to pick a member of that freshman class who would probably wind up as president, Kennedy was probably the least likely. He was so shy he could hardly tell you his name. One of the shyest fellows I'd ever seen." William Douglas, a family friend who was to later sit on the Supreme Court for more than thirty-five years, said Kennedy did not appear to have an anchor in, or a purpose to, his life. "He was sort of drifting. And when he started drifting, then I think he became more of a playboy," he said.[14]

By 1948, Kennedy decided he wanted to run for statewide office and began a four-year quest to visit Massachusetts's communities outside his district. "I would rather run for Governor or the Senate and lose and take a shot than go back and serve another term as a Congressman," he said. A Massachusetts highway map was placed on Kennedy's apartment wall in Boston with pins marking each community he visited. Kennedy told the aide that when the map was packed with pins he would be ready for a statewide race. The congressman frequently left Washington, D.C., on Thursday evening, spent the weekend traveling around his state, and then took an overnight train from Boston to Washington on Sunday night so he could resume his congressional duties on Monday. This version of long distance weekend commuting was quite unusual at the time.

Kennedy was not certain what office he was going to run for in 1952. The incumbent Democratic governor, Paul Dever, was debating whether to run for reelection or challenge Republican senator Henry Cabot Lodge. As a practical matter, Kennedy had to defer to Dever but he fumed as Dever agonized. Finally, on Easter Sunday, April 6, 1952, Dever told Kennedy he was running for reelection as governor. Jack declared his Senate candidacy the next day. This set up one of the most watched political races of the year—Kennedy versus Lodge. They were both young, ambitious, handsome, moderate, wealthy, and the scions of famous families. "Rarely in American politics have hunter and quarry so resembled each other," wrote historian James MacGregor Burns, later a Kennedy aide and biographer.[15]

Kennedy ran a textbook race, utilizing his father's money, his brother Robert's management skills, and his own team of political operatives. They ran a tough, disciplined, and organized operation. Kennedy tried to separate himself from Dever and other state Democrats. He tapped nearly three hundred secretaries to manage his operations across the state. Among other duties, these aides helped arrange more than thirty Kennedy Campaign Teas that attracted 75,000 women, an innovation that Lodge initially ridiculed but later came to realize significantly bolstered the Kennedy campaign. Kennedy hammered Lodge from all directions: from the left on social policy and from the right on foreign policy. He accused Lodge of shifting positions, for poor attendance in the Senate and for being more interested in globetrotting than tending to the needs of Massachusetts. This was a bold, even audacious, charge from the globetrotting Kennedy, whose attendance in the House was far from stellar. "Kennedy will do more for Massachusetts" was his campaign theme. Lodge belatedly realized the gravity of the threat that Kennedy posed to his Senate career. As Dwight

Eisenhower's campaign manager, Lodge had been preoccupied for most of 1952 in helping Eisenhower win the Republican presidential nomination over Robert Taft. He didn't focus on his Senate reelection bid until late in the summer, well after the Kennedy campaign had shifted into high gear.

On November 4, 1952, Eisenhower cruised to an easy win over Democrat Adlai Stevenson, winning 39 of 48 states and capturing Massachusetts by 208,000 votes. Even with Eisenhower's strong showing in the Bay State, Kennedy managed to defeat Lodge by slightly more than 70,000 votes, capturing 51.4% of the vote. Kennedy attributed his win to hard work. "I worked a lot harder in Massachusetts than did Senator Lodge. He was working for General Eisenhower and I think that he felt that would take care of his Massachusetts position," he said at the time. Eight years later, Kennedy described his win over Lodge more vividly. "I just buried Lodge. I don't think he was tough enough, Lodge, because he didn't do the work. He had every advantage in '52. I mean that was a very long shot. Nobody wanted to run against him."[16] Their paths would cross again.

Timing, they say, is everything. Democrats suffered punishing defeats that year, losing the presidency and both chambers of Congress. The party was looking for a fresh face and a new voice. It was looking for a star.

IV

When Kennedy arrived in the Senate in January of 1953, he was determined to follow through on his campaign pledge to help rebuild his state's economy in the context of major regional renewal. He instructed his staff, led by a new aide Ted Sorensen, to assemble a detailed program to revive the New England economy. He outlined this program in three lengthy speeches on the Senate floor that May. Each lasted for more than two hours and was packed with specifics. These were Kennedy's first substantive Senate addresses, and he presented, in near agonizing detail, a plan to rebuild his region. "Machinery is old; management is old; methods are old. Too often government, management, and labor have resisted new ideas and local initiative," he said. Kennedy's New England agenda sought to diversify and expand commercial and industrial activity in struggling communities, prevent further business decline and relocation, ease the pain caused by unemployment and recession, and identify national challenges that should be addressed simultaneously with his plan. "The theme of this program, if it may be boiled down to a single sentence, would be the importance of the federal government in the preservation of fair competition in an expanding economy."[17] Kennedy also made good on a campaign pledge to establish a regional caucus comprised of the twelve New England senators to meet regularly and discuss common challenges and opportunities. The group first met in March of 1954 and developed legislation to help New England's textile, fishing, and small business sectors as well as programs for seniors, veterans, and farmers.

Kennedy garnered regional and national attention when he announced in January 1954 that he was supporting a significant and controversial initiative: the construction of the Saint Lawrence Seaway. Building a seaway to link the Atlantic Ocean to the Great Lakes had been under discussion for decades. Northeast ports and American railroad interests had staunchly opposed this project. During his time in the House, Kennedy had opposed the seaway but had left open the possibility that he might eventually support it. Advocates on both sides of the issue inundated the new senator with calls and letters. "There appears to be a great deal of conflict with respect to the truth about the effect of the Saint Lawrence Seaway on New England," Kennedy wrote to one petitioner, adding that he was reviewing studies on how such a seaway would affect the Port of Boston, the cost of consumer goods, and national security matters.

After much deliberation and political calculation, Kennedy announced that few issues had troubled him as much as this one, and he was going to back the seaway. His support was, in large part, because he was certain that, regardless of what the U.S. decided, Canada would build the seaway, and it would be better for America to be part of the project. He said his decision was based on a broad view of the national interest. "I know of no direct economic benefit to the economy of Massachusetts or any segment thereof from the Seaway. But I am unable to accept such a narrow view of my functions as United States Senator . . . Where federal action is necessary and appropriate, it is my firm belief that New England must fight for those national policies," he declared.[18] Some analysts and politicians said Kennedy's new position reflected his future political ambitions. "I knew Jack was serious about running for president back in 1954, when he mentioned that he intended to vote for the Saint Lawrence Seaway," said Tip O'Neill, who had won Kennedy's House seat and later became Speaker of the House. "But Jack wanted to show he wasn't parochial and that he had a truly national perspective."[19]

When Kennedy entered the Senate, he was assigned to the Labor and the Government Affairs committees. He enjoyed the former and disliked the latter, in part because it was led by Senator Joseph McCarthy, a Republican from Wisconsin whom Kennedy realized had become politically explosive and increasingly toxic. Kennedy plunged into labor issues, the one domestic topic that truly engaged him. He assembled a top-flight team of experts including future luminaries Archibald Cox and Arthur Goldberg, and they drafted a major bill in 1958 that eventually was approved by Congress in 1959. The final legislation required changes to the management and financial disclosure practices of unions. It put more constraints on union elections and finances than Kennedy had preferred but he was widely praised for his ability to understand the nuances of labor issues and to draft a complex bill. Democratic senator Paul Douglas of Illinois said Kennedy's work in the arcane world of labor policy showed "a man with a truly first-rate intellect."[20]

Kennedy was cautious in some areas of domestic politics, most notably civil rights and the Senate's rebuke of McCarthy. On civil rights, Kennedy supported legislation to protect voting rights and end segregation and racial discrimination. But he often appeared reluctant, tactical, and cautious. He supported the thrust of civil rights legislation but stayed at the periphery of the reform effort. Senator Douglas, a civil rights champion, said Kennedy declined to attend meetings of senators pushing for civil rights reform. He seemed fearful of alienating either northern liberals who supported comprehensive legislation or southern conservatives who opposed a strong bill, believing both groups would be critical to his future political ambitions. Kennedy ultimately cast several votes that angered civil rights champions but also voted for compromise bills in 1957 and 1960 that became law. He supported a Senate motion to refer sweeping, House-passed civil rights legislation to the Senate Judiciary Committee on procedural grounds but it had the clear effect of derailing the bill for a year. He also supported a controversial jury trial amendment favored by Southern lawmakers that required a jury rather than a judge trial for criminal contempt cases involving civil rights disputes. Many liberals strongly opposed this amendment.

Kennedy's stance toward McCarthy was also cautious. The polarizing senator was a Kennedy family friend and had considerable support in Massachusetts's Irish Catholic community. Both factors persuaded Kennedy to be careful in his dealings with the senator whose unsubstantiated allegations about communist conspiracies and infiltration of the American government and society helped define the era. After McCarthy badly overreached in 1954 by attacking the army, and his incendiary techniques were fully exposed during the explosive Army-McCarthy hearings, the Senate voted 67 to 22 that December to condemn McCarthy for behavior that brought discredit to the Senate. At the time of the vote Kennedy was recovering from back surgery and did not vote on the resolution, nor did he express his views on the matter through a voting procedure called pairing, in which absent senators with differing views on a matter register the vote they would have cast. Decades later Sorensen accused Kennedy of ducking the McCarthy issue intentionally saying, "I was—and remain—disappointed by his inaction."[21]

Kennedy was captivated by what he called "the high realm of foreign affairs." He found foreign policy both deeply consequential and highly interesting. His two overseas trips in 1951 to Europe, Asia, and the Middle East while a House member deepened this interest in international affairs and expanded his contacts and understanding of issues. When he entered the Senate Kennedy immediately plunged into serious foreign policy debates even though he did not initially have a committee platform that gave him standing.

Saigon was one of the most consequential of all the destinations in Kennedy's 1951 travels. He met with American and French diplomats, military leaders, and journalists. He left the city convinced that the French were playing a losing hand in their effort to retain control over Indochina. He argued this perspective forcefully when he entered the Senate and joined a 1953 debate on a foreign aid bill. American financial support to France, he declared, should be structured to encourage that nation to give the three states of Indochina—Cambodia, Laos, and Vietnam—their freedom and independence. "The conditions are not now present in French Indochina that would permit a victory, regardless of the steady increase in

U.S. assistance since 1950. Continuation of an obviously fruitless campaign will certainly be more likely to result in the French withdrawing," Kennedy warned.[22]

In the spring of 1954, on the eve of the final communist assault on the French fortress at Dien Bien Phu and the start of the Geneva Conference that would eventually partition Vietnam, Kennedy said the United States should rethink its dutiful support of France in Indochina. It would be a big mistake, he declared, for the U.S. to "pour money, materiel, and men into the jungles of Indochina without at least a remote prospect for victory." France, he said, was reluctant to continue its war in Indochina without greater aid from the United States but warned this would be tantamount to throwing good money after bad. "I am frankly of the belief that no amount of American military assistance in Indochina can conquer an enemy which is everywhere and at the same time nowhere, an 'enemy of the people,' which has the sympathy and covert support of the people."[23]

After the French defeat at Dien Bien Phu in May of 1954, its subsequent withdrawal from Indochina, and the partition of Vietnam, the Eisenhower administration strongly backed the leader of South Vietnam, Ngo Dinh Diem. Kennedy now also championed American support of South Vietnam and Diem. He began to speak of a "Diem miracle," and became an informal member of a pro-Diem group called the American Friends of Vietnam. Kennedy gave a keynote address to this group on June 1, 1956, urging generous support of Diem for both moral and strategic reasons. "Vietnam represents the cornerstone of the Free World in Southeast Asia, the key-stone in the arch, the finger in the dike." The success of South Vietnam was critical for America, Kennedy contended. "This is our offspring. We cannot abandon it," he said.[24] The senator's shift from a shrewd critic of France's folly in Indochina to his full-throated backing of American sup-port for Diem and South Vietnam continues to perplex historians and is often explained as political expediency and opportunism.

Kennedy startled the American foreign policy establishment in the summer of 1957 when he delivered several much-discussed speeches on the Senate floor criticizing France's increasingly bloody war in Algeria. He said the war should be viewed as a desperate effort to maintain a colo-nial empire in North Africa—a project the United States should persuade France to abandon. He was reluctant to criticize a friend but added that friendship often meant conveying unpleasant truths. "Did we not learn in Indochina, where we delayed action as the result of similar warnings, that we might have served both the French and our own causes infinitely better had we taken a firm stand much earlier than we did? Did that tragic episode not teach us that, whether France likes it or not, admits it or not, or has our support or not, their overseas territories are sooner or later, one by one, inevitably going to break free and look with suspicion on the Western nations who impeded steps to independence?"[25] He urged France to negotiate an agreement with Algeria for its independence. Kennedy's stinging critique of France's Algeria policy provoked reprimands from Secretary of State John Foster Dulles, former Secretary of State Dean Acheson, and former Democratic presidential nominee Adlai Stevenson. All argued that American officials, including senators, should not criticize an ally over an internal matter. But Kennedy did not back down and said America had the responsibility to challenge allies when they were pursuing self-defeating policies. "The worldwide struggle against imperialism, the sweep of nationalism, is the most potent factor in foreign affairs today. We can resist it or ignore it, but only for a little while; we can see it exploited by the Soviets, with grave consequences; or we, in this country, can give it hope and leadership and thus improve immeasurably our standing and our security," he said.

Kennedy visited Poland in 1955 and was impressed by the spirit of the Polish people and their evident desire for more independence from the Soviet Union. Kennedy was critical about the disparity between the Eisenhower administration's soaring liberation proclamations to the captive peoples of the Warsaw Pact and its meager efforts to provide assistance to Poland and other nations in Eastern Europe. The senator argued that more flexible American foreign assistance programs would allow for more generous aid from the U.S. to nations such as Poland. He proposed educational funds, people-to-people exchange programs, expanded trade, and technical assistance to Poland. "Other satellites, we may be sure, are watching—and if we fail to help the Poles, who else will dare stand up to the Russians and look westward?"[26] The Eisenhower administration agreed with Kennedy in concept but did not work actively to support his initiative to overhaul the Battle Act that was the key statute that limited American foreign assistance programs. Some of the administration's Republican allies on

Capitol Hill said Kennedy's plan would be tantamount to providing aid to Communist nations.

Senator Kennedy often seized on foreign policy as a bludgeon with which to hit the Eisenhower administration and outline his own view of the world. He blasted the administration's New Look security policy, charging that it underfunded the defense budget and relied too heavily on nuclear weapons. He rebuked the administration for uncertainty in the Middle East, timidity in Eastern Europe, lack of imagination for Latin America, paralysis regarding the rise of China, indifference to India, and inept responses to crises in Berlin and the Formosa Straits. He seized on a so-called missile gap, alleging that Eisenhower's defense budgets had allowed the Soviet Union to surge ahead of the United States and put the nation in great danger. "Their missile power will be the shield from behind which they will slowly but surely advance—through Sputnik diplomacy, limited brush fire wars, indirect non-overt aggression, intimidation and subversion, internal revolution, increased prestige or influence, and the vicious blackmail of our allies. The periphery of the Free World will slowly be nibbled away," Kennedy charged in a Senate speech on August 14, 1958.[27]

V

Kennedy secured a seat on the Senate Foreign Relations Committee in January of 1957, a coveted assignment that gave him a platform to study foreign policy more rigorously and to speak more authoritatively. He had sought the placement since he first entered the Senate in 1953. Both he and his father lobbied the Senate Democratic leader, Lyndon Johnson, for Kennedy to be seated on this prestigious panel. Finally, at the start of 1957, Kennedy was selected to fill an opening on the committee. This was a plumb assignment for a senator still in his first term. Ironically, Kennedy joined the committee just as his political ambitions were beginning to soar, and he was spending less time in Washington and more time on the road. Consequently, he was not a committee stalwart. The chairman of the Senate Foreign Relations Committee, William Fulbright, griped that when Kennedy came to hearings he spent much of his time at the end of the dais signing autographed pictures of himself for campaign purposes.

One historian scrutinized Kennedy's attendance record during the final two years of his Senate tenure and calculated that he attended 24 of 117 committee meetings in 1959 and only 3 of 96 in 1960.[28] A story made the rounds that Kennedy grudgingly accepted a subcommittee chairmanship of the Foreign Relations Committee only after being assured that he would only be required to schedule a few hearings.

Still, Kennedy's limited participation on the Senator Foreign Relations Committee is revealing. While he tended to give lofty speeches on the Senate floor and on the campaign trail, in the committee he was willing and able to get in the weeds and discuss complex policy issues and debate highly technical legislative language. For example, in January of 1957 the committee worked for weeks on legislation authorizing the so-called Eisenhower Doctrine in the Middle East. This bill gave the administration authorization for American military and economic cooperation with Middle Eastern nations to block communist expansion in the region. Kennedy was an alert and perceptive participant in these committee debates. He asked penetrating questions about the justification for freezing Egyptian assets in the United States, probed the reasons why communism was gaining popularity in the Middle East, and offered an alternative resolution that raised provocative questions about national sovereignty, governance of the Suez Canal, development of economic resources, and the repatriation of Arab Palestinians. When several Republicans opposed his alternative, Kennedy observed that all of its principles had been drawn from public statements made by President Eisenhower, Secretary of State Dulles, congressional resolutions, or UN Security Council declarations the U.S. had supported. He knew his alternate resolution was unlikely to pass but believed the committee's deliberations had become both narrow and imprecise.

A revealing glimpse of Kennedy can be gleaned by studying the transcript of a subcommittee meeting on Africa he chaired in June of 1959.[29] The subcommittee heard from Paul Nitze, who had just returned from a fact-finding mission to Africa on behalf of the Council on Foreign Relations. With only one other senator in attendance, Frank Church of Idaho, the session was more like a policy seminar than a formal committee hearing. Kennedy was an astute, curious, and witty interlocutor, seeking insights into developments in Guinea, Liberia, Nigeria, and Kenya. He asked Nitze about the strength of communism in Africa and was bemused to learn that some of Africa's Communists had studied in Paris and London. "The London School of Economics—and these fellows almost all to a man have had a Marxist orientation," he quipped. He examined the role of France in West Africa and sought assessments of several African leaders and the quality of American embassies and diplomats. "I think this is terribly important. We do not know anything about it but we are very interested," Kennedy told Nitze, admitting that his subcommittee had just begun to explore these issues. But there is no record that Kennedy's subcommittee delved further into the topic. Kennedy moved on to other things.

VI

Kennedy's political career took on a new life in 1956, largely due to non-Senate events, including the publication of *Profiles in Courage*. As a result of the success of his new book and the Pulitzer Prize it would win the next year, Kennedy was becoming known as the Senate's leading historian and scholar and was asked to chair a special high-profile Senate committee to determine the five "most outstanding" senators in American history. In the keynote speech at that year's National Book Award banquet in New York, Kennedy argued that writers and politicians should join forces, adding that for many of the nation's founding fathers, "books were their tools, not their enemies." He said the link between the two worlds had been severed and needed to be repaired, asking, "Where are the scholar-statesmen of yester-year?"[30] It was quite a change from the average student he had once been. A few months later he delivered the commencement address at Harvard and argued that the political and academic communities needed to respect each other in order to learn the language of the other. "What we need are men who can ride easily over broad fields of knowledge and recognize the mutual dependence of our two worlds," he said, no doubt thinking of himself in that role. "If more politicians knew poetry and more poets knew politics, I am convinced the world would be a little better place in which to live on this commencement day in 1956."[31]

Later that summer, Kennedy became the star of the Democratic National Convention. He narrated the opening film, *The Pursuit of Happiness*, nominated Adlai Stevenson to be the party's candidate for president, and narrowly missed out at winning the vice presidential spot, which went to Senator Estes Kefauver of Tennessee. Nevertheless, he became the most popular Democratic surrogate on the campaign trail that fall. Over the course of five weeks, Kennedy traveled 30,000 miles and gave 150 speeches in 24 states. He campaigned for Stevenson but still managed to present himself as a fresh face and voice of the Democratic Party.

Just weeks after Stevenson's defeat in November, Kennedy decided to run for president in 1960. "If I work hard for four years, I ought to be able to pick up all the marbles," he told his aide Dave Powers. But he also knew he had to improve as a candidate. "I've learned you don't get far in politics until you become a total politician. That means you've got to deal with the party leaders as well as the voters. From now on I'm going to be a total politician," he said.[32]

Thus began a four-year campaign for president that often kept him away from the Senate. Kennedy gave scores of speeches in 1957 and intensified this pace throughout the next three years. He took to the road in 1958 and delivered more than 200 speeches while building a national organization. Preparing a formal campaign for the Democratic nomination, Kennedy traveled almost nonstop in 1959 and 1960 and logged more than 110,000 air miles in those two years. He presented himself as a youthful, modern, progressive Democrat who was steeped in, and respectful of, American history—a young man with gravitas, a scholar-statesman.

VII

Senator Kennedy had grown into a riveting force on the political landscape. He had changed during his eight Senate years. He filled out physically and displayed a robustness that contrasted with the shy and sickly congressman he had once been. He deepened his views on foreign and domestic policy and sharpened his speaking and writing skills with the important assistance of his aide Ted Sorensen.

John F. Kennedy was six feet tall, 170 pounds, with a slender waist and a large head, reddish brown hair, green-grey eyes, and a year-round suntan. He was a cool and detached man with a highly compartmentalized life. He had a large tight-knit family, a bevy of former navy and school friends, a score of devoted long-time policy aides, a so-called Irish mafia of political advisers, and a long line of amorous interests who were not his wife. Sometimes these worlds intersected, but not often.

Kennedy projected a calm self-confidence and dignified self-assurance. He was not a backslapper. Few described him as warm or kind. Charlie Bartlett, a reporter and longtime friend, said Kennedy was "not in love with humanity," adding he could be distant and easily grew bored with people. He was often self-focused and entitled, Bartlett said, but he added that there was "something very luminous" about him. Richard Goodwin, an aide, said Kennedy was "almost exotically glamorous." Journalist Rowland Evans, like many others, was mesmerized by Kennedy. "Jack was simply the most appealing human being I ever met."[33]

Kennedy was a controlled man, especially in public. Clark Clifford, a longtime family lawyer, said Kennedy "kept a tight rein on his personal emotions, enjoying immensely the company of many people from all ways of life, but never allowing intimacies to go beyond a certain point, and never losing control of his own emotions." Clifford was struck by Kennedy's remarkable grace and formidable political skills. "He knew how to win friends and charm people as well as anyone who has practiced the art. But beyond his appeal and elegance lay a very retentive mind, a quick intellect, and a pragmatic and useful cynicism regarding events and people. Unlike most politicians, he did not respond well to excessive and empty flattery that is such a large part of normal political discourse, and he looked for deft ways to deflate or deflect it. His wit, much of it highly sardonic, was justly celebrated," said Clifford.[34]

Kennedy's humor was dry, deadpan, acerbic, and sometimes self-deprecating. One aide, George Ball, observed that Kennedy enjoyed his own jokes more than those of others. Kennedy biographer James MacGregor Burns said he did not "lose himself in laughter," adding that his sense of humor tended toward "a light needling, slightly ironic banter such as one often meets in war or in other times of stress." Burns agreed that Kennedy kept his emotions under tight wrap and apparently had never lost himself in a passionate, unrestrained love affair, despite his extramarital engagements. "I'm not the tragic lover type," Kennedy once said.[35]

There was a dashing quality to Kennedy. Harry McPherson, a seasoned Washington observer, described Kennedy on the Senate floor as "elegant and casual, he sat in the back room, his knees against his desk, rapping his teeth with a pencil and reading *The Economist* and *The Guardian*. He was treated with affection by most senators, but he was ultimately elusive, finding his way in other worlds outside the chamber. Mythically wealthy, handsome, bright, and well connected, he seemed to regard the Senate grandees as impressive but tedious. In turn, he was regarded by them as something of a playboy, a dilettante." McPherson, an aide to Lyndon Johnson in both the Senate and the White House, added that Johnson saw Kennedy as "the enviably attractive nephew who sings an Irish ballad for the company, and then winsomely disappears before the table-clearing and dishwashing begin."[36] A writer for *The Progressive* magazine likened Kennedy to a popular visiting university professor who wows students and faculty wives with his charm and dash but stays clear of the grindingly hard work of academic life.

Historian Arthur Schlesinger Jr. described Kennedy as a voracious reader with a deep love of American and British history. He characterized the senator as practical, ironic, skeptical, and inquisitive. Kennedy wanted to know how things worked, and did not like vague answers. According to Schlesinger, "He was a man of action who could easily pass over to the realm of ideas and confront intellectuals with perfect confidence in his capacity to hold his own."[37]

His privileged upbringing and glamorous life did not prevent Kennedy from knowing tragedy. The deaths of his elder brother Joe and sister Kathleen, along with the serious physical pain he suffered for much of his life, gave him a stoic, unflinching quality. "There is always inequity in life. Some men are killed in war and some men are wounded and some men never leave the country . . . Life is unfair," Kennedy once said.[38]

Kennedy had the ability to look at events objectively, often with irony and detachment. His wife said her husband would have made a good judge, even-tempered and composed as he was. One journalist said Kennedy often employed "shattering understatement." There are only a few examples on record of him losing his composure. Evelyn Lincoln recalled a deeply distraught Kennedy who, in August 1960, had lost his voice as he prepared for the tough fall presidential campaign. Uncertain when he would regain it, Lincoln said he was "completely unnerved. He paced the floor, brushed his hair back a hundred times and kept hitting his fist on the table." Another aide, Richard Goodwin, described a campaign incident in which Kennedy's motorcade got lost for a long time in the Bronx, throwing his schedule into disarray in the final precious days of the presidential campaign. Kennedy returned to his hotel furious. He retreated to a private room to get ready for a reception. However, unable to control his anger, he walked out into the reception in his underwear and berated the driver. "Then, his anger abated, seemingly oblivious to the unbelieving stares of his reception guests, Kennedy returned to the bedroom, closed the door, and began to revise his speech," Goodwin recalled. "Less than thirty minutes later, clad in evening dress, the tall, handsome senator emerged and began his rounds of the suite, greeting each guest with a friendly handshake and a quip, totally controlled, his calm, amiable presence dominating the room."[39]

Kennedy was a demanding boss who was used to having things when he wanted them. Lincoln said she quickly learned "that if he wanted something done, he wanted it done immediately. He liked to have people around him available at all times. When he called, whether it was ten o'clock in the morning or twelve o'clock at night, he wanted to be able to reach you." Kennedy rarely offered compliments. Pierre Salinger worked on Kennedy's presidential campaign and later in the White House and said Kennedy inspired devotion despite his "bristling temper, his cold sarcasm, and his demands for always higher standards of excellence."[40]

He was not a skilled administrator and thought in terms of people, not organizations or systems. He disliked large meetings, preferring small group conversations and the quiet delegation of tasks. He sometimes gave two people the same project, not always intentionally. He occasionally grew frustrated at his own disarray and that of his staff. "Damn it, Ted, we need to get more organized," he once snapped at Ted Reardon, an aide, during a campaign trip.

Although few would describe Kennedy as profound, almost everyone described him as practical and probing. He preferred written to oral briefings. He enjoyed reading history and biography, and often found books better companions than people. He once said that if he were sitting on a plane he would prefer reading a good book to chatting to the person sitting next to him. He wondered if this were the right temperament for a politician, and compared himself unfavorably to Hubert Humphrey. "I'd be delighted if I had Hubert Humphrey's disposition. He thrives on this period. He loves to go out and campaign for five days. It's a lot of work."[41]

Despite his penchant for being alone with a good book, there was a restless quality to Kennedy. "Kennedy was a very impatient man. He didn't want to be bored," said aide Harris Wofford. "Life with him was always so fast," Jackie once said. Journalist Mary McGrory described Kennedy as demanding and selfish while simultaneously charming. "Either you informed him or you amused him. Otherwise he turned away," she wrote. "He had a gift for making one come to the point," observed Joe Alsop, a prominent columnist and Kennedy friend.[42]

Lyndon Johnson envied Kennedy's political skills but was underwhelmed by his accomplishments as a senator. From Johnson's perspective, Kennedy never said or did anything of importance in the Senate but was bolstered by his glamour and his Pulitzer Prize. Johnson's view of Kennedy, while clouded by their political competition, was consistent with other senators. Hubert Humphrey said Kennedy was talented but never fully engaged in the world of the Senate. Even his own staff saw Kennedy as a solid but not a stellar senator. "John Kennedy was not one of the Senate's great leaders," Sorensen said, adding he was never a "full-fledged member of the Senate's inner circle."[43] Kennedy said his presidential ambitions were fueled by his frustration about the inability of a single senator to accomplish much. But he was also an ambitious man who simply wanted to reach the top of his profession.

Part of his mid-tier performance as a senator would stem from the serious health problems Kennedy suffered during his Senate years. He was absent from the Senate for more than seven months, from October of 1954 to May of 1955, while recovering from two major back surgeries. He was also sick for long periods between 1955 and 1957. During the fall of 1957, he spent more than three weeks in the hospital due to urinary tract infections, back and stomach pain, and weight loss. While he complained only rarely, pain and illness wore him down and sapped his spirits. "I wish I had more good times," he told his wife, who interpreted this comment to be a reference to his health. She recalled him coming home from work tired and often sick. "He'd walk around the Senate looking wonderful and tan in his gray suit and then he'd come home and go in a hospital bed."[44]

But Kennedy was tough and determined to push through his pain to achieve his ambitions. When the 1960 campaign began he knew it was possible he would fail to get the Democratic nomination. Speaking to friends at a dinner party in January of 1960, just days after he had formally launched his presidential campaign, Kennedy acknowledged that he had no idea how the campaign would turn out. "Everybody reaches a natural level. It's possible my natural level is the Senate . . . We'll know in six months," he mused.[45]

Kennedy told his friends that a defeat for the presidency would be difficult to deal with and he would "have to pick up my life" and find something else to do professionally. He observed that in politics the margin is very narrow between those who succeed and those who don't. "Like life," he added. But he ended his rumination with determination and even excitement. "How could it be more interesting than this sort of checkerboard chess struggle of the next seven months . . . How could it be more fascinating than to run for president under the obstacles and hurdles that are before me?"[46]

SIX

PRESIDENT EISENHOWER TRANSFERS POWER

I

While Dwight Eisenhower did not look forward to relinquishing the presidency on January 20, 1961, throughout his tenure he had occasionally assembled lists of whom he deemed to be credible successors. These names included associates from business, the military, and sometimes even politics—a profession he did not hold in high regard. Richard Nixon was almost always on these lists, but rarely near the top. Senator John F. Kennedy was, of course, never on these lists, not even at the bottom. In the summer of 1960, Eisenhower told an aide he could not imagine handing over the presidency to that "whippersnapper" Kennedy.

The verdict of the American people on Election Day forced the outgoing president to not only contemplate but prepare for this indignity. After

Nixon conceded the election on November 9, Eisenhower sent Kennedy two telegrams. The first was a brief statement of congratulations and the second was a longer note in which he vowed to cooperate in the orderly transfer of power and proposed how to do it. The president didn't like to use the word "transition" because it connoted a sharing of power during this ten-week interregnum. A "transition" was not something that interested Eisenhower. But he was constitutionally obligated to "transfer" presidential power on January 20, 1961.

The president's two cables to Kennedy began one of the most poignant and challenging chapters in Eisenhower's life as he prepared to hand over the government to Kennedy, deal with complicated governing challenges, attend to personal affairs, say goodbye to his cabinet and staff, and deliver a final message to the country. The transition for Eisenhower began with a ten-day vacation in Georgia and ended with a snowy, eighty-mile car ride from the White House to his home and farm in Gettysburg, Pennsylvania, where he and Mamie retired. Most of Eisenhower's ten weeks were spent in Washington but also included a few brief trips. It was a bittersweet time. Eisenhower was variously nostalgic, angry, frustrated, magnanimous, petulant, proud, and wary. He was suspicious of the new president, protective of his own legacy, ambivalent about retirement, and determined to get his affairs and those of the country in order. "I want to leave this place as much a going concern as possible," he told his chief of staff, Wilton Persons.[1]

There was not very much about the 1960 presidential campaign that pleased President Eisenhower. He didn't like Kennedy's attacks on the administration, his own vice president's often lackluster campaign, and especially Nixon's ineffective response to Kennedy's criticisms of the past eight years. Eisenhower lamented the power of TV, the gullibility of the American people to "sentiment and emotion" and the shallowness of the televised debates. The outcome of these debates did nothing to warm him to this new media.

Speaking with his son John in the Oval Office on the morning after the election, the somber president said the verdict was a repudiation of all he had tried to do the previous eight years. Reeling from the results, Eisenhower was not even sure he wanted to go through with his long-planned golfing vacation to Augusta National Golf Club. But his son insisted that he go, "almost shoving me on the plane," Eisenhower later recalled. Before leaving Washington the president sent a note to Nixon, congratulating him on running a good campaign and explaining why he would not be there to greet him on his return to the capital. "This afternoon I am starting off to Augusta," Eisenhower began. "While it seems ridiculous for me to be speaking of fatigue when I know what you and Pat have been through in these many weeks, I am nevertheless feeling a great need to get some sunshine, recreation and rest."[2]

Several of the president's golf and bridge friends met him at National Airport in Washington and flew down to Augusta with him. On the flight, one friend, Ellis Slater, recalled Eisenhower sitting across the bridge table saying that Nixon's loss was the "biggest defeat" of the president's life. Eisenhower tried to shake his gloom during the ten-day golf and hunting trip, but later acknowledged there were "lugubrious post mortem discussions" about the campaign in Augusta.[3] But Eisenhower was a resilient man and was fortified by his time away. His spirits revived, he steeled himself for the task ahead.

Eisenhower was determined that the transfer of power would be conducted professionally and in the best interests of the country. He wanted to leave a functioning government and help the new administration get up and running—within limits. He was, unabashedly, a Kennedy critic. He opposed Kennedy's agenda, doubted the senator was ready to be president and believed that voter fraud may have been a factor in the Democrat's victory. Eisenhower ridiculed Kennedy's conception of the presidency, didn't believe he knew how to run a government and was certain he did not understand the nuances of national security challenges. Eisenhower was also convinced that Kennedy would blame him for future failures and take credit for successes that were the result of Eisenhower's policies. He did not want senior members of his administration to accept positions in the new administration. When he learned that Douglas Dillon, his undersecretary of state, was being considered as the treasury secretary, Eisenhower urged Dillon in several conversations and in a letter not to take the job. He warned that Dillon would "become a scapegoat of the radicals" in the incoming administration and was angry when Dillon disregarded his advice and accepted the Treasury post. When Eisenhower received the resignation letter of John McCone as chairman of the Atomic Energy Commission he applauded him for not staying on with Kennedy, convinced that holdovers from the Eisenhower administration would mostly be used as foils by the new team.

II

Eisenhower, a participant in a tense and angry transition with Truman eight years earlier, did not want to repeat the experience. President Truman had worked closely with General Eisenhower in the final months of World War II and for several years after the war when Ike was in high ranking military posts. However, when Eisenhower decided to run for president in 1952, one of the central themes of his campaign was the assertion that the Truman administration had created a horrible mess in Washington. This mess, in Ike's telling, was characterized by both incompetence and venality. He also hammered Truman's foreign policy as weak and flawed, citing the stalemated war in Korea as grim evidence of the administration's ineptness. Not surprisingly, Truman did not take kindly to Eisenhower's campaign criticisms, unleashed his own rebukes at Ike, and dismissed as demagoguery Ike's vow to visit Korea soon after the election. They had a frosty meeting at the White House after the November election, and there was limited cooperation between the two men during the transition in late 1952 and early 1953. Eisenhower blamed Truman mostly for that fraught changeover but almost certainly realized that he was not blameless for the tensions.

Clearly, handing the presidency over to Nixon would have been easier— after all, he had just been there by Eisenhower's side for the past eight years. But now Eisenhower was preparing to welcome the youngest, and, he thought, the greenest president in history.

On July 1, four months before the election, Eisenhower and his cabinet reviewed Cabinet Paper 60–110, which outlined how executive branch authority would be transferred to the next administrataion. White House budget director Maurice Stans led the discussion and also described a special project that was being organized by the Brookings Institution to facilitate the transition. The president was determined the coming transfer would go smoothly but was skeptical about the Brookings project that involved regular meetings between representatives of the two campaigns, the White House, executive branch departments, and policy experts. He was wary of any project that brought outsiders too deeply into the work-ings of his government. Eisenhower didn't think Nixon needed guidance from the project and doubted the Democratic nominee, who would be decided in the coming weeks in Los Angeles, would be interested in it while actively running for president. Eisenhower supported additional intelligence briefings for the presidential candidates. He also believed the eventual president-elect should get more comprehensive national security briefings than had been provided in the past. Eisenhower told his cabinet that he was confident the exchange of power would go well if Nixon won. However, if the Democrat were to win, the administration would have to take great care, "so there would be no risk of disaster during the transition."[4]

Persons, the White House chief of staff, assured the president that the cabinet paper would be refined to reflect the president's concerns. On November 3, less than a week before the election, Persons and Eisenhower discussed the transition in the context of a possible Kennedy win despite Eisenhower's aversion to it. He and his senior staff and cabinet knew they had to prepare for all outcomes.

When the results were clear, Eisenhower telegrammed Kennedy, pledging to work with him. "I stand ready to meet with you at any mutu-ally convenient time to consider problems of continuity of government and orderly transfer of Executive responsibility on January 20th from my administration to yours. In the meantime—or even in lieu thereof—in order to facilitate and prepare for this transfer, I would be happy to have one of your assistants meet with my principal staff assistant, Wilton B. Persons, to whom I am assigning coordinating responsibility. He will be prepared to make arrangements by which representatives designated by you could meet with the present heads of the Executive Departments."[5] The president also suggested meetings between Kennedy's staff and the White House budget office regarding government administration and budget issues and also between Kennedy representatives and the secretary of state for foreign policy updates. Kennedy sent a gracious reply to Eisenhower, thanking him for his commitment to cooperation and designating Clark Clifford as his representative to work with Persons. Kennedy said he was eager to meet with Eisenhower.

Eisenhower convened his cabinet on November 9, the morning after the election and before he left for Augusta. They formally approved cabinet paper, CP 60–110/1—"Preparatory Arrangements for Turn-Over of Executive Responsibility," which was then transmitted by the president to the heads of departments and agencies. The paper pledged the outgoing administration would cooperate with the incoming team with the "double objective" of facilitating an orderly transfer of responsibility on January 20, 1961, while also "maintaining until then, without compromise, Executive authority and responsibility in this Administration. Under the Constitution, there can be no 'sharing' of responsibility with the new Administration prior to that time."

The cabinet paper drew clear boundaries between the current administration and its successor. "Contact by representatives of the President-Elect within the Executive Branch is to be limited and controlled. Normally, no more than one designated representative, who may of course be the individual intended for appointment to the Cabinet post in the new Administration, should be in contact in any Department . . . Obviously there is to be no general movement into the Executive Branch by personnel from the Administration to come."[6]

Eisenhower emphasized to his cabinet that Persons would be the initial and primary point of contact between the incoming and outgoing administrations. The president did not want Kennedy's government-in-waiting to take over, or wander into, the Eisenhower administration until the final moment. The reason for Eisenhower's acute sensitivity to this issue is not evident apart from his determination for orderly government and his dislike of Kennedy's campaign and by extension the candidate and now president-elect.

III

The mechanics of the transition were placed in the hands of Persons and Clifford who became central, albeit behind-the-scenes, players in the ensuing drama. They were very different men. Clifford was a smooth Missourian and revered Democratic operative who was now a prominent Washington lawyer. He was widely credited in Democratic circles for helping organize President Harry Truman's stunning upset in 1948 over the Republican presidential candidate, Thomas Dewey. Clifford was considered a shrewd man and a skilled operative. Persons was an affable military man with an Alabama drawl who had spent much of his professional life working on Capitol Hill as the military's liaison to Congress. He was respected and well-known in the Washington political world including by Clifford. He was understated and controlled and spent his entire career effectively operating behind the scenes.

Persons and Clifford met on Monday, November 14, at the White House for their initial face-to-face meeting to discuss the transition. The meeting ran for more than two hours and focused on their broad approach to the transition and addressed several immediate issues. Clifford said Kennedy respected that Eisenhower would be in full charge of the government until January 20, and his team only sought necessary background information on key issues so they could better understand the mechanics of running the White House and the executive branch. Clifford understood the president's desire not to have a multitude of outsiders going through the departments and agencies during this period.

Clifford asked if Kennedy could send an office manager to examine the organizational structure of the Eisenhower White House. Persons consented and emphasized the importance of Kennedy moving quickly to select the secretaries of state, defense, and treasury; a White House budget director; and a staff secretary. Persons informed Clifford that Treasury Secretary Robert Anderson and Undersecretary of State Douglas Dillon were about to travel to Bonn to meet with top officials in West Germany on critical international economic issues: the U.S.'s growing balance of payments deficit and a potential gold crisis. Persons said the administration wanted to brief Kennedy on the matter but was not trying to force his hand. Persons also asked how the Eisenhower administration should deal with foreign governments seeking to contact Kennedy.

The two men set up a meeting between Kennedy and Eisenhower about ten days after Thanksgiving, which would involve a private session between the president and the president-elect followed by a larger meeting with senior officials of Eisenhower's administration. They discussed how to arrange daily briefings for Kennedy by the CIA and the State Department, ensuring that he had the same intelligence as Eisenhower. This was in marked contrast to what Eisenhower received from the outgoing Truman administration. Persons and Clifford briefly touched on the best way to arrange FBI background checks and security clearances for Kennedy appointees so they could review classified materials.

Persons and Clifford provided a general summary of their first meeting to Anne Wheaton, the deputy White House press secretary, who briefed reporters. From that point on they worked quietly behind the scenes, keeping their principals informed, and avoiding the press. The two men largely withdrew from public view for the duration of the transition although they were far from idle.

Several days after the first Persons-Clifford meeting, Eisenhower instructed Persons to keep a careful written record of the transfer. This procedure was a departure for Persons, who tended to operate orally and was not a careful notetaker during his White House years. The president, however, believed written records provided clarity and precision and were useful if disputes later arose. Person's frequent "memos for the record" are the best chronicle of the transition from the perspective of the Eisenhower administration. They reveal what topics were discussed, the views of each side, and what follow-up was needed. For Eisenhower, this extensive paper trail established a record and preempted later finger-pointing by his successor if something were to fall through the cracks.

As the transition unfolded, Persons and Clifford typically met two or three times a week in person and exchanged several phone calls each day. Persons was often joined at these meetings by White House counsel Dave Kendall while Clifford was sometimes accompanied by Ted Sorensen, who was poised to be a leading official in the Kennedy administration. Persons and Clifford dealt with matters large and small—from the future employment of the White House secretaries to the status of arms control negotiations. Persons repeatedly encouraged Clifford to push Kennedy to name key people who would make the transfer simpler and more effective, reiterating the need for secretaries of state, defense, and treasury, as well as a national security adviser and an office manager. Clifford signaled that he was doing all that he comfortably could in this regard.

While Persons knew that Clifford was hardly a neophyte to the federal government, he reminded him of the many complex activities the White House engaged in especially those the new team needed to prepare for such as scheduling daily appointments, drafting presidential speeches and messages, congressional communication, interacting with the national party apparatus, managing the National Security Council, keeping in daily contact with the State and Defense Departments and the CIA, monitoring scientific developments, and overseeing trade negotiations.

William Hopkins, the White House executive clerk and a civil servant, frequently attended the meetings, seeking instructions from the new administration on its plans regarding White House support personnel, office space, and the White House budget. Hopkins provided the Kennedy team with detailed briefing books on the current White House staff and maps of the West Wing and Executive Office Building office layout. He was very concerned about the future employment fate of the "career girls" in the White House—the three dozen or so secretaries who answered phones, typed letters, filed papers, and usually remained in place as presidents came and went.

Persons instructed the outgoing White House staff on how to dispose of the mountains of reports and files that this paper-generating administration created. He told White House officials they could retain their personal documents but had to hand over all other official documents. These would be collected and eventually sent to the Eisenhower Presidential Library in Abilene, Kansas. Robert Gray, the cabinet staff secretary, offered Eisenhower guidance on how to deal with cabinet papers. The president could keep personal and political papers generated for cabinet meetings but should leave copies of other documents for the incoming administration. Persons also instructed the various cabinet departments and agencies to prepare briefing books to help the incoming administration understand each department's structure, budget, statutes directing its affairs, and relationships with relevant congressional committees. Persons described his memo as a "checklist, not a mandate—a guideline as to points which might be considered for inclusion." Persons told department heads that the purpose of their briefing books was "distinctly not to involve the recipient in matters of current agency operations but only to look beyond January 20."[7]

As Persons and Clifford oversaw the tedious but important details of transferring government authority they also focused on preparing for the first one-on-one meeting between Eisenhower and Kennedy. The two men had met briefly in 1945 when Ike was a commanding general and Kennedy traveled to the war zone with the navy secretary, James Forrestal. They had been in large group gatherings during Eisenhower's presidency but had never held a private meeting. Both Kennedy and Eisenhower approached the first encounter with wariness and attention, recognizing the importance to the nation—and to themselves—of achieving a smooth transfer of power.

On November 28 the White House officially announced that the president and president-elect would meet on December 6 at 9:00 A.M. Persons, after consulting with Eisenhower, proposed to Clifford a carefully organized meeting. The president would meet Kennedy at the North Portico of the White House and then escort him to the Oval Office for a private meeting that would last for a "duration agreeable to themselves." The two men would then confer with the president's secretaries of state, defense, and treasury, as well as Persons and Clifford. At the end of the meetings, Hagerty, Eisenhower's press secretary, and Pierre Salinger, Kennedy's press aide, would issue a statement. Kennedy would then leave the White House and speak to the press outside the West Wing. Clifford told Persons that this proposed arrangement was "completely agreeable" to Kennedy.

Both Persons and Clifford conferred with their principals and other top officials to discuss what each hoped to accomplish in the meeting. Meticulously organized briefing books were assembled for Kennedy and Eisenhower by their staffs. Kennedy wanted to discuss the crises in Berlin, Cuba, and the Far East, specifically China and Formosa. He also wanted to solicit Eisenhower's views on overhauling the National Security Council, the Pentagon, and White House operations. He was eager to hear the president's confidential assessments of French president Charles de Gaulle, British prime minister Harold Macmillan, and German chancellor Konrad Adenauer. The president was prepared to talk about these topics as well as recent developments regarding NATO, the United States' worsening balance of payments situation, and a gold crisis, which he partly attributed to Kennedy's expansive and expensive campaign promises. The president also had other topics in mind: redeployment of U.S. troops in Europe, disarmament talks with the Soviet Union in Geneva, the structure of the White House staff, and challenges in the Congo, Laos, and Algeria.

IV

On Tuesday, December 6, the president arrived in the Oval Office at about 8:00 A.M. and had meetings with his son, with Persons, and with

Hagerty. Just before 9:00 A.M. he strolled over to the North Portico of the White House.

Kennedy had returned to Washington the previous evening from his family compound in Palm Beach. Chronically late for events and meetings during his presidential campaign, Kennedy was determined to be punctual for his first session with Eisenhower. As it happened, his borrowed white Lincoln limousine approached the White House so early that morning that Kennedy ordered his driver to circle around the block to kill time and avoid an embarrassingly premature arrival.

When Kennedy arrived at the North Portico at 9:00 A.M. he was met on the steps by Eisenhower. More than two hundred reporters and cameramen jostled for the best view of the encounter between the seventy-year-old president in his brown suit and the forty-three-year-old president-elect in blue pinstripes. Eisenhower had arranged for a military honor guard comprised of representatives from the army, navy, air force, marines, and coast guard. The Marine Band played "Stars and Stripes Forever" as Kennedy arrived. "Good morning, Mr. President," Kennedy said as he approached Eisenhower, who was at the top step, looming more than a foot above Kennedy. "Senator," Ike responded with a smile and offered his hand, looking down on Kennedy in an optic that was almost certainly not accidental. "I'd have come down there, but these photographers wouldn't let me," he quipped. The two men paused a minute for the cameras and then Eisenhower snapped "okay" to the press and ushered Kennedy inside. He gave Kennedy a quick walking tour of the White House, pointing out the indoor swimming pool and introducing Kennedy to several of the ushers.

The two met alone for nearly two hours in the Oval Office and then joined Eisenhower's three senior cabinet members in the Roosevelt Room: Secretary of State Herter, Secretary of Defense Gates, and Secretary of the Treasury Anderson. Kennedy knew Herter from Massachusetts politics, and Gates and Anderson mostly by reputation. Persons and Clifford also attended the larger group meeting and Hagerty and Salinger stopped by twice for guidance on the joint statement.

According to later accounts, the two men reviewed challenges facing the United States in Berlin, the Far East, and Cuba, discussed Pentagon reform, the operations of the National Security Council, and the personalities and predilections of de Gaulle, Macmillan, and Adenauer. Eisenhower gave Kennedy a private twenty-minute briefing on the balance of payments issue and then his treasury secretary addressed the same topic for forty-five minutes in the larger group discussion, giving Kennedy more information on the topic than he wanted to absorb at the time. Eisenhower urged Kennedy to think carefully and move deliberately before overhauling the Pentagon and reorganizing the White House's operations. The two men covered many topics that December morning but the president cautioned his successor that they were only skimming the surface of very complex challenges facing the nation.[8]

Eisenhower and Kennedy issued a statement after the meeting that blandly reviewed some of the subjects that were discussed. "There was of course full understanding that under the Constitution the President of the United States maintains sole jurisdiction for the conduct of the Government until his successor is inaugurated," the statement said. The men declared that their talks provided "a better foundation for our representatives who are working on the necessary orderly transfer of Executive responsibility from one Administration to another." They included a positive assessment of the transition. "The progress to date of this work has been most satisfactory. We believe that through such orderly processes the continuity of Government affairs will be assured and our people will continue to demonstrate that they are united in the nation's leadership toward peace."[9]

The three-hour meeting ended shortly after noon. Eisenhower returned to his office routine. He jumped into back-to-back meetings with the National Agricultural Advisory Council and members of the Civil War Centennial Commission. During this time Kennedy remained on the White House grounds, talking to the press outside the West Wing. Standing in the December cold without a jacket, Kennedy was swarmed by reporters, several standing almost at his elbow. He praised Eisenhower's graciousness and professionalism and repeated that the president was fully in charge until January 20. Kennedy said Eisenhower had been "extremely generous in the time that he gave to the discussion of the problems that the United States now faces and will face in the coming months." Kennedy noted that he and Eisenhower spoke privately for longer than he expected before meeting with the others. "The president was extremely helpful. He has been very careful in the arrangements that he had made to make it easier for the new Administration to assume the responsibilities. He has gone to great pains. They have given us every cooperation and the meeting this morning was an extension of that cooperation." He parried a question about which challenges were most pressing. "I wouldn't attempt to assign a priority," he said. Asked about a possible overseas trip to attend a NATO meeting before the inauguration, Kennedy said, "No, I have got a lot of problems here in Washington."[10]

Kennedy sent a note to Eisenhower a few days later expressing appreciation for "the precision and frankness" of the president's views. He added that he was greatly impressed by Herter, Gates, and Anderson, praising their "high quality and devotion to public service." Eisenhower told his aides he was impressed by Kennedy and later said that Kennedy displayed "unusual good taste" during the meetings. "I was struck by his pleasing personality, concentrated interest, and receptiveness."[11] Ike said he found Kennedy a serious and thoughtful student, but then added a dig. "He had no idea of the complexity of the job at that time."

The meeting helped break the ice between the two men although Eisenhower actually took a first step about a week earlier when he sent Kennedy a note congratulating him on the birth of his son, John F. Kennedy Jr. "Dear Senator Kennedy," Eisenhower began, not yet able to bring himself to refer to him as the president-elect. "Mrs. Eisenhower joins me in warm congratulations to you and Mrs. Kennedy on the birth of your son. We add also our good wishes to your little daughter on her approaching third birthday." Kennedy responded warmly. "My dear Mr. President: Mrs. Kennedy and I wish to express our great appreciation to you for your generous note to us on the birth of our son. It was indeed heartwarming to receive these kind words from Mrs. Eisenhower and yourself. With every good wish."

Eisenhower sent Kennedy a note on December 19 in which he admonished himself for an oversight. "I regret it did not occur to me, earlier, to offer you as President-Elect one facility that might be of some possible use, namely the use of a governmental plane." Eisenhower said that if Kennedy wished to use a plane the administration would arrange it. "On the other hand, should you decide otherwise, I would hope that the existence of this suggestion and this letter itself might be held confidential. For this reason, I have marked the letter personal." Kennedy responded to Eisenhower in a letter on his Senate stationery. "My dear Mr. President: Thank you for your very generous thought in regard to the use of the plane. Fortunately,

I have been able to use the same plane that carried us through the fall and as I do not plan to travel very much between now and the 20th of January I believe it will serve us very satisfactorily."[12]

After the Eisenhower-Kennedy meeting and with Christmas approaching, Clifford sent Persons a warm note on December 21 thanking him for "the full and complete cooperation you have extended to me in our joint endeavor. You have not only made the operation efficient and effective, but it has also been exceedingly pleasant. When I contemplate what this task might have been without the unique contribution you have made to it, I shudder at the shambles it might have been." Clifford offered Persons Christmas greetings and wishes for a happy New Year.[13]

In his private interactions with Kennedy and in his public statements, Eisenhower was determined to be constructive and generous. In one staff meeting he said he wanted to avoid coming across as "fatherly or professorial" to Kennedy, reasoning this would make the younger man less likely to heed his advice. However, privately to his friends and staff, Eisenhower was more skeptical of Kennedy and his team. Still smarting from Kennedy's campaign attacks on his administration, Eisenhower ripped into many of his appointments, particularly Dean Rusk to head the State Department. He was incredulous that Kennedy would prominently feature Frank Sinatra and Sammy Davis Jr. in his inaugural festivities, apparently believing the entertainers were too frivolous for this august occasion. Eisenhower was especially critical of Kennedy when conversing with his bridge and golf friends at Augusta during brief visits in December and January. The president and his friends took turns deriding Kennedy's support for expensive government programs and the quality of nominees who would populate the new administration. Eisenhower remained convinced and even preoccupied that Kennedy was prepared to take credit for all of the positive things that happened in United States during the first weeks of his presidency while blaming any mistakes on the departed Eisenhower administration.

V

Even as the mechanics of transition were being attended to, Eisenhower and his team still had to deal with running the federal government while managing serious international challenges in Laos, Cuba, Berlin, and elsewhere. While Eisenhower had hoped for a period of calm between Election Day and the inauguration, it did not turn out that way. Statutory requirements, domestic challenges, and international events were impervious to America's electoral calendar.

After nearly eight years at the helm, the business of government was familiar to Eisenhower and his team. The president was required by law to submit a final budget before leaving office. In the final weeks of his presidency, Eisenhower, a longtime and relentless proponent of fiscal discipline and balanced budgets, conferred extensively with Treasury Secretary Anderson and Budget Director Maurice Stans. They spent hours going over the federal budget, refining estimates for the current 1961 fiscal year, making proposals for the 1962 budget, and framing the plan in the context of his eight years in office.

Initial estimates by the White House and Treasury showed that small deficits were likely in both 1961 and 1962. However, any shortfall would be small and could easily be estimated away by using different and quite plausible assumptions on spending and revenues. Eisenhower was initially conflicted. He thought that a budget that projected deficits would send a warning to Congress and the American public that even with a fiscally prudent administration the dangers of deficits were real and a threat to the nation. Alternatively, Eisenhower feared that if his budget projected a deficit and the final result was even a small surplus, Kennedy would get credit for this apparent improvement even though he had done nothing to bring about the result. Ultimately, Eisenhower, prodded by Persons, decided that his budget would predict a small surplus for both the current 1961 and the coming 1962 fiscal years. Stans drafted a memo on December 12, the title of which framed the issue and presented the conclusion: "The Symbol and Strategy of a Balanced Budget For 1961 as well as 1962." Stans reasoned that the spending and revenue estimates were uncertain and there was much to be gained by projecting even small budget surpluses. Eisenhower's 1961 federal budget estimated the nation would spend $78.9 billion and take in $79 billion in revenues. For fiscal year 1962, Eisenhower proposed $80.9 billion in spending and $82.3 billion in revenues. Democrats derided these projections as creative accounting but Eisenhower shrugged off the criticisms and portrayed himself as a steadfast protector of the public purse.[14]

On January 18 the administration released a separate, brief economic report. In it the president emphasized the underlying strength of the economy and acknowledged it had slowed some in 1960, but predicted it was poised to strengthen. "Because action to maintain balance and to consolidate gains was taken in good time, we can look forward, provided public and private policies are favorable, to a period of sound economic growth from a firm base." Eisenhower recommended a balanced federal budget for the 1962 fiscal year, giving the treasury secretary the power to increase a long-term interest rate, targeting federal programs to areas with persistently high unemployment, and amending the Employment Act of 1946 to make reasonable price stability a goal of the federal government as well as strong growth.

Eisenhower's State of the Union address, which he submitted in writing on January 12 rather than deliver personally before a Joint Session of Congress, was his broadest explanation and defense of his record as president. It appeared to be written for historians. The outgoing president observed that it was his constitutional duty to assess the State of the Union, noting that in the past this was also an occasion for him to chart the future course of the nation and offer fresh proposals. "This time my function is different," he wrote. "The American people, in free election, have selected new leadership which soon will be entrusted with management of our government. A new president shortly will lay before you his proposals to shape the future of our great land." He said that in his final State of the Union report he wanted to thank Congress for "devotion to the common good and your friendship" and to review events and his record over the past eight years.

The world, the president argued, had undergone profound changes since he assumed office but the United States had forged ahead under a constructive foreign policy seeking peace, liberty, and well being, for others as well as Americans. He reminded the nation that since the Korean truce, "Americans have lived in peace in highly troubled times." Eisenhower defended his administration's policies in Iran, Guatemala, Suez, Lebanon, Formosa, and West Berlin. He touted the mutual security arrangements he helped build and strengthen, including the Southeast Asia Treaty Organization, NATO, the Organization of American States, the Central Treaty Organization, and the Australia, New Zealand, United States Security Treaty. He cited his Atoms for Peace proposal, which led to the creation of the International

Atomic Energy Agency. Under Eisenhower, the United States had also supported the doubling of capital for the World Bank and a 50% capital increase for the International Monetary Fund. "Our great moral and material commitments to collective security, deterrence of force, international law, negotiations that lead to self-enforcing agreements and the economic interdependence of free nations should remain the cornerstone of a foreign policy that will ultimately bring permanent peace with justice in freedom to mankind," he wrote, seeking to bring cohesion to these initiatives.

Eisenhower, still displeased about Kennedy's attack on his defense policies in the 1960 campaign, declared that America's military was an awesome force. "For the first time in our nation's history we have consistently maintained in peacetime, military forces of a magnitude sufficient to deter and if need be to destroy predatory forces in the world. Tremendous advances in strategic weapons systems have been made in the past eight years," he declared.

But he was aware the future would be challenging, and the United States would face large defense expenditures for an indefinite period to come, probably for decades. Eisenhower warned that this money needed to be spent carefully. "Every dollar uselessly spent on military mechanisms decreases our total strength and, therefore, our security." He cautioned against crash spending in which each move by the Communists, however innocuous, triggered an American overreaction. "The 'bomber gap' of several years ago was always a fiction, and the 'missile gap' shows every sign of being the same," he wrote in a sentence that seemed specially earmarked for his successor. His position was that the nation needed a fully adequate and steady level of effort, designed for the long term.

Eisenhower noted that his administration helped shift the American economy from a war footing to peacetime stability. The American economy had passed the half-trillion-dollar mark in gross national product early in 1960 and its output of goods and services was now nearly 25 percent higher than it had been in 1952. The president wrote, "These have been times for careful adjustment of our economy from the artificial impetus of a hot war to constructive growth in a precarious peace. While building a new economic vitality without inflation, we have also increased public expenditures to keep abreast of the needs of a growing population and its attendant new problems, as well as our added international responsibilities."

Eisenhower celebrated major infrastructure developments and under-scored two: the construction of the Saint Lawrence Seaway, which opened the heartland of America to ocean commerce, and the landmark Interstate and Defense Highways Act that contemplated 41,000 miles of roads, about a quarter of which was already open to traffic. And there were achieve-ments to celebrate in agriculture, the environment, education, health and welfare, housing and urban development, and finally, veterans programs and civil rights, where advances were made, especially in voting rights and the integration of schools. He noted that the first consequential federal civil rights legislation in eighty-five years was passed by Congress in 1957 and 1960 at the urging of his administration. "This pioneering work in civil rights must go on. Not only because discrimination is morally wrong, but also because its impact is more than national—it is worldwide."

All of this, Eisenhower declared, had been accomplished in the context of fiscal discipline that led to balanced budgets and the largest tax cut in history in 1954, with almost two-thirds of its benefits going to individuals in the low-income brackets. Eisenhower said the nation had accomplished much of what he had set out to do eight years earlier: a stronger mutual security program, more robust global trade and commerce, the truce to end the Korean war, a powerful military deterrent, fiscal discipline, an effective internal security program, conservation of natural resources and reduced government interference in agriculture, and civil and social rights. But the president also acknowledged continuing challenges in foreign policy in Berlin, Laos, Cuba, and across Africa. And there was still an unfinished domestic agenda that envisioned more jobs, steadier economic growth, a sound dollar, improved balance of payments, and advances in agriculture, health, and education programs. "Our goal has always been to add to the spiritual, moral and material strength of our nation. I believe we have done this. But it is a process that must never end."[15]

VI

During the transition weeks, Eisenhower received reports from several task forces. The National Goals panel had been suggested by Illinois businessman Chuck Percy several years earlier but only began its work in

February of 1960. After a fitful start the panel issued a thirty-one-page report on November 27, 1960.

The report sketched out broad goals for domestic and foreign policy and called for fiscal responsibility. Eisenhower received the report respectfully and hosted the task force members at a December 5 luncheon to discuss their findings. But at that point there was little he could do with their insights in the final weeks of his presidency, beyond publicizing them. As Eisenhower escorted the panel's chairman, Henry Wriston, out the North Portico door he acknowledged the sounds of workers building platforms for the coming inaugural parade. "I feel like the fellow in jail who is watching his scaffold being built," he said.[16]

Eisenhower also received a report from Mansfield Sprague, who had chaired a task force to study the psychological aspects of U.S. foreign policy. The panel had suspended its deliberations during the campaign because leaks were beginning to occur and the panel members wanted to avoid getting pulled into the campaign debate. Now that the work was done, Eisenhower had to determine whether it would be more effective for the findings to be submitted as an official report or transmitted to him as a letter. According to minutes of his meeting with Sprague, Eisenhower did not want to provide the incoming administration with "a vehicle to make unfounded charges against the present administration at a time when there would be no voice to defend the administration." He decided to have the report sent to him as a letter and not printed as an official document. This would allow Eisenhower the flexibility to decide whether to keep the material for himself or to personally transmit it to his successor. Eisenhower was concerned, the minutes say, that the new administration could "take such a document and use it to ridicule and attack its predecessor. He said that so far he saw no reason to be too optimistic on such a score. If good ideas were found in it, the new group would take them and give no credit. But if they find any chance, they will cut us up."[17] Clearly Eisenhower felt continuing skepticism toward, and even distrust of, his successor. Kennedy's relentless campaign attacks on the Eisenhower administration clearly angered the president and suggest why Ike was so wary about his successor and suspicious of his motives on many matters.

★

VII

As 1960 drew to a close Eisenhower held several discussions with senior Republican Party officials to discuss the future of the GOP in the aftermath of Nixon's loss to Kennedy. Eisenhower wanted to make sure the party was planted in the political center. He did not want it to move either sharply to the left, as Nelson Rockefeller wanted, or dramatically to the right, as Barry Goldwater preferred.

On December 28 the president met with Nixon, Senator Thruston Morton (also the chairman of the Republican National Committee), Bryce Harlow (Eisenhower's top legislative aide), and Persons. Harlow took extensive notes and wrote a long memo recapping the meeting. Eisenhower said he wanted to help rebuild the party after Nixon's credible, but unsuccessful, race against Kennedy. He was concerned that congressional Republican leaders weren't interested in the views of others. Eisenhower said he was resolved to stay active in party matters and might host a meeting or two a year with party officials, former cabinet members, and business supporters. But he insisted, according to Harlow's account, that he had no desire to become a "male Mrs. Roosevelt." This apparently referred to Eleanor Roosevelt's high profile involvement in Democratic affairs in the years after her husband had died.

Eisenhower confessed that he had initially planned to retreat from public life after leaving the White House but was now leaning toward a different approach. He intended to publish articles to elaborate on his middle-of-the-road political philosophy. The president believed most Americans thought of themselves as moderates and the Republican Party should reach out to them and make a stronger appeal to labor and business. He bemoaned that the party's outreach to African Americans had yielded so few electoral rewards and that, despite an earnest effort these past eight years, Republicans lost, rather than gained, African American support. Eisenhower said nobody was more sincere than he in trying to help black Americans but he was convinced that it was wrong to rely entirely upon the law for remedies to discrimination. He was proud of his efforts to quietly push for intergration through moral pleas and quiet persuasion.

The president also criticized Kennedy's emerging cabinet. He warned that Douglas Dillon, a senior State Department official in his

ABOVE: President Eisenhower poses with a group of senators in March of 1953, less than two months after being sworn in as President. The newly elected junior senator from Massachusetts, John F. Kennedy, stands at the end of the front row on Eisenhower's far right. The two men had little direct contact during the eight years that Eisenhower was president and Kennedy was a senator. *Courtesy of the Dwight D. Eisenhower Presidential Library, Museum, and Boyhood Home.* BELOW: Senator John Kennedy and Vice President Richard Nixon meet in Florida the week after the 1960 presidential election in which Kennedy narrowly defeated Nixon. Kennedy requested the meeting, hoping it would help confirm to the country that he had won the election despite allegations of voting irregularities. *Courtesy of the Richard Nixon Presidential Library.*

Kennedy and his new vice president, Lyndon Johnson, meet in Texas shortly after the election. The pair's victory marked a significant role change for both men. Kennedy was now the boss and Johnson the underling. *Courtesy of the LBJ Library, photo by Frank Muto.*

ABOVE: Kennedy confers with Clark Clifford at the Kennedy home in Palm Beach, Florida, following the election. A Washington lawyer and Democratic operative, Clifford played a critical role during the ten-week transition as Kennedy's chief liaison to the Eisenhower administration. *Courtesy of the John F. Kennedy Presidential Library and Museum.* BELOW: Kennedy autographs a book for a nun. Kennedy's campaign and election sealed his celebrity status. As the nation's first Roman Catholic president, he was especially popular among America's Catholics. *Courtesy of the John F. Kennedy Presidential Library and Museum/Associated Press.*

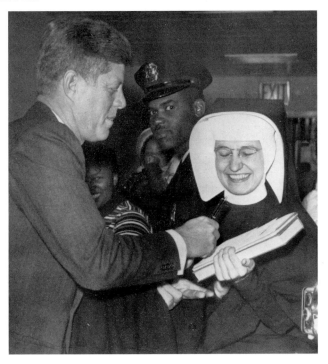

ABOVE: President Eisenhower greets Senator Kennedy at the North Portico of the White House on December 6, 1960, their first meeting after the election. Doubtless Eisenhower enjoyed the image of him towering over, and looking down on, his successor. *Courtesy of the John F. Kennedy Presidential Library and Museum.* BELOW: Eisenhower and Kennedy confer in the Oval Office on December 6, 1960. The two men had a lengthy, private conversation before participating in a larger meeting. Kennedy prepared carefully for the sessions and Eisenhower was impressed by the senator's respectful demeanor and nuanced understanding of the issues. *Courtesy of the John F. Kennedy Presidential Library and Museum.*

ABOVE: Kennedy announces the appointment of Dean Rusk as his secretary of state at a press conference at the Kennedy home in Palm Beach, Florida. Although this was one of Kennedy's most important appointments during the transition, he had known Rusk for only a week before nominating him to be the nation's top diplomat. *Courtesy of the John F. Kennedy Presidential Library and Museum/Associated Press.* BELOW: Eisenhower delivers his televised farewell address from the Oval Office on January 17, 1961. The president—and former five star general—surprised many Americans by warning of the dangers of the country's large military-industrial complex.

ABOVE: Kennedy speaks to reporters outside the White House following his meeting with Eisenhower on January 19, 1961, the day before his inauguration. The press briefing followed Kennedy's second, and final, session with Eisenhower before he was sworn in as the 35th president of the United States. *Courtesy of the John F. Kennedy Presidential Library and Museum.* BELOW: President and Mrs. Eisenhower bid farewell to members of the White House staff on January 20, 1961. During the ten-week transition, Dwight and Mamie Eisenhower expressed their gratitude to those who had served them during the previous eight years. *Courtesy of the White House Historical Association.*

Eisenhower and Kennedy prepare to head to the U.S. Capitol on Inauguration Day. The two men and their wives first met at the White House for coffee and were then driven down Pennsylvania Avenue to the inaugural ceremonies. *Courtesy of the Dwight D. Eisenhower Presidential Library, Museum, and Boyhood Home.*

President Kennedy delivers his inaugural address as Eisenhower and Jacqueline Kennedy look on. For many, this image of the youthful and energetic Kennedy and the elderly and weary Eisenhower clearly captured the transfer of power that had just occurred. *Courtesy of the Library of Congress.*

ABOVE: A heavy coat of snow drapes Lafayette Park and the parade reviewing stands. Nearly nine inches of snow fell the day before the inauguration, throwing Washington into disarray. *Courtesy of the John F. Kennedy Presidential Library and Museum.* BELOW: As Kennedy delivers his inaugural address, Dwight Eisenhower, Lyndon Johnson, and Richard Nixon look on. A singular moment in time that captures past, present, and future—four presidents who shaped American politics for decades. *Courtesy of the John F. Kennedy Presidential Library and Museum.*

administration, was being set up for failure if he took the job as the treasury secretary in the Kennedy administration. He was skeptical of Kennedy's nominee to be defense secretary, Robert McNamara, saying he took the job because of the prestige of running the Pentagon. McNamara, he argued, was not well versed in the challenges facing the Department of Defense. Morton, as the party chairman, worried that between four hundred and five hundred experienced Republicans would be leaving government when the Eisenhower administration ended, and said the party apparatus should help them find jobs and keep them in the Republican network. The president strongly agreed.

The conversation on the future of the Republican Party ultimately turned to the last presidential campaign. Nixon blamed his defeat on voter fraud, an ill-advised commitment by his vice presidential running mate, Henry Cabot Lodge, that they would appoint a black man to their cabinet, and, even with this, lackluster support among black Americans for Republicans. Eisenhower rather indelicately noted that some of his friends were convinced the televised debates with Kennedy hurt Nixon. He was right, but the comment had to sting his vice president who had just narrowly lost the election to succeed Ike.[18]

VIII

In the ten weeks between Election Day and Kennedy's inauguration, Eisenhower had to deal with a complicated world and make consequential decisions. On December 5, about six weeks prior to Inauguration Day, the president decided to officially suspend nuclear arms talks in Geneva with the Soviet Union after consulting with his secretary of state and others on his national security team. The talks were making no progress as the Soviets appeared determined to wait to deal with the next administration. So the negotiations, which began in October of 1958, were recessed until February. Before announcing the suspension of the talks, Secretary of State Herter told the president that he would first inform Kennedy's representatives before officially notifying America's key ally, Great Britain, and the Soviet Union. Herter informed Eisenhower through a memo to Persons that he felt certain Kennedy would agree with the decision to suspend the talks until his administration was in power.[19]

Eisenhower also had to decide how the United States should vote on a UN resolution before the inauguration that would formally oppose colonialism. He was inclined to back the resolution, seeing it as a valuable way to signal support to Third World nations who were ending decades of colonial rule. However, the president eventually acceded to the plea of British prime minister Harold Macmillan who argued the text of the resolution was sharply and he believed inappropriately critical of the United Kingdom. Eisenhower instructed the American ambassador to the UN to abstain. The president also reviewed a host of issues related to the deployment of American nuclear weapons that would be considered at an upcoming NATO meeting in Paris.

Eisenhower had hoped to pass on to Kennedy a desk in the Oval Office that was clear of foreign policy crises. But the world did not cooperate, and he was determined to offer specific, even controversial, recommendations to his successor.

The president had been struggling with the problem of Fidel Castro and Cuba ever since Castro took power in 1959. Eisenhower's initial wariness of Castro quickly shifted to skepticism and then outright hostility. Now he objected to almost everything that Castro did. He opposed the political executions in Cuba, Castro's failure to hold elections, confiscation of U.S.-owned property, criticisms of the United States as an imperialist power, and Castro's praise of communism and embrace of the Soviet Union.

Eisenhower responded to Castro on several fronts. Most significantly, in March of 1960 he authorized the CIA to begin exploring ways to oust the Castro regime. In July of that year Congress authorized the president to reduce the amount of sugar Cuba could export to the U.S., and Eisenhower did so sharply. The administration later canceled Cuba's quota under the U.S. Sugar Act and in October imposed a partial embargo on U.S.-Cuba trade.

Just weeks before Eisenhower was to leave office, Castro ordered a dramatic reduction in the number of American diplomats in the U.S. embassy in Havana, requiring most of the American diplomats to leave Cuba within forty-eight hours. This was the last straw for the president. On January 3, 1961, Eisenhower formally terminated American diplomatic relations with Cuba, saying the island nation's behavior was unacceptable. "This calculated action on the part of the Castro Government is only the latest of a long series of harassments, baseless accusations, and vilification," Eisenhower declared. "There is a limit to what the United States in self-respect can endure. That limit has been reached. Our friendship for the Cuban people is not affected. It is my hope and my conviction that in the not too distant future it will be possible for the historic friendship between us once again to find its reflection in normal relations of every sort. Meanwhile, our sympathy goes out to the people of Cuba now suffering under the yoke of a dictator."[20]

As the CIA trained Cuban exiles in Guatemala for a possible invasion Eisenhower advanced a project of regime change that his successor would have to deal with. "So, to the incoming administration, we left units of Cuban refugees busily training and preparing hopefully for a return to their native land," Eisenhower later wrote. "Because they had as yet been unable to find the leader they wanted—a national leader known to be both anti-Castro and anti-Batista—it was impossible to make specific plans for a military invasion. However, their hatred of Castro, their patriotism, and their readiness to sacrifice for the restoration of freedom in Cuba could not be doubted."[21]

Eisenhower briefed Kennedy on Cuba during their December 6 and January 19 meetings, and told Kennedy that strong American action was needed soon to oust the Castro government. In their second meeting, Kennedy asked Eisenhower point-blank if the U.S. should support guerilla operations in Cuba. "To the utmost," Eisenhower declared, insisting it was the incoming president's responsibility to "do whatever is necessary" to oust Castro, adding, "We cannot have the present government there go on."

IX

Another brewing foreign crisis was, from the president's perspective, even more urgent and imminent: Laos. Eisenhower had been focused on Southeast Asia for most of his presidency, convinced that it was strategically critical. His attention to the region intensified after the French were driven out of Indochina in 1954 and the Geneva Accords temporarily divided Vietnam into North and South and gave Laos its independence. With French withdrawal, the United States devoted significant resources to the region, sending substantial military and economic assistance to President Diem in South Vietnam and to various pro-Western groups in Laos.

Eisenhower devoted more time in 1959 and 1960 to discussing Laos than Vietnam during National Security Council meetings. The president referred to Laos as the "cork in the bottle" that could determine the fate of Southeast Asia. Using another metaphor, he saw the country as a domino and warned its fall into Communist control would have cascading negative implications for the Western position in Southeast Asia.

Eisenhower was determined that the outcome of the country's long and messy insurrection against the Boun Oum royalist government would not be a victory by either the Pathet Lao communist forces or the neutralists. He feared the neutralists would likely establish a coalition government in which the Communists would participate and eventually dominate. The president was frustrated by conflicting intelligence reports he received in the fall of 1960 about war in Laos and spent long hours in conferences with the National Security Council and with military experts trying to determine America's options in that country. Eisenhower struggled to understand the political scene that was complex and fluid, with several factions maneuvering for power.

The fighting in Laos intensified in the middle of December with all-out civil war a distinct possibility. Eisenhower was especially troubled that the Soviet Union was intervening to support the Pathet Lao. Eisenhower debated American options that included deploying U.S. combat troops, dispatching the Seventh Fleet, instructing the CIA to wage a proxy war against the Pathet Lao, and even threatening the use of tactical nuclear weapons. "We cannot let Laos fall to the Communists even if we have to fight with our allies or without them," Eisenhower said.

The president sought a common front with the British and French but both were more comfortable with a neutralist government than was Eisenhower. In a stern letter to de Gaulle, he wrote, "There is also growing evidence of substantial intervention of indeterminate proportion from North Vietnam," adding the West must make it clear to the Soviet Union that it would not be allowed to control Laos.

When Eisenhower and Kennedy met in early December, Laos was a second-tier issue. By their January 19 session it was the top item on Eisenhower's list. He described it as the most pressing foreign policy problem

Kennedy would have to confront. He forcefully argued that neither a neutralist nor a communist government was acceptable in Laos, and that Kennedy should be prepared to send in American forces unilaterally to prevent this. "As the administration came to a close, we left a legacy of strife and confusion in Laos," Eisenhower later acknowledged. "This I regretted deeply. But we left also, I believe, a correct policy of supporting the Boun Oum government. We were ready to stand by against oppression from the outside."[22] Eisenhower had also directed the CIA to defend the sitting government in Laos and it launched a fierce bombing campaign against insurgents opposing the regime.

X

Throughout the ten weeks of the transition, President Eisenhower was also deeply distressed by the United States' balance of payments deficit and the declining value of the dollar in relation to gold. He had been monitoring the situation with his economic and national security team for months.

As a general rule, they knew that a balance of payments surplus by a country was typically seen as an indication of a strong economy with effective fiscal, monetary, and trade policies, while a nation with chronic balance of payments deficits is viewed as evidence of a struggling economy with poor policies.

The U.S. balance of payments deficit under Eisenhower was partly the result of American generosity and the success of the post–World War II economic order. Portions of the large American defense budget were spent overseas to deploy and support troops. Additionally, the U.S. government provided substantial economic aid, initially to allies in Western Europe and Japan in the wake of its surrender, and later to emerging nations in the Third World. American businesses were investing dollars overseas and short-term capital was also flowing out of the U.S. in search of higher interest rates elsewhere.

All of this resulted in a balance of payments deficit that had grown in the late 1950s. Eisenhower was convinced the U.S. needed to do something about it. From his perspective, the deficits from 1945 to 1957 were small and of little concern. But after 1957, they had grown and became more troubling. As America's balance of payments problem worsened many overseas investors were cashing in their dollars for gold. Between 1958 and 1960 the U.S. lost $5 billion, or nearly one quarter, of its gold supply. The president believed that this was partly due to the fear of, or speculation against, a possible devaluation of the dollar. He blamed the "glittering promises" of Kennedy and other Democrats on the 1960 campaign trail for making a chronically bad situation acute. He believed the foreign investor's perspective was that if the U.S. dollar was to be radically devalued, it was better to cash in dollars for gold now.

Eisenhower met with his advisers the day after the election to discuss the way ahead. Treasury Secretary Anderson warned that if people around the world lost confidence in the dollar and sought to convert claims to gold, the Free World's monetary system would collapse. Anderson presented Eisenhower with recommendations on how to deal with the crisis. On November 16 Eisenhower released his plan. The U.S. would cut overseas spending, push exports, negotiate deals to get other nations to reduce tariff and quota restrictions, and urge other countries to spend more on defense and long-term foreign assistance programs.[23]

The president instructed Persons to inform Clifford about the severity of this problem and the details of his plan. Clifford briefed Kennedy but he did not want to get directly involved. Kennedy asked Paul Nitze, a veteran diplomat, to meet with Eisenhower administration officials on his behalf and to keep him updated.

Kennedy was given an earful on the balance of payments issue during his December 6 meeting with Eisenhower followed by a detailed briefing from Anderson on January 10 that examined the challenge in detail.

The central message that Eisenhower and his team was trying to impart to the new administration was that addressing the balance of payments challenge required a two-pronged strategy: tough economic measures to stem the outflow of dollars overseas and clear political signals that Kennedy would run a disciplined fiscal policy in the United States.

Throughout the transition, Eisenhower thought Kennedy was trying to minimize the balance of payments problem. Conversely, members of Kennedy's team believed the president-elect was actually becoming obsessed by the problem, perhaps due to the torrent of information he was receiving on the matter from Eisenhower as well as from his own father, Joe Kennedy. In the first months of his administration, Kennedy offered a detailed balance of payments proposal that was substantially based on the Eisenhower plan.

XI

Eisenhower managed to close out his presidency with one foreign policy victory: an agreement with Canada resulting in the Columbia River Basin Treaty. The United States and Canada had been studying joint development of the water resources of the Columbia River basin for nearly two decades. The agreement authorized the construction of four dams to provide power and flood control for areas of British Columbia and the Pacific Northwest. President Eisenhower and Canadian prime minister John Diefenbaker signed the treaty at the White House on January 17, 1961.

Diefenbaker called it an historical milestone in Canadian-American relations. He praised the accord and Eisenhower, whom he called one of "the great leaders of the legions of freedom in the darkest days of war." Eisenhower no doubt appreciated Diefenbaker's wide-ranging accolade but focused his remarks on the agreement. "The signing of this treaty marks the culmination of a long effort—indeed 16 years long—between Canada and the United States to reach a common ground of agreement on the development of the Upper Columbia," he said, adding that concluding the accord in his final days as president provided great personal gratification and satisfaction.[24]

XII

As the final weeks of his presidency wound down, amid everything else, Eisenhower found himself dealing with a rush of personal and professional matters before leaving the White House.

The president wanted to get his presidential papers in order. The Eisenhower administration kept extensive records over its eight years and the president wanted to understand which documents belonged to him and which should be left behind. Persons, after consulting with legal counsel, instructed White House staffers that they could retain personal documents but that all documents of an official nature should be handed over to the staff secretary who would in turn forward them to the Eisenhower Library in Abilene.

Eisenhower also attended to his own financial affairs, continuing to make modest investments with his friends Cliff Roberts and Aksel Nielsen during the waning months of his presidency. During the transition, Nielsen gave Eisenhower several updates on real estate opportunities. In early January, Eisenhower sent a check of $2289.99 and then a separate one of $160.00 to Nielsen for property investments in Colorado. On January 4, Eisenhower received a letter from the Turnpike Land Company informing him that he had missed the company's annual stockholder's meeting. "Dear Mr. Eisenhower," the letter began. It noted that the company's business meeting scheduled that day had to be postponed until January 9 because only 55.69% of the stock issued was represented and under the company's bylaws 66% of the stock issued needed to be represented. "You are urged to attend or represent your stock by proxy in order that your company may conduct such business as is required by the annual meeting of stockholders," the letter admonished.[25] Eisenhower scrawled a note at the bottom of the letter, asking Ann Whitman if he had sent his proxy to Nielsen. She said he had, so his obligation to the Turnpike Land Company had been fulfilled.

Eisenhower also grew interested in organizing his future office at Gettysburg College that would be his base of operations after January 20th. The president of the college offered Eisenhower the use of his official residence as Eisenhower's future office. Ike took several brief trips to Gettysburg during the transition to inspect the space, and asked his military aide, Robert Schulz, to take a leave of absence after January 20 to help him get established in Gettysburg. Eisenhower's secretary, Ann Whitman, also agreed to join him at first and was later succeeded in Gettysburg by another White House secretary, Rusty Brown.

As his presidency wound down, Eisenhower received inquiries from publishers about writing his presidential memoirs. He informally decided to go with Doubleday, which had published his World War II memoirs. Although he would not sign his contract until March of 1961, Eisenhower and his son John met several times with top Doubleday executives to discuss the project. John Eisenhower later said that he was not certain his father had initially intended to write presidential memoirs, but he felt compelled to respond to the 1960 campaign. Kennedy's criticisms of Eisenhower's record needed to be answered and his his eight years as president placed in their proper perspective. John urged his father to get as many documents from his White House staff before leaving office so these records could serve as the foundation of his book.[26] The president sent his secretary of state, Christian Herter, a letter asking for brief written answers before January 20 to a number of factual questions about the administration's foreign policy record and the major changes that had occurred in the world during his presidency. The document did not need to be lengthy but accuracy was essential. Ultimately each cabinet department was instructed to submit a 3,000-word summary of its accomplishments during the previous eight years. Eisenhower drew heavily from these documents when assembling his memoirs.

Eisenhower had been contemplating his post-presidential retirement status for several years, wondering if he should request the return of his rank as general of the army that he relinquished in 1952 when he decided to run for president. He may have wanted to regain his army rank out of pride based on his stellar military record but there were also practical motivations. As a retired general, Eisenhower would be allowed several support staff, and he had grown very dependent on his orderly, John Moaney, and his top aide, Bob Schulz, to take care of his daily needs. Eisenhower contemplated special legislation that would give him a hybrid retirement status in which the prerogatives of a general and president were blended. His legislative chief Bryce Harlow began working on this with Congress near the end of 1960. The legislation accomplishing this was passed in the spring of 1961 and signed into law by President Kennedy. Eisenhower regained the five-star rank he had resigned in 1952. The law entitled him to an annual $25,000 presidential pension and $50,000 for office expenses and salaries for three military aides but he would not be paid the compensation due a general of the army.[27]

Dwight and Mamie Eisenhower came up with a plan on how to spend the initial months of their retirement. They decided to go immediately to Gettysburg for a few days, allow Dwight to take a brief hunting trip in Georgia, and then travel together by train to Palm Desert, California, for a six-week visit. Eisenhower resisted making any further firm commitments for projects or travel until after July 1, 1961. He felt the need for six months of relaxation and a flexible schedule. He told his publisher that he aspired to spend some time in a "vegetable state" after leaving the presidency, as he had been working at a breakneck pace at least since 1941.

During this transition time Cliff Roberts, in his capacity as chairman of Augusta National Golf Club, tried to delicately ascertain Eisenhower's need for office space at Augusta National after leaving the presidency. The club had given him use of both a special cabin—called Mamie's Cabin—and an office during his frequent visits to Augusta as president. Roberts wondered if Eisenhower would need an office there after January 20. Roberts said the club wanted to "preserve your desk as a keepsake" and was committed to finding acceptable working accommodations for him in the future. "The main thing is for you to let me know, as near as you can, your Augusta National office requirements during, say, the next ten or twenty years," he wrote to the seventy-year-old retiring president.

Eisenhower responded by saying he would like to have an office to use during his visits to Augusta, but would try to not use it during the Masters Tournament each April when it could be used by the tournament committee. Eisenhower continued to experience the complex demands of the presidency during his final weeks in office. Shortly after the election, he learned from his secretary of state that Ambassador Michel Gallin-Douathé of the Central African Republic had been denied food service at a Baltimore restaurant because of his race. The president was saddened and embarrassed. "Dear Mr. Ambassador," the president wrote, "I have learned with deep regret that so soon after our friendly meeting on November third you were the victim of a most unfortunate incident on your way back to New York. I want you to know how sincerely I deplore this incident." The president hoped the ambassador would "judge this regrettable incident, which reflects the attitude of only a minority of the citizens of this country, in its proper perspective."[28]

Even with the demands of the presidency and the transition, Eisenhower took time to write a twelve-page letter to his British friend, Hastings Lionel Ismay, about his impressions of Ismay's new memoir about World War II. Eisenhower's review was revised several times to fine-tune his assessment. "I am fascinated by your book," he began. "Indeed I have become something of a local promoter for your volume and I am missing no chance to tell my friends that they owe it to themselves to read such an accurate, behind the scenes account concerning much of the thinking, planning, and incidents of

World War II." Ismay's book seemed to catapult Eisenhower back in time, and he commented in significant detail on Ismay's description of the complex Allied effort to defeat Hitler. "Right here I decided I have written enough," Eisenhower said on page twelve of his letter. "After all I merely wanted to say that in my estimation you have written the outstanding book of World War II Memories. Congratulations—and I hope a million people get to read it."[29]

Several weeks later, the president received a warm note from Ismay about Eisenhower's substantial legacy. In response, Eisenhower confided to his friend his ambivalence about leaving the White House. "You are characteristically understanding of the emotions that crowd my mind these days. I appreciate beyond words your comments concerning what I have tried earnestly to do. The verdict on my efforts will of course be left to history, and I don't have to worry about it now—but it is wonderful to know of your approval."

Eisenhower declined an offer from a friend, Clarence Francis, an executive at Studebaker, who proposed offering the president the car of his choice if, after leaving office, he would pose for a photo in a Studebaker with Mamie and his grandchildren. Eisenhower thanked Francis for the offer but declined it firmly. "I simply cannot agree to anything that could have commercial value for any industrial firm. I have been forced to decline many suggestions, most of them involving glittering offers of directorships with no duties, on the ground that I have never allowed my name or picture to be used for any purpose that has advertising value, except for charitable purposes." He acknowledged Francis's offer was extended out of kindness. "But I am committed to adhering to a policy, the violation of which would cause me difficulty and embarrassment in the future."[30] He also declined a suggestion by Aksel Nielsen that he sit on the board of directors of United Airlines after leaving the presidency. Nielsen told him the board was comprised of a "really swell bunch of fellows," adding that by sitting on the board the former president would also have use of an executive plane. Eisenhower flatly declined. "I do not see how I can possibly accept membership on the Board of any commercial company," he wrote, adding, "Won't you please express my appreciation to those who were responsible for the suggestion?"

But Eisenhower was not averse to getting involved in nontraditional activities during the waning weeks of his presidency. In early December he sent a letter to Mohammad Ayub Khan, president of Pakistan, with a generous and unusual offer. He had learned that the Pakistani president was planning to convert the greens on the golf course at Rawalpindi from sand to grass and was experiencing difficulty in locating the plant materials best suited to the climate and soil. The president informed his Pakistani counterparts that in the United States, Tifgreen, a type of Bermuda grass, had been developed that the U.S. Department of Agriculture believed was ideal for this purpose. "Accordingly, I am taking the liberty of sending you enough nursery stock to develop a culture which, in the course of a year, should provide enough grass for eighteen greens. I hope you will accept this small gift as a token of my appreciation of the cordial hospitality you accorded to me and my party on our visit a year ago." He listed several officials who could help Pakistan in the care and propagation of the Tifgreen stock, adding, "I certainly hope that you will find the grass satisfactory for your use." [31]

Throughout the transition the president had days packed with varied, even discordant, activities. For example, on Monday, December 5, the President began his day with breakfast with House Republican leader Charlie Halleck, met with Undersecretary of State Douglas Dillon, and accepted the credentials of several overseas ambassadors arriving in Washington. Then, according to the White House log, the president was presented with a white tiger, a gift to the children of the United States from India, which was destined for the National Zoo. Still later that morning, Eisenhower presented the Collier Trophy, an award for developing, testing, producing, and putting into operation America's first intercontinental ballistic missile, the Atlas, which had a range of five thousand miles. The president met briefly with a man who had received the State Department's Superior Service Award and then had lunch with the members of his Commission on National Goals. That afternoon he discussed the Pentagon budget for over ninety minutes with budget director Maurice Stans and Secretary of Defense Tom Gates. Later, the president had an off-the-record conversation with Senate Republican leader Everett Dirksen, held several other meetings with aides, and returned to the residence.

There were poignant and personal matters to attend to during this time. Eisenhower attended a lunch on December 16 for the reunion of his West Point Class of 1915 at the Army-Navy Club. He stayed for two hours and saw old friends including General Omar Bradley. As the holidays approached, Eisenhower made time to visit with his ailing orderly, John Moaney, whom he had known and relied on for decades. Though the ill health of his friend no doubt affected Eisenhower, he could not let up in his duties as the final weeks of his presidency approached. In early January, the president attended his final troop inspection at Fort Gordon, Georgia. Speaking from the reviewing stand on the parade ground, Eisenhower said the military was part of his identity. "Although I call myself a civilian— and even sometimes a politician—I am still by law Commander in Chief and therefore I feel part of you," he said to the troops. "This is the last review I shall ever receive in my life. I have been part of such ceremonies during this half century. None has been more meaningful than this one." He waxed nostalgic about the military. "My heart will always be filled with admiration for you, and there will be in my soul a certain nostalgia as I see a uniform, whether it be a single solider on the streets or when I see a unit marching in a parade."[32] However poignant the moment, Eisenhower was not overwhelmed by sentimentality. He immediately flew from Fort Gordon to Augusta with several friends and they managed to get in eighteen holes at the fabled course before dark.

On January 9, the president attended Richard Nixon's forty-eighth birthday party at the Mayflower Hotel in downtown Washington. Eisenhower spoke fondly of his vice president, telling the guests that Nixon had been "one of the mainstays of the Republican administration and to me personally," adding that the vice president "has been not only an invaluable associate in Government but a warm friend." The president expressed gratitude. "I shall never cease to be grateful to him for his loyalty, his absolute readiness to undertake any chore, no matter what the inconvenience to himself and to his family—and whenever he has undertaken such a chore, to perform it brilliantly and to the credit of the United States of America."[33] As a testament to his respect for Nixon, Eisenhower did not duck out of the party early as he often did at other events. "The President remained throughout the dinner," according to his official schedule.

While Eisenhower's calendar remained full during these ten weeks, his schedule also chronicles the inexorable ebbing of power. An increasing number of his appointments were valedictories. He attended holiday and farewell parties, arranged picture-taking sessions at the White House with staff and friends, and handed out medallions with his likeness, a Roman emperor–like gesture that even he found awkward. He was deflated to be leaving the White House on terms that were less than triumphant. "We could not help a vague feeling of rejection, that the American people had disapproved of our efforts over the past years," his son John said.[34] Eisenhower was touched by a warm note that he received from the staff at Augusta National and sent a cable in return in which he said their note was "a bright spot in a day that is darkened by Laos, packing, and snow that prohibits a journey to the golf course."

Beginning in late December and extending into January the president received in relentless succession cabinet and staff resignation letters effective on January 20. They were colleagues, friends, and loyal members of his administration. It was a sad ritual for all.

His cabinet secretaries and their spouses held a farewell dinner for the president and his wife on January 11 and Eisenhower presided over his final cabinet meeting on January 13. At that meeting, Eisenhower posed for photographs with his cabinet and senior staff. They discussed the state of the world and the administration's accomplishments. Adhering to tradition, each cabinet member purchased his own chair in the Roosevelt Room from the U.S. government. The price was $88.00. Cabinet members and White House staff pitched in and bought the president's chair for him. Nixon and the president spoke at this final official gathering and Eisenhower got choked up as he concluded, managing only to wish his colleagues "good luck" before leaving the room. He and Mamie then went to Camp David for their final weekend as president and first lady.

Eisenhower held a farewell press conference on January 18 in which he highlighted his administration's successes, touted the smoothness of the transition, defended his role in the 1960 presidential campaign, and dismissed a question about whether the press had been fair to him with a derisive quip. "Well, when you come down to it, I don't see what a reporter could do much to a President, do you?" Eisenhower's 193rd—and final— press conference as president ran from 10:00 A.M. to about 10:30 and ended with a standing ovation from more than three hundred reporters who attended.

★

XIII

Eisenhower gave his official farewell to the American people on January 17 in a televised address. He had begun soliciting and debating ideas about how to leave the public stage since the spring of 1959. He was intrigued by the magisterial farewell address of his hero, George Washington, and instructed his speechwriter, Malcolm Moos, to begin assembling ideas for his eventual parting remarks. "I want to have something to say when I leave here, and I want you to be thinking about it," Eisenhower said to Moos. "I'm not interested in capturing headlines, but I want to have a message and I want you to be thinking about it well in advance." Moos took this as a suggestion that "we should be dropping ideas into the bin, to get ready for this."[35]

That spring Moos sent Eisenhower and his brother Milton a tentative proposal for thirteen speeches the president might deliver during the rest of his presidency, including a farewell address. The other twelve speeches would deal with America's purpose in the world, foreign economic policy, transportation policy, Latin America, defense, Abraham Lincoln and the Republican Party, and foreign policy. In a letter to Milton that May, the president mentioned several of the proposed speeches but zeroed in on the farewell. Eisenhower said he did not have a "fixed idea that I should deliver a so-called 'farewell talk' to the Congress, even if that body should invite me to do so." But he added that if he were to give such a talk before Congress, his remarks should not be partisan but rather "emphasize a few homely truths . . . A collateral purpose would be, of course, merely to say an official 'goodbye'."

Moos later brainstormed with another aide, Ralph Williams, about a farewell speech. They met on October 31, 1960, and one of the themes that resonated with Williams was "the problem of militarism—for the first time in its history, the United States has a permanent war-based industry." Williams had glanced at some aerospace journals and was struck by how many companies marketed and sold military hardware. He also reviewed a study about people retiring from the military at a young age and taking senior jobs in the defense industry. Moos also reflected on how much scientific research was driven by grants from the federal government.

Williams sent Moos some ideas and Moos assembled a draft speech that he sent to the president after the November 1960 election. However,

Eisenhower did not review it until early December. The draft included themes and initiatives important to him throughout his presidency, as well as an issue Ike had thought about but had not publicly elaborated on: the growth of a permanent arms industry in the United States. "I think you got something here," Eisenhower told Moos after reviewing the draft speech.

This was just the beginning of a more intense phase of editing and revising that involved Moos, the president, and Milton. Eisenhower was an aggressive editor who liked to begin with what Williams called "completed staff work"—a full and polished draft—before he went to work. Eisenhower would then take a pencil and mark up the draft. He would cross out phrases, scrawl marginal notes, and would often dictate two or three pages of additional material to be worked into the draft. Important Eisenhower speeches, according to Williams, often went through up to fifteen drafts. "I always thought that things got better up until the fourth or fifth draft, and after that it was straight downhill . . . But it was always an endless iteration; back and forth; back and forth; back and forth," Williams recalled.[36] Moos contends that Eisenhower left his original draft of the farewell address "substantially intact," but in fact the president and Milton spent hours reworking the speech and it was ultimately revised through nearly thirty drafts.

At 8:30 P.M. eastern time on Tuesday, January 17, Eisenhower delivered a speech that expressed many familiar themes but contained several surprising warnings.

Dressed in a brown three-piece suit, the president sat at his Oval Office desk in front of drawn curtains. He spoke into two large, conspicuous microphones and looked straight at the camera for most of his remarks, occasionally glancing to the right and left, looking at his son John and a special guest, Republican Senate Leader Everett Dirksen, who watched from inside the Oval Office. He periodically referred to his twenty-six-page reading text that was heavily underlined and included a handwritten introduction and conclusion. His delivery was halting and tentative and, typical of his public speaking style, he stumbled over several words.

Eisenhower began by thanking the radio and TV networks for giving him the opportunity to address the nation on various occasions over the past eight years. Now, after decades of public service it was time to say goodbye. "This evening I come to you with a message of leave-taking and farewell, and to share a few final thoughts with you, my countrymen. Like every other citizen, I wish the new President, and all who will labor with him, Godspeed. I pray that the coming years will be blessed with peace and prosperity for all," he said.

The president urged the White House and Congress to work together to advance the national interest and find agreement on the large issues of the age. He described his own relationship with Congress, "which began on a remote and tenuous basis" when a senator appointed him to West Point a half century earlier but had grown close and cooperative in subsequent years. "So, my official relationship with the Congress ends in a feeling, on my part, of gratitude that we have been able to do so much together."

Eisenhower then underscored the historical moment. America was now ten years "past the midpoint of a century that has witnessed four major wars among great nations. Three of these involved our own country." The United States was now preeminent, respected for its wealth, power, and military strength. But it would be judged, the president said, "on how we use our power in the interests of world peace and human betterment."

The president noted that America faced a formidable adversary— international communism—that would not be vanquished soon or easily. "We face a hostile ideology—global in scope, atheistic in character, ruthless in purpose, and insidious in method. Unhappily, the danger it poses promises to be of indefinite duration," the president cautioned. The nation, Eisenhower said, needed to prepare itself for the long haul, to gear up for "not so much the emotional and transitory sacrifices of crisis, but rather those which enable us to carry forward steadily and surely, without complaint the burdens of a prolonged and complex struggle—with liberty the stake." The U.S. needed to respond to this challenging world, the president emphasized, but not with crash programs or frenzies of spending. He warned of a "recurring temptation to feel that some spectacular and costly action could become the miraculous solution to all current difficulties." These warnings appeared directly aimed at Kennedy who Eisenhower believed was mesmerized by grandiose projects.

He urged policymakers to carefully consider competing priorities, arguing that "each proposal must be weighed in the light of a broader consideration: the need to maintain balance in and among national programs—balance between the private and public economy; balance between the cost and hoped for advantages; balance between the clearly necessary and the comfortably desirable; balance between our essential requirements as a nation and the duties imposed by the nation upon the individual; balance between actions of the moment and the national welfare of the future."

Eisenhower said the country has constantly faced threats that were new in kind or degree and he elaborated on two threats that he believed commanded serious reflection. First, the U.S. had been compelled by events to create a large and permanent arms industry and "this conjunction of an immense military establishment and a large arms industry is new in the American experience." The president said the pervasiveness of this coupling was difficult to exaggerate. "The total influence—economic, political, even spiritual—is felt in every city, every State house, every office of the Federal government. We recognize the imperative need for this development. Yet we must not fail to comprehend its grave implications." He then delivered words that startled the nation. "In the councils of government, we must guard against the acquisition of unwarranted influence, whether sought or unsought, by the military industrial complex. The potential for the disastrous rise of misplaced power exists and will persist. We must never let the weight of this combination endanger our liberties or democratic processes."

Eisenhower then issued a second warning: that the continuing scientific-technological revolution was altering the concept of research and invention and a new technocratic elite was emerging. "Today, the solitary inventor, tinkering in his shop, has been overshadowed by task forces of scientists in laboratories and testing fields. . . . Partly because of the great costs involved, a government contract becomes, virtually, a substitute for intellectual curiosity. For every old blackboard there are now hundreds of new electronic computers." The president said citizens had to stay alert to the danger that public policy could become the captive of this scientific-technological elite.

Eisenhower moved toward familiar ground as he delivered an impassioned plea for stewardship and generational responsibility. He implored Americans to "avoid the impulse to live only for today, plundering, for our own ease and convenience, the precious resources for tomorrow. We cannot mortgage the material assets of our grandchildren without risking the loss of their political and spiritual heritage. We want democracy to survive for all generations to come, not to become the insolvent phantom of tomorrow."

America should approach the rest of the world respectfully, seeking peace. "Disarmament, with mutual honor and confidence, is a continuing imperative. Together, we must learn how to compose differences, not with arms, but with intellect and decent purpose." He regretted that lasting peace was not in sight. "Happily, I can say that war has been avoided. Steady progress toward our ultimate goal has been made. But, so much remains to be done."

Eisenhower thanked the American people for the opportunities given to him for public service, beginning with his days as a soldier and now as their president. Eisenhower then offered a prayer for the world. "We pray that peoples of all faiths, all races, all nations, may have their great human needs satisfied . . . That the scourges of poverty, disease, and ignorance will be made to disappear from the earth, and that, in the goodness of time, all peoples will come to live together in a peace guaranteed by the binding force of mutual respect and love."

Then he took off his glasses and looked steadily into the camera. "Now on Friday noon I am to become a private citizen of the U.S," he said. "I am proud to do so."[37]

More than seventy million Americans watched Eisenhower's farewell address on television, including Kennedy, who viewed it alone at his Georgetown house before heading to a party at his sister Jean's house for Hollywood and Broadway celebrities.

The press coverage of Eisenhower's speech was extensive and respectful. "Eisenhower's Farewell Sees Threat To Liberties in Vast Defense Machine," a *New York Times* front page headline declared. The article said Eisenhower had cautioned Americans to be vigilant against dangers to their liberties that were implicit in a vast military establishment and a permanent arms industry unparalleled in peacetime. Noting that Eisenhower's speech "brought down the curtain on fifty years of public service," the article added, "This warning against the political potential of the huge military-arms production apparatus by the President came as a surprise to many in the capital. A more sentimental leave taking had been expected from the old soldier." The paper included a special page one insert, "Prayer By President," that quoted Eisenhower's prayer.

"Ike Warns of Dangers In Massive Defense," declared a *Los Angeles Times* headline. The New York *Daily News* was less reverent: "Beware of

Eggheads, Munitions Lobby: Ike." A *New York Times* editorial focused on Eisenhower's presidency rather than this speech. "Dwight Eisenhower will retire from office with the respect and goodwill of his countrymen. Few presidents in the history of the United States have had a more secure hold on the affections of the American people." An *Atlanta Constitution* editorial said the president had delivered an important speech. "President Eisenhower's Farewell Address to the nation Tuesday night was not only his best speech, but it was one of the best speeches by any American political leader in recent years. It was good to hear the President state the case so forcefully, so understandably and so eloquently . . . There was dismay in his speech and there was hope. Both were justified. The speech, we repeat, was a good one. It belongs in the history books. Now we await Mr. Kennedy's inaugural address, which, we hope and expect, will take its place beside it. Farewell and hail."

A *Wall Street Journal* editorial said Eisenhower's farewell expressed some new themes but also displayed the president's familiar wisdom. "President Eisenhower would not be Mr. Eisenhower if he had not accompanied his farewell, the other evening, with something more than a mere goodbye. So he spoke also of thoughts that troubled him. And the American people, who have so often listened to this man, might do well to listen again." The *Journal* op-ed went on to observe that Eisenhower was troubled "by things that pass unnoticed by so many others," adding it would be wise to study his concerns. "As is so often the case with this man, Mr. Eisenhower's wisdom is seemingly so simple—we are almost tempted to say so obvious—that to self-styled sophisticates it may sound like just another homily out of a discarded copybook. Certainly, the problems that trouble Mr. Eisenhower are not to be met by assigning them to a 'task force' for diagnosis and treatment. Yet it seems to us that the simplicity of Mr. Eisenhower's farewell thoughts is elemental."

Several days later, the *New York Times* published "The Military-Industrial Complex: An Analysis" by Jack Raymond, a reporter. The article sought to probe and interpret Eisenhower's newly coined term. It reported that nearly 59% of the $81 billion federal budget was spent on national security, a sum that exceeded the annual corporate profits of all American companies. Raymond also referred to a study by a House committee that revealed that 726 former top-ranking military officers were employed by

100 top defense contractors. The article used charts to chronicle trends in military spending, the size of the defense budget in relation to the entire federal budget, the number of federal civilian employees in the Pentagon, the size of the arms industry, and the federal funds devoted to science. It concluded that "few suggestions have been put forward to deal with the combined, subtle, real but unmeasurable influence of what Mr. Eisenhower described as the 'industrial-military complex'."[38]

An editorial in *The Nation* offered a backhanded compliment to the president. "For eight years, Mr. Eisenhower has depressed his fellow Americans by a seeming inability to grasp the major problems of his era; but now in the closing days of his Administration he spoke like the statesman and democratic leader we had so long hungered for him to become. That is sad, but it can be said that he handed the torch to Mr. Kennedy with an honesty and resolution rarely equaled by previous retiring presidents. And Mr. Kennedy seems to us too intelligent to overlook the urgent accents of his predecessor's farewell."[39]

Walter Lippmann praised the president and his often somber message. In a syndicated column titled "Eisenhower's Farewell Warning," Lippmann praised the president for "rising above the issues which divide the parties and were the material of the election campaign" and dealing with a "question never before discussed publicly by any responsible official, which is of profound importance to the Nation's future." Lippmann added, "Surely, it is impressive that the old soldier should make this warning the main theme of his Farewell Address."[40]

Looking back on the speech in his presidential memoirs, Eisenhower defended his decision to "include a sobering message in what might otherwise have been a farewell of pleasantries." He said, "This was, at the end of my years in the White House, the most challenging message I could leave with the people of this country."[41]

SEVEN

PRESIDENT-ELECT KENNEDY PREPARES

I

W hen John Kennedy returned to his family's compound on November 9 after his victory press conference at the Hyannis Armory he knew a busy time lay ahead. But he likely had no idea of how rushed, crowded, and even frenetic the ensuing ten weeks would be. This was due to both the tremendous amount of prepatory work that was required for the project ahead and Kennedy's working style, which was intense but not always orderly or methodical.

Between November 9, the day after the election, and his inauguration on January 20, 1961, Kennedy had to keep his eyes on, and defeat any, recount effort waged by his challenger, Richard Nixon. He had to ensure his election was certified by the Electoral College, meet with President

Eisenhower and coordinate with the outgoing administration, create a transition organization, form a government, select a cabinet and White House staff, forge a policy agenda, resign from the Senate and advance a successor, get his personal finances in order, sell his Washington home, and support his wife as she prepared to give birth to their second child.

In the midst of all this Kennedy also managed to narrowly avert an assassination attempt. A deranged man, Richard Pavlick, drove from New Hampshire to Kennedy's Palm Beach home and prepared to slam Kennedy's car with his own vehicle, which contained seven sticks of dynamite. Luckily, Pavlick passed up a clear opportunity to kill Kennedy on December 11. Kennedy was leaving home to go to church, and his wife and daughter Caroline were at the door of their house seeing him off. Pavlick did not want to assasinate Kennedy in front of them so he waited for another chance. His plot was discovered several days later and he was arrested before he tried again to kill the incoming president.

Kennedy aides Ken O'Donnell and David Powers insisted he was calm when he got the news. "When we told Kennedy about the plot, he was completely fascinated by it, wanted to know all about Pavlick and the details of his confession, and he asked to see a copy of the letter he was carrying, which charged that the Kennedys bought the presidency and the White House. But Kennedy was not a bit upset or worried by the ugly incident. It merely intrigued him," they later recalled.[1] Ted Sorensen offered a similar account. He said that Kennedy mentioned during a lunch "with a touch of humor" about the assassination attempt uncovered the week before. "The President-Elect seemed more intrigued than appalled by the man's ingenuity in planning a motiveless murder, and then he dismissed it from his mind and returned to work," Sorensen recalled.[2]

Kennedy's ten-week transition was ad hoc, improvisational, and messy. Due more to restlessness than reason, Kennedy was frequently on the move, traveling between his residences in Hyannis Port, Palm Beach, Washington, and Manhattan. In Palm Beach he operated out of his father's white stucco mansion on Ocean Drive. In New York he stayed at the family's two-floor penthouse suite in the Carlyle Hotel. In Washington, he mostly worked out of the red brick federal home in Georgetown that he shared with Jackie and their daughter, and later, infant son. But even in Washington his transition lacked a central command station.

Meetings took place at his home on N Street, his suite at the Senate Office Building, the Democratic National Committee offices, his old campaign headquarters in the Esso Building at the foot of Capitol Hill, Clark Clifford's law offices, and conference rooms at the Brookings Institution. "His 'office' was the living room or library of whichever home he inhabited at the time—Palm Beach, Georgetown, or the Carlyle Hotel penthouse— and his 'office' continually throbbed with activity," recalled Sorensen. "While the Senator interviewed one prospective appointee, another waited in the bedroom, sometimes along with a Kennedy aide waiting to brief the president-elect and a delegation invited to see him. Press and Secret Service clustered outside, telephones rang constantly inside."[3]

When Kennedy met with his top advisers on November 10 in Hyannis Port, he assigned projects. Sorensen was charged with assembling a policy program and drafting statements and speeches, Pierre Salinger with heading up the press team, and Ken O'Donnell with arranging Kennedy's appointments. Clark Clifford and Richard Neustadt were designated as transition advisers and would help plan the ensuing ten weeks. Clifford was also to be Kennedy's liaison to the Eisenhower administration. Sargent Shriver, Kennedy's brother-in-law, would lead the search for high level appointees and Lawrence O'Brien would help find jobs in the federal government for loyal Democrats who supported the campaign. Kennedy's brother Robert, who had managed his brother's campaign, remained an all-purpose problem solver and sounding board. His brother Edward and his father Joe weighed in on various matters, his father with his trademark forcefulness. His brother-in-law Steve Smith kept track of finances. Everyone had their work cut out for them.

This was a time when Kennedy's multiple worlds, usually carefully compartmentalized, came together, sometimes meshed, but often clashed. His campaign team, Senate staff, congressional colleagues, the Democratic establishment, and his academic brain trust all tried to position themselves for the coming administration. "The intimate camaraderie of the campaign dissolved, displaced by the harsher reality of divergent ambitions, a muted struggle between strangers, cast together by the coincidence of mutual service to Kennedy's pursuit. The war was over. The occupation had begun," recalled aide Richard Goodwin.[4] Evelyn Lincoln noticed and tried to stay clear of turf battles between Kennedy's Senate and campaign staffs.

There is no record of a Kennedy master plan for the transition. For the exhausted senator there was an initial period of rest and recuperation followed by a focus on top-level appointments, then a shift to his policy agenda, and lastly attention to inaugural events and his inaugural speech. But this may put too tidy a face on an operation that was making it up on the fly.

Kennedy's spirits ebbed and flowed during this period. Exhausted from the grueling campaign, he spent most of the first two postelection weeks in Palm Beach sleeping, reading, golfing, conferring with aides, and watching movies at night under the stars on the patio of his home. He then became more focused on the tasks at hand, but there were moments of feeling overwhelmed. Lamenting to his father about all the things he was juggling, Joe did not offer sympathy, snapping to his son that votes were still being counted in Illinois, a shorthand way of saying that if Kennedy didn't want the burdens of the presidency there was a defeated rival who would eagerly exchange places with him.

But as appointments and policies started to come together, Kennedy's anticipation grew. When his friend Charlie Bartlett mentioned he had received an inaugural invitation, Kennedy quipped, "It almost makes you think it is going to happen." But the ever-controlled Kennedy could not admit to euphoria. When asked by reporters the day before he was sworn in if he was excited, Kennedy admitted only that he was "interested."

Two meetings in particular capture some of the complexity Kennedy was facing during this period.

On November 14, Kennedy traveled from Palm Beach to Key Biscayne to meet Nixon. Kennedy had arranged the get-together with the help of his father and former Republican president Herbert Hoover. While the Kennedy team portrayed his visit to see Nixon as an act of statesmanship and magnanimity, this was a charitable interpretation of the meeting. Kennedy, his top aides later acknowledged, saw the meeting with Nixon as a crucial step in confirming his win and cementing in the public's mind the fact that Kennedy had won the presidency fair and square, albeit by a tiny margin, negating any serious threat of a recount.

Speaking to reporters after the session at Nixon's hotel, Kennedy described their encounter as a "very cordial meeting." He recalled that he and Nixon had a long personal history. They entered Congress on the same day and had served on the same House Labor and Education Committee. He insisted he had been "anxious to come here today and resume our relationship, which had been somewhat interrupted by the campaign." Kennedy said the two men discussed the problems facing the nation and reviewed the past campaign "from a professional point of view." He joked that Nixon declined to disclose how he managed to win the fiercely contested state of Ohio, adding that Nixon was probably withholding that information for a rematch in 1964. Kennedy sidestepped questions about a job for Nixon in his administration, a possible recount in key states, or Nixon's political future. Kennedy said he expected another meeting with Nixon during the transition but they had not yet set a date. Asked if he was pleased with his session with the vice president, Kennedy said "very." There was no elaboration. However as he returned to Palm Beach, Kennedy offered a less guarded account of the session. He told O'Donnell that Nixon did most of the talking and the discussion was labored and uncomfortable. Kennedy did not leave the encounter with a generous view of his rival. "It was just as well for all of us he didn't quite make it," he said, referring to Nixon's near victory.[5]

A few days later, Kennedy traveled to Lyndon Johnson's ranch in Texas for a courtesy visit and to discuss the vice president–elect's future role. Kennedy was less than delighted to learn that an early morning hunting trip was on the agenda. He had never gone deer hunting before, had no desire to do so, and never did again. When he was rustled out of bed before dawn by O'Donnell he grumbled, "This is ridiculous. It's still dark outside." Overcast skies, occasional rain, and the sound of thunder did not boost Kennedy's spirits as he and Johnson traversed the rocky hill country northeast of the ranch. The hunting expedition lasted more than seven hours and included an inspection of Johnson's ranch and cattle—both of which were probably of little interest to the urbane Kennedy. Kennedy killed the first two deer, Johnson the final two, and the four animals were "processed for consumption at home," according to the press pool report. "Both men looked weary after their day in the field. Kennedy wore a brown tweed sport jacket, blue woolen shirt, and gray slacks. Johnson wore more typical ranch attire including western books and hat."[6]

O'Donnell returned to the ranch about an hour ahead of the others and Congressman Torby Macdonald, a Kennedy friend from Massachusetts who was part of the group, returned to the ranch with a Band-Aid on the bridge of his nose, apparently caused by the backfiring of his gun. The men cleaned up, and Kennedy and Johnson had dinner with several Texas political leaders. Kennedy learned that it was the Johnson's twenty-sixth wedding anniversary and had arranged for a small gift that he presented with gracious remarks. He happily headed back to Florida the next day and was ready to really relax before getting down to work.

II

In the days following the election Kennedy and his top advisers examined separate memos drafted by Richard Neustadt and Clark Clifford on how to structure the transition. Neustadt, a Columbia University professor, had written a well-received and provocative book, *Presidential Power,* that resonated with Kennedy. A plea for strong presidential leadership, Neustadt's book argued that the presidency, in the hands of a purposeful and creative leader such as Franklin Roosevelt, could be a powerful and positive force for good. By name and with examples, Neustadt derided Dwight Eisenhower's presidency, arguing that Ike was passive and reactive whereas Roosevelt was aggressive and forward leaning. This was music to Kennedy's ears.

During the campaign Senator Henry "Scoop" Jackson, in his capacity as the Democratic National Committee chairman, had asked Neustadt to write a memo on presidential transitions. Jackson liked Nuestadt's draft, which he received on September 15 and arranged a breakfast meeting a few days later with himself, Neustadt, and Kennedy at Kennedy's Georgetown home. Kennedy flipped through the paper during the meal, asked questions, was intrigued by Neustadt's views, and sought additional information. Neustadt was already assisting Clark Clifford on a transition project for Kennedy. Neustadt asked Kennedy how he should coordinate his work with Clifford's. "Don't," Kennedy said. "I can't afford to have only one set of advisers on anything."

Later that fall, Neustadt drafted another transition memo on staffing the White House and was invited to join Kennedy's campaign entourage a few days before the election. He delivered his memo to Kennedy on the candidate's plane on November 4 but urged Kennedy not to read it until after Election Day. However, Kennedy reviewed at least part of the paper during the flight and told Neustadt he especially appreciated learning about FDR's approach to staffing the White House. He learned that FDR's staff was constantly generating new ideas and that Roosevelt was at the center of a bold and highly creative policy generating operation. "That Roosevelt stuff was fascinating. Absolutely fascinating," he said. Neutstadt believed Kennedy was especially attracted to how Roosevelt relied on multiple sources of information and expanded the power of the presidency.[7]

Kennedy's assignment to Neustadt did not reflect a lack of confidence in Clifford, who was arguably the leading informal adviser to Kennedy's political operation. Clifford had known Kennedy for years and had done sensitive legal work for him and the Kennedy family. In early August of 1960, shortly after Kennedy won the presidential nomination, Kennedy invited Clifford to breakfast at his home. He wanted to pick Clifford's mind on past presidential campaigns, especially Truman's stunning upset victory in 1948. "Tell me about the one we won," Kennedy said and listened intently as Clifford regaled him with 1948 campaign stories. Then Kennedy shifted the conversation. He was beginning to think about what he would do if elected in November. Kennedy was aware that he and his inner circle were knowledgeable about the legislative branch but had no direct experience in the executive branch. He asked Clifford to prepare a "takeover" paper he could use to think through the challenges he would face immediately after the election. "I don't want to wake up on November 9 and say what do I do?" he confided. Clifford agreed and began reading, thinking, and drafting an outline. Kennedy also asked Clifford to participate on a small campaign advisory group with Senator Albert Gore Sr. and Senator William Fulbright to provide Kennedy with an outsider's perspective on his campaign. Clifford also represented Kennedy on a special Brookings Institution transition project in which representatives of the Democratic and Republican presidential campaigns brainstormed with academic experts about the complexities of exchanging presidential power. In addition, Clifford took part in a task force chaired by Senator Stuart Symington on reorganizing the Pentagon.[8]

Clifford worked diligently on these various political and policy projects throughout the fall, but the transition memo was especially dear to his heart, allowing him to draw from his experiences in government, law, and Washington politics. He solicited ideas from former colleagues in the Truman administration including David Lloyd, who sent him a detailed draft memo for Clifford to use in developing his own submission to Kennedy. Clifford tweaked his transition memo right up to Election Day. On November 9, Kennedy called him from Hyannis Port and said, "Clark, could you send that takeover memo of yours up here? Looks like we're going to need it." Later that day, a Secret Service courier came to Clifford's law office in downtown Washington and picked up his thirty-one-page document bound in heavy green paper and flew it to Hyannis Port. "My dear Mr. President," Clifford's cover letter began. "In accordance with your instructions, I attach hereto Memorandum on Transition." He also enclosed three reports from the Brookings Institution project. "I shall be able to confer with you or your staff at any time suiting your convenience. You have my sincerest congratulations on the magnificent job you have done. Respectfully yours, Clark Clifford."

Clifford's memo urged Kennedy and his team to move forward with speed and determination, declaring that it was "important to realize that pockets of resistance to the president inevitably tend to grow up in the Departments, in Congress, and in the Party, and the president-elect should consolidate the reins of power and leadership in his own hands, as soon as possible." He counseled urgency and focus. "The first problem of the new Administration, of course, is to get off the mark quickly with its New Frontier program, and this objective has been kept in mind in framing the suggestions that follow." Clifford's memo urged the president-elect to work cooperatively with the outgoing Eisenhower administration, seize control of the executive branch, work closely with Congress, and take control of the Democratic Party. He outlined initial legislation for Kennedy to promote in the early days of his presidency to generate a sense of momentum, including medical care for the elderly, minimum wage, housing, urban renewal, and education legislation.[9]

In Kennedy's first postelection press conference on November 11, he referred to Neustadt and Clifford as his transition advisers. They were to play important, but different, roles in the ensuing ten weeks. Neustadt, with his academic background in history and public administration, wrote detailed papers on staffing and government reorganization. Clifford served as Kennedy's primary link to the Washington establishment and the Eisenhower administration. When Kennedy received a telegram from Eisenhower after the election inviting him to assign someone to work on the transition with Wilton Persons, his chief of staff, Kennedy asked Clifford and he immediately agreed. Sorensen presented Kennedy with a draft response to Eisenhower. Kennedy showed his considerable political skills in reshaping the cable by removing several assertive, even demanding, clauses and inserting gentler, more indirect ones. At the end, he penciled out "President elect" and signed it "Senator."[10] The telegram thanked Eisenhower for his courtesy and his commitment to a smooth transfer of power. Kennedy's words to the sitting president were respectful and polite but not obsequious. "I look forward to meeting with you and again to express my appreciation for your cooperation," he said.

Clifford was a St. Louis native, former Truman staffer, respected Washington lawyer, and Democratic operative. He was smart, smooth, and savvy. Tall, elegantly dressed, and poised, he knew how Washington worked. He combined shrewdness and tact with a quietly charismatic personality. Clifford, Arthur Schlesinger Jr. observed, was "a man of unusual ability and discretion, concealing a sharp and quick mind under a big-man-on-campus exterior."[11] He was detail-oriented and organized and methodically worked through his handwritten to-do lists. He took careful notes during meetings, listing the topics discussed in numerical order, but his notes offer little commentary and rarely connect topics. They offer few clues about what he was really thinking but provide a reliable record of topics discussed during these meetings.

Clifford had an easy and respectful relationship with Kennedy, whom he called "Jack" up to the day of his inauguration and perhaps even later in private conversations. In fact he had to jot a note to remind himself to call Kennedy "Mr. President" when Kennedy met Eisenhower at the White House after the election. He was deferential to Kennedy but also could speak to him directly. When Kennedy received a transition report from Brookings, Clifford urged Kennedy to send a reply to Robert Calkins, the think tank president. "You will want to have Mrs. Lincoln write Mr. Calkins thanking them for their assistance and cooperation," Clifford wrote.

Not everyone was convinced of Clifford's profundity. "I am never certain whether Clark Clifford is a genius in making the complex sound simple or in making the obvious seem profound, but either way he is a genius," a Kennedy aide quipped.[12] Clifford knew everyone in political Washington, including Persons, Eisenhower's chief of staff, whom he liked and respected. Persons called Clifford after he had been named to head the Kennedy transition team and invited him to the White House to begin their joint effort.

III

As was typical for Clifford, he carefully prepared an agenda for his first session with Persons. He wanted especially to explore how the initial meeting between Eisenhower and Kennedy should take place, including its timing and format, and whether a joint statement should be issued after it concluded. He suggested they review how to deal with urgent matters that might come up during the transition that required the outgoing administration to get the views and even the concurrence of Kennedy. Clifford was eager to learn what instructions Eisenhower had given government departments and agencies about cooperating with the incoming administration. And he was eager to ensure that Kennedy received timely foreign policy and intelligence briefings from the State Department and the CIA.

Clifford also wanted to nail down an arrangement for setting up ongoing meetings between key players in both administrations. He asked permission for a Kennedy representative to visit the White House to better understand its daily operations. A veteran of past governments, Clifford recalled that the Bureau of the Budget, a unit of the Executive Office of the President, compiled a file of the campaign promises of both major party candidates. "A copy of this memorandum should be obtained," Clifford reminded himself in a note. Clifford assumed each cabinet-level department would prepare a memo describing the organization and its principal staff for the new secretary and he wanted copies of each. He needed lists of all the jobs the new president would be able to fill both in the White House and the cabinet departments, including job titles and salaries. He also wanted to arrange a personal meeting with Maurice Stans, the director of the Bureau of the Budget, to see what other documents and reports might be available and helpful.

Clifford took a taxi to the White House Northwest Gate on Monday, November 14, for his first transition meeting with Persons. The guard did not know him so Clifford brandished his ten-year-old White House pass that had not seen action during the Eisenhower years. The pass had expired but he was eventually recognized by a staffer and waved through. He met Persons in his White House office. They shook hands, sat for a photo, exchanged pleasantries, and then got to work. Clifford found Persons easygoing, open, and cooperative. "Persons was a fortunate choice," he recalled later. "I had known him for years, and respected him as a thorough, careful, and nonpartisan military officer with an easygoing and attractive manner." He added that their first meeting was cordial and productive, and "set a tone of low-key cooperation that was to last through the transition period." They reviewed the problems of the 1932 and 1952 transitions and vowed to do better. Both agreed that neither would hold press conferences or conduct interviews. Their work would be private, diligent, and discreet. "There was no tension, no fireworks, no ego problems. I was to meet regularly with Persons for the next two months and speak with him on the telephone on a daily basis, without ever encountering a single difficulty," Clifford recalled.[13]

At that first meeting they methodically worked through the agendas each had prepared. They agreed that Eisenhower and Kennedy should meet after Thanksgiving. Both would check the schedules of their principals to schedule it shortly after the holiday. "One meeting will probably be sufficient in the absence of a national emergency," Clifford later told Kennedy. Clifford and Persons discussed a joint statement issued by Eisenhower and Kennedy after their meeting and decided to review the one issued by Eisenhower and Truman eight years earlier for guidance. Clifford learned that Eisenhower had recently sent a letter of instructions to federal departments and agencies on how to proceed with the transition, especially how to deal with members of the incoming administration. Persons promised to give him either the letter or a summary of it. "This will be useful in ascertaining the framework within which the transition is to be conducted," Clifford told Kennedy.

The two men set up a procedure for Kennedy to receive daily briefings from the State Department and CIA. They arranged for a courier to bring foreign policy and intelligence updates to Kennedy wherever he was and to schedule briefings with the CIA director as Kennedy needed them. They also set up the process by which the FBI would conduct background checks for Kennedy nominees as well as an arrangement for a special clearance procedure for those dealing with atomic energy issues.

Persons and Clifford devised a method for contact between the incoming and outgoing teams—a matter of considerable sensitivity and concern to Eisenhower, who was was suspicious of Kennedy on many levels. The president did not want incoming Kennedy officials roaming the halls of federal agencies before January 20. They agreed that when Kennedy selected a cabinet secretary or a senior White House adviser, Clifford would contact Persons who would then arrange a meeting between the Kennedy nominee and his counterpart in the Eisenhower administration. After the initial encounter the two would be permitted to arrange subsequent meetings for themselves and their staffs.

Persons assured Clifford that departmental briefing papers would be provided to Kennedy nominees as they were appointed. He also agreed to forward lists of jobs to be filled by the new administration, including a document prepared by the Civil Service Commission along with 475 White House staff, Executive Mansion, and White House grounds positions. William Hopkins, executive White House clerk, provided a layout of the White House and Executive Office Building offices that were designated for the White House. Clifford and Persons also discussed Kennedy's appointment of a staff secretary to begin examining White House operations, drawing on the expertise of Hopkins and the current staff secretary, Andrew Goodpaster who would ultimately be asked to remain in the White House for the first few months of the Kennedy administration.

Clifford, delighted with his first meeting with Persons, conferred the following day with Stans, the budget director, and then met again with Persons at the end of the week. During that first week of direct contact with the Eisenhower administration, Sorensen also met with both Persons and David Kendall, chief counsel in the Eisenhower White House.

IV

Clifford then traveled to Palm Beach for several days of meetings with Kennedy and other top advisers. Clifford later said that Kennedy wanted to "know in rather complete detail how far we had reached at this point, and what subjects we had covered." Clifford spelled out the procedures he and Persons had agreed to and handed Kennedy several volumes of job lists with extensive information on the job classifications, salary ranges, and current employees. Kennedy's meetings with his top advisers in Palm Beach the week of November 21 helped drive the agenda and set the tone for the coming weeks. They reviewed tentative dates for first messages to Congress, legislative priorities and possible executive orders, the use of formal task forces and informal working groups to fashion their policy agenda, how to find the right people for important jobs, possible candidates for key positions, the liaison procedure with the Eisenhower administration, and the future structure of the Kennedy White House. Clifford urged Kennedy to move quickly to appoint a White House budget director, saying that office was an important arm of the president and should be used to the fullest extent. Clifford recalled staying up well past midnight one evening discussing possible candidates for top cabinet jobs with Kennedy, Sorensen, Shriver, O'Brien, and others.[14]

Kennedy confirmed during these meetings that he had decided that he did not want a chief of staff, a view supported by both Clifford and Neustadt. Kennedy felt a chief of staff diluted the power of the president by limiting the flow of information into the Oval Office. Kennedy also wanted a smaller White House staff than Eisenhower had. But Kennedy was less certain if he wanted to cut back on both White House staff and the executive offices of the president, which included the budget office, the Council of Economic Advisors, the National Security Council, and other agencies.

The following week Clifford had an extensive conversation with Kennedy to review the progress of the transition. Kennedy was considering Robert Lovett, who had worked in sensitive diplomatic and administrative posts under several presidents, for several cabinet positions. Clifford had learned that Lovett's health would not allow him to accept a top post but he was available to meet with Kennedy to discuss other candidates and the broader challenge of forming a government. Kennedy was narrowing his options for some cabinet secretary nominations: Governor Luther Hodges of North Carolina for commerce, Governor Abe Ribicoff of Connecticut for health, education, and welfare, Congressman Stewart Udall of Arizona for interior, and Washington lawyer Arthur Goldberg for labor. He had several ideas about where his brother Robert Kennedy might serve, including the number two job at the Pentagon or a senior position at the State Department. "He has received a substantial amount of advice against making Bobby the attorney general. I told him I would consider some additional names for the attorney generalship and would be prepared to consult with him," Clifford wrote in a memo about his November 30 conversation with Kennedy.[15]

Clifford helped prepare Kennedy for his December 6 meeting with Eisenhower in the Oval Office. He and Persons arranged the logistics of Kennedy's arrival, the format and topics to be discussed, and the statement that would be issued after. Clifford implored Kennedy to be punctual for the meeting that was expected to focus heavily on foreign policy. To prepare Kennedy, Clifford asked respected Washington lawyers George Ball and John Sharon to create a briefing book for Kennedy. It was a succinct and carefully organized document, providing facts, recommendations, and questions pertaining to NATO's nuclear policy, Laos, Latin America, Cuba, Congo, disarmament and nuclear test suspension talks, budget policy, the balance of payments issue, and the outflow of U.S. gold.

After Kennedy and Eisenhower's private meeting they were joined by senior members of Ike's cabinet. Secretary of State Herter discussed nuclear testing and targeting—and the importance of the Polaris system for America's defenses, the recessed UN arms talks, upcoming international meetings involving NATO and CENTO, disarmament talks with the Soviet Union, a possible Kennedy-Khrushchev summit in the spring, and challenges in Congo, Berlin, Laos, Algeria, Israel, and Cuba. Treasury Secretary Anderson gave a detailed presentation on the balance of payments problem, described its history and the approach of the Eisenhower administration explaining, "No President has ever had this problem before . . . This is not an administration problem but it is a world problem." Defense Secretary Gates discussed, and even celebrated, the administration's military reforms declaring, "Maybe we are in too good shape." The president then spoke and said that once Kennedy appointed a National Security Council director that person should meet with the outgoing NSC chief, Gordon Gray.[16]

Persons called Clifford after the meeting and said Eisenhower was very impressed with Kennedy. Kennedy offered more restrained praise of Ike in his remarks to Clifford, but Clifford responded graciously to Persons.

At this time, Clifford wrote about the transition to a friend, Charles Loring. "The task is awe-inspiring in its immensity but I am getting excellent cooperation from the present Administration and I believe we will be able to effect the transition more effectively and efficiently than it has ever been done before." As the Christmas holidays approached, Clifford took stock of what had been achieved to date. In a December 23 "Dear Jack" letter to Kennedy, Clifford offered an upbeat assessment. "I am immensely pleased at the progress that is being made. Your Cabinet selections have received universal acclaim and you are off to a wonderful start. All is going smoothly at this end. I send best wishes for a very merry Christmas and the happiest of New Years. Respectfully yours."[17]

Clifford continued to press ahead in the new year. Persons told him that every department and agency would have an acting head in place when Eisenhower departed office in the event that Kennedy nominees had either not been named or confirmed by the Senate. Clifford received detailed reports on each major department from the McKinsey consulting firm as part of the Brookings transition project.

Kennedy's second meeting with Eisenhower would be on January 19, one day before he was to take the oath of office. Eisenhower's White House counsel, Dave Kendall, said that Kennedy should be prepared to review with the president important White House emergency procedures, special operations, and the technical aspects of using nuclear weapons. "The above would be discussed by the president with Mr. Kennedy alone. The purpose of discussing President Eisenhower's list when alone is that there will be things that will come out and that he will raise that have not been discussed in the presence of some of the Cabinet officers who would be present at the larger meeting," Clifford told Kennedy.

Clifford attended the January 19 meeting and again took extensive notes. His account describes Eisenhower's grim warnings about the problems related to Laos and Cuba. Eisenhower argued that Laos was the key to Southeast Asia and the U.S. should do all within its power to prevent that nation from falling under communist control. Eisenhower also briefed Kennedy on the administration's work to confront Castro in Cuba. "Ike says we should support guerillas to the utmost" in Cuba, Clifford wrote in his notes of the session, adding, "We are helping train forces in Guatemala."

Clifford would later say that he felt Eisenhower had unfairly pressured Kennedy on Laos and Cuba. "This discussion was a real turning point, I thought. This was the handing over of the baton: in a few hours Laos—and everything else—becomes the new President's problem. With no warning, his predecessor was raising the possibility of deploying American troops overseas." He noted that Eisenhower had not sent U.S. combat troops into Indochina in 1954 to help France during its bloody fight to save its embattled position at Dien Bien Phu. And yet "on this last day in office, he was taking a far tougher stand than at any time during the previous eight years . . . This new line in Southeast Asia—far tougher than he had taken on his own watch—cast a shadow over the early decisions of the next Administration. Its consequences, moreover, affected Vietnam and even Cuba."[18]

V

Kennedy had assumed that staffing his government would be interesting, possibly even fun. But he actually found it difficult, complicated, and time-consuming calling it "damn hard work." But he realized it was deeply consequential and he came to believe that putting the right people into the right jobs constituted about 75% of his transition challenge. He immediately grasped part of the problem. He knew many high-quality people but they were largely inhabitants of the world of partisan electoral politics with a smattering of associates from academic communities in the Northeast. He did not have a vast network of contacts from Wall Street, corporate America, foundations, the military, or diplomacy—the communities that are critical to staffing the top ranks of the federal government.

Shortly after the election, Clark Clifford identified the scope of the challenge. Kennedy and his team needed to select eighty top-level nominees and four hundred to five hundred second-tier appointments. These were the people who by managing the operations of the massive federal government could make or break his presidency. Additionally, there were about 1,200 third-tier support jobs that Kennedy could also fill without civil service exams. "Where am I going to find that many good people?" he asked his staff.

Kennedy quickly settled on a two-pronged effort. First, he tapped his brother-in-law Sargent Shriver to head up the so-called Talent Search. Shriver would lead the effort to find what he called "the brightest and the best" and what Kennedy on the campaign trail had referred to as a "Ministry of Talent." Kennedy also selected a top political aide, Lawrence O'Brien, to head the effort to find jobs for loyal Democrats who helped his campaign. Shriver's team began with positions and sought out people; O'Brien's team began with people and looked for jobs for them. Shriver concentrated on recruitment, O'Brien on placement. But the Shriver and O'Brien teams were part of the same broad effort. Both worked primarily out of offices at the Democratic National Committee in downtown Washington. Shriver's team sought stars who were loyal to Kennedy and O'Brien's team looked for good Democrats who were competent and would reflect well on Kennedy and his administration.

Shriver was an amiable, exuberant, Chicago businessman who was married to Kennedy's sister Eunice. He had worked for the Kennedy family for years, running the Merchandise Mart, a massive commercial facility in Chicago. Shriver was never part of the family's inner circle, which was comprised of Jack, Robert, Ted, Joe Kennedy Sr., and in-law Steven Smith. However, Kennedy admired Shriver's wide network of contacts and respected his drive, energy, optimism, and ability to get along with people. He was a sensible choice to find high-level talent for Kennedy's New Frontier.

Shriver assembled a team of primarily Kennedy Senate staffers that included Harris Wofford, Adam Yarmolinsky, Louis Martin, and Tom Farmer. They met at the Mayflower Hotel on November 14 and spent the following weeks working either from Shriver's hotel suite or the Democratic National Committee offices in Washington. While Shriver ran a free-wheeling operation, there was some specialized talent acquisition. Shriver scoured the business community, Wofford the academic world, Yarmolinsky concentrated on law schools and foundations, and Martin focused on the African American community.

Shriver clearly understood the kind of people his brother-in-law liked and wanted surrounding him: young, aggressive, discreet, nonideological, unemotional, and terse; mostly men, preferably between the ages of thirty and fifty. Mary Bundy, the wife of senior Kennedy aide McGeorge Bundy, referred to Kennedy's top team as "The junior officers of World War II come to responsibility." Kennedy liked thinkers and doers, people who were interested in ideas and could deliver results. Shriver briefly brought in a consultant from IBM to give his search a more rigorous quality but there was quick mutual acknowledgment that the arrangement would not work. The IBM consultant defined accomplishment in terms that were not directly relevant to Shriver's search—how fast a person's income rose and how many people worked under him. Yarmolinsky developed an evaluation tool that was more useful—an "index of excellence" in which candidates were assessed on the basis of judgement, integrity, toughness, and devotion to Kennedy's agenda. But those were, of course, subjective qualities. For example, Kennedy's agenda was evolving and would be difficult to understand, let alone be devoted to. Toughness was often in the eye of the beholder and did not lend itself to precise definition. Yarmolinsky's index shaped evaluations but was not used religiously. Shriver and his colleagues referred to it as they made thousands of phone calls to generate names, check references, and conduct interviews. Files were assembled on candidates but a lot of information was scribbled on napkins, envelopes, and hotel stationery.[19]

While Shriver's recruiting effort aspired to be national, many detected a decidedly East Coast bias. Someone quipped the New Frontier seemed to end on the banks of the Hudson River or even the Charles. To be sure many candidates lived in Cambridge, home to Harvard and MIT. Orville Freeman, a University of Minnesota graduate and Kennedy's eventual nominee to head the Department of Agriculture, joked that he may not have gotten his job if Harvard had a School of Agriculture, suggesting Kennedy would have tapped a professor from there.

There was some effort to find highly qualified women for key positions. Margaret Price, a campaign aide, drafted a report about women who had served in previous administrations. She argued that women should not be appointed to the Kennedy administration because of their gender but they also should not be discriminated against for this reason. She observed that more than one third of American women were in the labor force, meaning many good candidates were available. She also said the new administration should not limit women to only those jobs women had held in previous administrations. Price noted that Woodrow Wilson was the first president to make significant appointments of women and that Franklin Roosevelt "continued and expanded" on Wilson's record by appointing several women as top diplomats, and importantly Frances Perkins, the first female cabinet secretary. Price argued that Truman furthered this trend, selecting the first woman ambassador, federal communications commissioner, and U.S. treasurer. According to a survey by the Republican National Committee that Price cited, Eisenhower named 175 women to high-level appointments, including Oveta Culp Hobby as the first secretary of health, education, and welfare. Price suggested Kennedy consider naming a woman to head the Department of Labor or serve as postmaster general.[20]

Shriver's team worked across the hall from O'Brien's, and their efforts overlapped and intermingled, creating a kind of friendly competition for top-level talent. O'Brien was joined by the DNC chairman John Bailey and two of Kennedy's Senate staffers, Ralph Dungan and Richard Donahue. O'Brien was a political operative from Springfield, Massachusetts, who had worked on Kennedy's first Senate campaign in 1952, his reelection race in 1958, and had done much of the grassroots legwork for the 1960 presidential primaries. He joked that he did not feel like he was a natural fit in Kennedy's world. "I don't know what I'm doing with this crowd," he once said. "I didn't go to Harvard and I'm not athletic. I don't even play touch football."

Shriver and O'Brien's in-boxes were filled with letters of recommendation from party leaders and old friends. Minnesota Attorney General Walter Mondale recommended Freeman, the just defeated governor, to a top position. *Washington Star* columnist Mary McGrory recommended an obscure professor named Daniel Patrick Moynihan, whom she called "the pearl of great price," who "has been heretofore overlooked in the federal treasure hunt. His main interests are international labor affairs and transportation. He also knows a great deal about politics, especially the New York brand, but he says if he comes here it must be to do something for this country, not for one of its politicians."[21] Peter Briggs from *Ladies Home Journal* cabled an unconventional idea, suggesting the appointment of novelist Ernest Hemingway to be the American ambassador in Cuba.

Kennedy's initial hires were to his White House staff, and for those he drew heavily from his Senate staff and campaign team. Ted Sorensen was named counselor, Ken O'Donnell appointments secretary, Pierre Salinger press secretary, Larry O'Brien congressional liaison and personnel chief, and Ralph Dungan and Fred Dutton as staff assistants. Late in the transition, McGeorge Bundy was hired as Kennedy's National Security Advisor and he and his deputy, Walter Rostow, built a mini State Department at the White House. Senior staff members earned $21,000 per year and received an official commission from Kennedy. This was the letter Pierre Salinger received: "JOHN F. KENNEDY, PRESIDENT OF THE UNITED STATES OF AMERICA, To PIERRE E. G. SALINGER of California, Greeting: REPOSING special trust and confidence in your Integrity, Prudence, and Ability I do appoint you Press Secretary to the President of the United States of America, authorizing you, hereby, to do and perform all such matters and things as to the said place or office do appertain, or as may be duly given you in charge hereafter, and the said office to hold and exercise during the pleasure of the President of the United States for the time being." Salinger later said that his commission from Kennedy was prominently displayed in his office throughout his subsequent professional career.[22]

Kennedy wanted a smaller White House staff than Eisenhower's, which Kennedy felt was cumbersome and bureaucratic. He wanted a staff that was flexible and versatile and that would relate directly to him. He often used the analogy of spokes on a wheel, with himself at the center. When Kennedy heard an expansive account of what McGeorge Bundy's responsibilities would be as his chief foreign policy aide, Kennedy bristled, saying that he, as president, expected to retain "some residual functions."

He wanted his staff to work hard and stay out of the news. When Sorensen mentioned to Kennedy in December of 1960 that he was receiving speaking invitations and queries about magazine profiles, Kennedy offered clear advice. "Turn them all down. Not only will you not have time. Every man that's held a job like yours—Sherman Adams, Harry Hopkins, [Colonel] House, all the rest has ended up in the shithouse. Congress was down on them, or the president was hurt by them, or somebody was mad at them. The best way to stay out of trouble is to stay out of sight."[23]

After focusing on senior White House staff, Kennedy turned to selecting the ten members of his cabinet and top-level officials in the departments. He personally interviewed dozens of candidates and made scores of calls to check people out. Kennedy's most intense deliberations were over the four positions he considered most important: the secretaries of state, defense, and treasury, and the attorney general.

Kennedy's thinking about his cabinet was not always coherent or clear. He sounded out Robert Lovett about three very different cabinet jobs—state, defense, and treasury—all of which required different expertise. Kennedy considered Robert McNamara for two highly dissimilar jobs—secretary of defense and treasury—but McNamara said he had no interest in or qualification to run the Treasury. Initially, Senators Symington and Jackson were thought to be the leading contenders for defense secretary. But their ambivalence and Kennedy's desire for a fresh face propelled him toward McNamara, who had just been appointed president of the Ford Motor Company. Shriver went to Michigan to meet him and was greatly impressed. McNamara then traveled to Washington for a thirty-minute meeting with Kennedy. Kennedy offered him the job on the basis of this interview and a follow-up discussion, and McNamara accepted a few days later. Reporters pressed Kennedy to confirm that he had given one of the most important jobs in the American government to man he knew less than a week. He acknowledged this was so.

Kennedy conducted a more exhaustive search for secretary of state considering, at least briefly, former Governor Adlai Stevenson, Senator William Fulbright, Congressman Chester Bowles, and Ambassador David Bruce. He ultimately selected Dean Rusk, president of the Rockefeller Foundation, after he received strong recommendations from Lovett and former Secretary of State Dean Acheson and held a meeting with Rusk that Rusk himself did not think went very well. Acheson urged Kennedy to approach this appointment realistically. "You are not picking God when you choose a secretary of state," Acheson said. "You are making a choice between alternatives. You are looking for a man with the greatest number of assets and the fewest liabilities." Again, reporters pressed Kennedy to confirm that he had known Rusk less than a week when he selected him to the most high-profile job in his cabinet. He said this was so.

Kennedy named Douglas Dillon as treasury secretary. Dillon was a prominent Republican and respected internationally. Kennedy had known him for several years and had worked with him on issues in Dillon's capacity as Eisenhower's undersecretary of state. They shared a patrician reserve and a penchant for understatement. When asked by a reporter if he had given Dillon written assurances about his role in the new administration, Kennedy grew annoyed. He said that no president could or should "enter into treaties" with cabinet members.[24]

Kennedy's decision to select his brother as attorney general was convoluted, deeply controversial, and influenced heavily by his father. Both Jack and Robert Kennedy had serious misgivings about the arrangement for many reasons, not least of which was that Robert was in his early thirties and had never practiced law. Jack even asked Clark Clifford to travel to New York, meet with his father, and try to persuade him to drop the idea. Recalling the incident later, Clifford said he viewed this as "truly a strange assignment—the president-elect asking a third party to try to talk to his father about his brother." Clifford agreed to do what he could. He had a pleasant dinner with Joseph Kennedy and explained why he felt it would be better that Robert not become the attorney general. The senior Kennedy listened politely and then responded, "Thank you very much Clark. I am so glad to have heard your views. I do want to leave you with one thought, however—one firm thought. Bobby is going to be attorney general. All of us have worked our tails off for Jack, and now that we have succeeded I am going to see to it that Bobby gets the same chance that we gave to Jack." Clifford said the conversation stayed with him—and troubled him—over the years. "I would always remember the intense but matter-of-fact tone with which he had spoken—there was no rancor, no anger, no challenge . . . For a moment I had glimpsed the inner workings of that remarkable family, and despite my admiration and affection for John F. Kennedy, I could not say I liked what I saw."[25] The president-elect decided to go forward with Robert's nomination as attorney general. He joked to a friend that he would announce it at a predawn dash outside his Washington home and then duck back in before any reporter could ask a question. The actual announcement was slightly more elaborate than that, but also palpably awkward.[26]

There were scores of letters to Kennedy about who he should, or should not, appoint to key positions. More than a few sharply worded cables, many from private citizens, urged Kennedy not to appoint his brother as attorney general and others fiercely rebuked him when he did.

"Your choice of your brother as attorney general has caused me not only to regret my vote for you but to lose all respect for you," wrote Diana Gast from New Jersey. Thomas Ransjell of Jacksonville, North Carolina, found the appointment of Robert almost shocking. "I voted for you but I did not vote for your family. With all the good lawyers in the entire United States and you appoint your little brother as attorney general of this United States I think is a very disgraceful thing to do. I am sure thousands of others feel the same as I do." Clifton Grubbs, the Colorado chairman of "Professors for Kennedy" believed the selection of Robert would hurt Kennedy's policy agenda. He said, "simply too much is at stake and the time is too short for any of us to detract from the urgent business of getting the country back on the move. The Republican Party will hound us to death over this appointment and of all people Robert should know this." Harry Sufflebarger from Columbus, Ohio, was both sharply critical and deeply sarcastic. "Why not dear old dad for Postmaster General? That will pay off and keep it in the family. To think I voted for you."

Kennedy also took an interest in reshaping the corps of American ambassadors. He worked with Dean Rusk and Chester Bowles, who was appointed to be Rusk's deputy at the State Department, to find envoys who reflected the energetic spirit of the New Frontier. Bowles scoured the ranks of the Foreign Service to find young talent. He helped block the assignment of seven of Eisenhower's nominees to be ambassadors to newly declared African nations and eventually persuaded more than thirty other ambassadors to retire. Kennedy and Rusk promoted a number of career foreign service officers but also made some solid ambassadorial selections such as Professor Edwin Reischauer to Japan, veteran diplomat George Kennan to Yugoslavia, Ambassador David Bruce to the United Kingdom, and General James Gavin to France.

As Kennedy's initial Talent Search came to a close, the press focused on the youth, academic credentials, and professional background of Kennedy's nominees. *U.S News & World Report* looked closely at Kennedy's selections and did some calculations and comparisons. In 1953, twenty-two of Eisenhower's fifty most important appointees were businessmen. Among Kennedy's top fifty-one nominees, six came from the business world. The average age of the Kennedy group was forty-eight, whereas the average age of Eisenhower's appointees was a full decade older.[27]

The youngest member of the Kennedy cabinet was thirty-five, the oldest was sixty-two. All ten cabinet secretaries had college degrees—six with law degrees—five had political backgrounds, one came from organized labor, three from business and banking, and one from a philanthropic foundation. A cartoon depicted the Phi Beta Kappa ring as the current "key to the city." The magazine noted that sixteen in the top echelon of the new administration were Phi Beta Kappa, four had won Rhodes Scholarships, and one had won a Nobel Prize.

The Kennedy government reflected its leader. "There were no crusaders, fanatics, or extremists from any camp; all were nearer the center than either left or right," said Sorensen. "All spoke with the same low-keyed restraint that marked their chief, yet all shared his deep conviction that they could change America's drift. They liked government, they liked politics, they liked Kennedy, and they believed implicitly in him."[28]

Clifford found the Kennedy team impressive but cocky. "They were a competent and dynamic group, younger than the Truman or Eisenhower staff men. From the start, however, I was disturbed by one aspect of their general demeanor: with the exception of the president-elect himself, they behaved as though history had begun with them. They regarded both Eisenhower and Truman (and their own vice president) with something bordering on contempt."[29]

Goodwin, a Kennedy aide, reflecting later believed Kennedy made one fundamental mistake in some of his high-level selections. "Only later did I understand the often decisive principle of presidential appointment: The deficiencies of those one knows are also known; relative strangers, being remote from experience, appear unblemished."[30]

Some press accounts focused on how little Kennedy actually knew the members of his cabinet, which one reporter quipped was to be comprised of "nine strangers and a brother." This phrase was a play on an earlier description of Eisenhower's first cabinet as comprised of "eight millionaires and a plumber." (A new department, the Department of Health, Education, and Welfare was created in 1953 pursuant to a proposal by Eisenhower.)

VI

With Clark Clifford leading the transition effort and Sargent Shriver and Larry O'Brien running the talent search, Ted Sorensen took on the central role in assembling Kennedy's policy agenda. After fourteen years in Congress, Kennedy was conversant if not expert in domestic and especially foreign policy. He had taken specific policy positions in both the House and Senate and on the campaign trail. Typical of many presidential candidates, his campaign included many promises to many groups.

But the president-elect still needed to translate his numerous ideas into a governing agenda. Sorensen was clearly the man to help him. An intense midwesterner, Sorensen had been Kennedy's closest policy aide during his Senate career, helping Kennedy sharpen and express his ideas. Kennedy described him as his "intellectual blood bank." A contemporary journalist called Sorensen a "brilliant, bespectacled, and somewhat brittle egghead from Nebraska," adding, "to many he has seemed surly, highhanded, abrasive and abrupt." But he knew Kennedy's mind and moods better than anyone else. Sorensen shared many of Kennedy's intellectual traits and had a similar cast of mind but he lacked his boss's polish. Sorensen was on the campaign trail with Kennedy from the start and knew what issues animated the candidate and which drew the most enthusiastic responses from his supporters.

As Sorensen set out to assemble Kennedy's policy agenda, his first step was to catalogue what Kennedy had actually promised on the campaign trail. He instructed Richard Goodwin to create a specific record of what Kennedy proposed to do as president. Goodwin assembled one of the most revealing documents of the transition—a thirteen-page compilation of eighty-one campaign pledges. Goodwin scribbled a handwritten note to Sorensen at the top of the report. "Ted: Here is a listing of campaign promises w/some repetition, but not much. I did not repeat a promise if made several times. I planned to organize this by subject matter but I had no secretarial help and so I am sending it along as is. If you want it organized I have a copy to work from. Dick."[31]

Goodwin's pledge compendium was largely drawn from Kennedy campaign's speeches in chronological order. Consequentially, the candidate's procession of promises reflected the Democratic primary calendar more than a coherent policy agenda. Early in the list were a series of late winter and early spring promises that were clearly targeted at voters in Wisconsin and West Virginia, two critical early primaries. For Wisconsin voters there were policy pledges related to agriculture, forestry, and protecting fish in inland lakes. For West Virginians, there was a promise to increase defense contracts and enact a New Deal for their state. The Goodwin paper also lists pledges of a national scope: medical care for the elderly through Social Security, federal aid for education, funds for school construction and teachers' salaries, increased defense spending, support for a minimum wage increase, unemployment insurance expansion, Social Security benefits indexed to the cost of living, the creation of an Arms Control Research Institute, broad civil rights legislation, new hospitals, improved programs for the elderly, and the creation of a Peace Corps. Kennedy had promised to reverse "the disastrous high interest rate policies of the administration" despite the fact that most key interest rates were set by the Federal Reserve Board. He also pledged to clear slums, modify the Federal Housing Administration mortgage interest program, improve cooperative and public housing, and increase housing research.

In preparing Kennedy's policy agenda Sorensen also reviewed a list of expiring laws that would require responses and scoured the 1960 Democratic Party platform to remind himself of additional promises the party had made to voters.

During the campaign, Kennedy created several task forces to clarify his understanding of and ultimately his position on topics such as defense, foreign policy, agriculture, and natural resources. These groups issued their reports after the election. Adlai Stevenson chaired the foreign policy task force, the defense strategy task force was led by Paul Nitze, Congressman Frank Smith of Mississippi ran the panel on natural resources, and a Senate study on reorganizing the government's foreign policy machinery was coordinated by Senator Henry Jackson.

The Stevenson report was the most interesting and influential. Though it bore Stevenson's name, it was largely written by George Ball, a foreign policy expert in Stevenson's law firm. Ball consulted other authorities in the United States and Europe over the summer and fall and assembled a comprehensive study of American foreign policy. It was exactly the kind of document that Kennedy devoured. It was well written, carefully organized, and clearly distinguished short-term emergencies from longer-term challenges. The first section dealt with pressing matters such as the gold drain, the status of disarmament talks, tensions in Berlin, and a pending proposal to create the Organization of Economic Cooperation and Development as a way for Western nations to work together on economic matters. The second section dealt with longer-term challenges such as the need for a new trade strategy, economic development, NATO nuclear cooperation, and arms control. Kennedy was delighted when he finished reading the initial section of the Stevenson report. "Very good. Terrific. This is excellent. Just what I needed," he said.

The Stevenson report and several others convinced Kennedy and Sorensen that creating task forces was an effective device for generating ideas, identifying talent for the new administration, creating a sense of movement, and assuring the public that Kennedy was poised to be a serious president. This encouraged them to create additional task forces to examine specific foreign policy and domestic policy issues in more detail.

The result was the creation of task forces on Africa, Latin America, India, combating the U.S. recession, taxation, education, aiding West Virginia and other depressed areas, health care and Social Security, housing and urban affairs, space, disarmament, the United States Information Agency, foreign economic policy, distributing agricultural surpluses abroad, State Department personnel overseas, an Arms Control Research Institute, a Peace Agency, the minimum wage, regulatory agencies, civil rights, government reorganization, and natural resources development. Sorensen took the lead in setting up most of the task forces but Ball and his law partner, John Sharon, were also involved. In a few cases the expanding number of presidential task forces forced members to collide with each other, reflecting Kennedy's penchant for assigning similar activities to different people and groups. In a few instances the overlap was due more to confusion than intention.

Sorensen urged the task forces to limit their scope and submit clear and brief reports. "Let me emphasize once again that we are interested only in the most urgent and significant steps on which you think the next Administration must decide in its first sixty days, before there is time for an official study," he wrote to the task force chairmen. "Obviously only one—or at best a few—proposals have this kind of high priority—and if your Task Force concludes that its proposals are not of that priority and can be postponed, we trust that you will be frank enough to say so." Sorensen asked that recommendations be ranked in priority and the task forces focus on proposals that could be implemented during the first months of the new administration. "The more concise your report can be, the better," he said, adding that he would prefer reports in a form that they could easily be put into legislation. He also urged task force members not to make public comments about their work unless advised to do so by transition leaders. "These Task Forces will remain anonymous, and their reports confidential, unless I notify you to the contrary. We are still counting on having all reports in by the last of the year," he wrote.[32]

While several of the task forces adhered to Sorensen's request on length and scope, many submitted documents that resembled small books rather than policy memos. With an opportunity to shape the new administration's agenda, task force members unfurled ideas that had been germinating for years. More than a few concluded that an historic turning point had been reached in their specific policy areas and outlined their recommendations in enormous detail. Several task forces set out ambitious agendas for the entire 1960s.

Recommendations from several of the task forces were of immediate importance for the incoming administration. MIT economics professor Paul Samuelson chaired the panel on combating the recession. He argued the United States was still mired in a recession that was superimposed on an economy, which, in the last few years, was already sluggish. But he urged against despair. "With proper actions by the government, the contraction in business can be brought to a halt within 1961 itself and converted into an upturn." He urged the administration to think boldly and creatively. "Prudent policy now requires that we also combat the basic sluggishness which underlies the more dramatic recession. In some ways a recession imposed on top of a disappointingly slack economy simplifies prudent decision making." The goal for the coming year should be to end the recession, reinstate expansion and recovery, and adopt measures to make that expansion self-sustaining. "Indeed policy for 1961 should be directed against the background of the whole decade ahead," he said.

Samuelson urged the incoming Kennedy administration to be activist. "History reminds us that even in the worst days of the Great Depression, there was never any shortage of experts to warn against all curative public actions, on the grounds that they were likely to create a problem of inflation." The report urged vigorous and creative fiscal policy—but not a program of hastily devised public works or a surge in defense spending. The government should continue to fund foreign aid, education, urban renewal, health, and welfare, and expanded unemployment insurance, and if the economy did not recover the administration should consider a one-time tax cut. "A temporary reduction in tax rates on individual incomes can be a powerful weapon against recession," he wrote, adding that an effective package might cut three or four percentage points for all tax rates.[33]

Harris Wofford, Kennedy's Senate and campaign aide on civil rights, wrote a detailed report that was both impassioned and practical. He recommended that Kennedy propose little or no civil rights legislation in 1961 aside from the extension of the Commission on Civil Rights. Instead, Wofford argued Kennedy should focus on executive action. "You have power now to do more than you will be able to do on this problem in one year. If you make this a year full of executive action you can overcome the disappointment of Negroes and civil rights groups, although they will holler for a while."

Wofford said only the judiciary branch had been leading the charge for civil rights. "If the full power of the Federal Government can be brought to bear on this problem with intelligence and consistency, the racial bottleneck in our national life can be broken in one decade. If even two branches of government—the Executive and the Judiciary—would work together on this problem, the solution would be in sight." Wofford said the first executive order, coming soon after January 20, should state the principle that the entire U.S. government rejects discrimination. Other executive orders were needed to prohibit discrimination in federally assisted housing programs and to direct that federal aid to higher education be conditioned on policies of non-discrimination.

Wofford suggested Kennedy ask Congress to renew the Civil Rights Commission before the end of the session since it would expire in November of 1961 unless extended. He said Kennedy might also want to take some small but symbolic steps such as backing passage of the anti–poll tax constitutional amendment already supported by two-thirds of the senators.

According to Wofford, Kennedy needed to be aware of the importance of good optics on civil rights. "Even if you now decide on a course of executive action with practically no legislation this year it would be impolitic to announce or so acknowledge any such decision. Negro and civil rights groups are not yet adjusted to the idea of the primacy of executive action in this field. They have so long operated in the absence of presidential action, with all attention given to legislation, that they would greet such a decision as a sellout . . . Moreover, you probably need the possibility of Administration support for far-reaching legislation this session as a threat to use in the recurring negotiation with southern political leaders."

Wofford urged Kennedy to hire qualified African Americans for sub-cabinet jobs and appoint a black federal district judge in New York City. He emphasized the importance of keeping in contact with, and entertaining at the White House, top African American leaders such as Roy Wilkins, Martin Luther King, and Adam Clayton Powell. "But above all you should keep King and Wilkins with you, and they are warmly and strongly with you now," Wofford wrote.[34]

Some of the task force reports were more aspirational, focused on long-term goals rather than immediate crises. The Space Task Force chaired by Jerome Wiesner, also an MIT professor, examined ballistic missiles, scientific observations from satellites, exploring the solar system, military space systems, and the challenges of putting a man into low-earth orbit, and ultimately into deep space exploration. It criticized the Eisenhower administration's management of the space program. It also offered bracing statements, arguing that there was "the distinct possibility that planetary exploration may lead to the discovery of extraterrestrial forms of life. This clearly would be one of the greatest human achievements of all times."

The Space Task Force urged the U.S. government to play a more active role in manned space exploration and suggested the goal of human explo-ration that would eventually help define the Kennedy presidency. Because of the lag in the development of large boosters, it was unlikely that the U.S. would be the first nation to place a man into orbit around the earth. The panel nonetheless urged a robust American effort in space. "While the successful orbiting of a man about the earth is not an end unto itself, it will provide a necessary stepping stone toward the establishment of a space station and for the eventual manned exploration of the moon and the planets. The ultimate goal of this kind of endeavor would, of course, be an actual landing of man on the moon or a planet, followed by his return to earth," the task force report said.[35]

Kennedy and Sorensen had scores of ideas to consider and wrangle into a policy agenda. At a late December meeting in Palm Beach, Kennedy and his policy advisers reviewed more than 250 ideas gathered from the task forces, his campaign promises, and the party's platform. In early January Kennedy met with about a dozen task force chairmen individually as well as with some of their members. Kennedy studied the reports, some carefully. Most were eventually sent to the appropriate cabinet department or agency for consideration. By Inauguration Day, twenty-four of Kennedy's twenty-nine task forces had submitted their reports. Arthur Schlesinger Jr. said the overall effort was constructive. "It gave the men of the New Frontier an opportunity to work together in hammering out new policies. Out of the task force experience there came—for the president-elect and for those close to him—a freshened sense of programs, priorities, and of people."[36]

VII

From the first days of the transition, Kennedy affected an air of nonchalance about Republican threats to demand recounts in key states and to challenge the election's result in the courts. Kennedy decided the best strategy was to confidently declare victory, offer his best wishes to President Eisenhower and Richard Nixon, and act like the next occupant of the White House. He was especially eager to receive and acknowledge congratulatory messages from Eisenhower the day after the election and to meet with Nixon the following week in Key Biscayne.

But Kennedy was more concerned about sustaining and confirming his razor-thin victory than he let on, as suggested by terse responses to reporters' questions on the topic. When asked on November 14 after the Key Biscayne meeting with Nixon if the two had discussed the Republican recount threat, Kennedy offered a clipped, "We did not." Clearly aware of the effort and following it closely, Kennedy later chided Republican officials for working harder to alter the election's outcome after the November 8 voting than they did during the campaign.

Just two days after the election, Kennedy met with his top advisers in Hyannis Port. The fragility of the vote tally was the subject of intense discussion. Pierre Salinger said it was "assumed that there would be challenges because of the narrowness of the election" and Kennedy took the likely disputes seriously. "There was some thought that, if they challenged, there might even be a real question about who would become president and a whole mish-mash. So it was decided we should proceed full scale, so there would be no doubt in anybody's mind that we were confident we had won the election and we were going ahead with it." Salinger said the Kennedy campaign was worried that an election challenge "could tie up the presidency of the United States for a period of time which would make whoever was the winner of such a challenge in an untenable position." According to Salinger, Kennedy was determined to act like the winner and move forward to prevent his presidency from being crippled by uncertainty before it even got started.[37]

But Kennedy knew that he was not officially the president-elect until the Electoral College voted on December 19. He and his political and legal teams kept a careful watch on, and in close touch with, local leaders in the eleven states that Republicans were considering contesting. There were also concerns that some electors in key Southern states could withhold their support of Kennedy and throw the election into the House of Representatives. But on December 19 the Electoral College made John F. Kennedy the next president even as a dispute continued about the outcome of the election in Hawaii. Kennedy ultimately prevailed in the Electoral College, 303 to 219.

Kennedy gave considerable thought to when he should resign from the Senate and who his successor should be. Kennedy had been reelected in 1958 and his Senate term was slated to run until 1964. However, under Massachusetts law, the governor would appoint a new senator to replace Kennedy and that person would serve until the next statewide elections were held in 1962. Kennedy, as the outgoing senator, would not have a formal role in the appointment of his successor; it was the governor's responsibility and opportunity. However, as a practical matter Kennedy was the president-elect and the leading Democrat in his state, and would have considerable say in designating his successor.

Legally Kennedy could resign from the Senate at any time up to January 20, which meant that he controlled the timing of his resignation. This was relevant because Kennedy had a tense and uneasy relationship with the outgoing Democratic governor of Massachusetts, Foster Furcolo, whose term would end on January 5, 1961. Furcolo was to be succeeded by John Volpe, a Republican, who had defeated him in November. Furcolo apparently contemplated a scheme where if Kennedy resigned before January 5, Furcolo would resign as governor before his term concluded, then have the secretary of state assume the governorship for the final days of the term and appoint Furcolo to Kennedy's Senate seat. Kennedy had no interest in this arrangement not only because he did not want Furcolo to be his successor but also because he wanted a transitional figure to hold the Massachusetts Senate seat until 1962. This would allow either his brother Robert or Ted, who turned thirty that year, the minimum age for a senator, to run for JFK's old Senate seat in the state election. The Massachusetts secretary of state said he would not participate in the scheme, so Furcolo's hand was forced to appoint a Democratic placeholder.

Kennedy was publicly tight lipped about the political maneuvering in Massachusetts but was ultimately instrumental in persuading Furcolo to appoint Kennedy's Harvard classmate, Benjamin Smith, the former mayor of Gloucester, to the Senate seat. Smith planned to serve for the two years and not run in 1962. On December 22, once all the pieces were in place, Kennedy sent his Senate resignation letter to Furcolo and to the president of the Senate, Vice President Nixon. Under Senate rules, Kennedy was allowed to keep his Senate offices for an additional thirty days that his staff used to abet the transition.[38]

Another sensitive matter Kennedy contemplated during the transition was what to do with Lyndon Johnson when he became vice president. The two talked about Johnson's role in the new administration when they met in Texas on November 17 but there is no record of what was specifically discussed. In the ensuing weeks Johnson attended various transition meetings with Kennedy in Washington, Palm Beach, and New York. Johnson was quickly tapped to head up the space program and oversee federal government contracts for minorities. But this hardly seemed enough to keep the ambitious Johnson busy or happy.

As the retiring Senate majority leader, Johnson aspired to serve as Kennedy's legislative operator on Capitol Hill. He was widely regarded as a legislative master and far more skilled in orchestrating congressional levers of power than Kennedy. He was also reluctant to relinquish his longstanding ties to the Senate. Even as vice president, Johnson wanted to retain his chairmanship of the Senate Democratic caucus and continue to sit, unofficially, on the Senate Democratic Policy and Steering committees.

This unusual proposal was presented to Senate Democrats when they convened on January 3, 1961, and was met by considerable surprise, some anger, and only grudging support for the idea. A number of senators did not like Johnson and resented his years-long stranglehold on Senate power and perks. Even some Democratic senators who respected Johnson felt this proposed arrangement would violate separation of powers strictures. Johnson's future role was put to a vote among Senate Democrats and his proposal prevailed, forty-six to seventeen. But the opposition of seventeen of his former colleagues was seen as a striking repudiation of Johnson. He was angered and hurt by the vote, quietly dropped the idea, and largely withdrew from Senate affairs.

Johnson's staff drafted an executive order that delineated the incoming vice president's responsibilities and authorities. One of the earliest versions would have given Johnson unprecedented supervisory powers over the executive branch. Even the executive order draft that was finally sent to Kennedy envisioned a major expansion of vice presidential power. James Rowe, a longtime Democratic operative, called it the "most presumptuous document" that any vice president had ever presented to his president. Johnson also sought a sizeable increase in the vice president's staff and prized office space in the West Wing. Kennedy did not directly discuss the proposal with Johnson and never approved the draft executive order. Instead, he gave Johnson a letter that largely reaffirmed the historically limited vice presidential role. Johnson was never given a West Wing office but was sent across the street to the Executive Office Building to a nice suite that was far from the center of power in the Kennedy White House.[39] While Johnson had played a critical role in Kennedy's November election, the president-elect was unable or unwilling to soften his long-standing suspicion of Johnson. They had been political rivals much longer than they had been allies, and neither was comfortable with the other. Additionally, Kennedy's victory and coming ascendancy to the presidency represented a huge change in the power relationship between the two men. The junior backbencher was now the boss and the powerful Senate leader was now Kennedy's underling. The new relationship was destined to be awkward at best.

★

VIII

Kennedy enjoyed a friendly relationship with most of the reporters covering his transition. He liked reporters, considered several to be personal friends, and often enjoyed bantering and sparring with journalists. He realized the press could be a valuable instrument to assure the American public that the transfer of presidential power was unfolding smoothly and professionally. During the ten-week transition, Kennedy held nearly twenty press conferences, and his press secretary, Pierre Salinger, often briefed reporters twice a day. Kennedy met with reporters to announce cabinet selections from wherever he happened to be at the time: outside his Georgetown house, on his patio in Palm Beach, or at the Carlyle Hotel in New York. At these events, Kennedy posed for congratulatory handshakes and made brief remarks that he was more than willing to repeat if the press did not hear them clearly. He responded to questions but typically said little about policy matters and declined to comment about current events in the foreign policy realm. But Kennedy participated in the ritual in a way that helped reporters file plenty of stories to keep their editors happy.

Salinger met routinely with reporters wherever Kennedy was ensconced as well as in Capitol Hill briefing rooms and in a hotel conference room in Palm Beach, where reporters sometimes attended briefings wearing swimming trunks or Bermuda shorts. Salinger's press conferences often involved sustained verbal jousting as reporters tried to elicit information about future cabinet appointments, Kennedy's daily schedule, and his future transition travel plans. Reporters took special delight in correcting Salinger for misstating titles or handing out press releases with typos or factual errors. Usually good-humored and self-deprecating, Salinger could grow testy. When one reporter sought to correct his explanation about the staff structure in the Eisenhower White House, Salinger snapped, "I don't want to be helped because I know some things you don't. That might surprise you."

Kennedy enjoyed golfing in Palm Beach with several reporters but he grew grumpy about stories that calculated how frequently he golfed. He especially disliked newspaper pictures that showed him on the links. This was a sensitive topic because Kennedy and other Democrats had spent years berating Eisenhower for golfing so much. Reporters noted that Kennedy golfed more in Florida than Eisenhower ever did as president. In December, Salinger announced that photos of Kennedy on the golf course would not be permitted until after the inauguration. This displeased reporters, created a brief dustup, and generated several negative stories that chided the Kennedy team for secrecy and by implication hypocrisy. However, the press never stayed angry at Kennedy during the transition. He gave them reasonable access, a steady flow of news, and even hosted a small party for reporters and their wives at his Florida home on Christmas Day. And he was able to joke with reporters. During a briefing outside his Georgetown house he noticed that Bill Lawrence of the *New York Times* was wearing a Russian hat and quipped that it was good to know that TASS, the Soviet news agency, was covering the event. Reporters sometimes asked blunt questions that Kennedy usually deflected but he understood the ritual. There was one December press conference outside his Washington home that grew especially awkward. The briefing was called to announce that Adlai Stevenson was accepting the job of U.S. ambassador to the United Nations, but Stevenson, standing next to Kennedy, surprised reporters and annoyed Kennedy by saying that he not yet decided whether to accept the position. Kennedy stood by visibly displeased.

During the transition Kennedy and Salinger came to an important decision regarding the press. For the first time, live television coverage of presidential press conferences would be allowed starting in January with the new president. The decision came after an often tense negotiation with network executives and wire service and print reporters. These private talks took place in Palm Beach and over drinks at a Washington restaurant that Salinger described as "three hours of bombast and bourbon." After a stormy session in Palm Beach between Salinger and reporters, Kennedy teased Salinger that he could hear the angry comments of print reporters from several miles away. Salinger initially suggested that only some press conferences be televised but then acknowledged this was not a workable proposal since it was not possible to know in advance whether a press conference would generate news. There were also extensive discussions about whether the televised presidential press conference should be moved from the Indian Treaty Room in the Old Executive Office Building to a larger auditorium at either the Department of Commerce or the State Department. Of considerable concern to Salinger was whether reporters would preen before the cameras during press conferences and whether they should identify themselves by name and news organization when asking the president a question. Kennedy took a bemused, detached view on many of these matters, allowing Salinger to negotiate with the press and face its wrath.[40]

While Kennedy delivered only one formal speech during the transition, he published an essay that attracted considerable notice. He and Jackie graced the cover of the December 26 issue of *Sports Illustrated*. They were photographed standing on a dock in casual clothes with sailboats anchored behind them. "Sport on the New Frontier" was the cover article, but Kennedy delivered a far more bracing message in his essay inside the magazine called "The Soft American." In it Kennedy lamented physical decline of American youth. He argued that too many young Americans were neglecting their bodies and that "softness on the part of individual citizens can help to strip and destroy the vitality of a nation." Invoking the intellectual and physical vigor and rigor of classical Greece, Kennedy said Americans needed to get in better shape—for their own good and the good of the nation. "For the physical vigor of our citizens is one of America's most precious resources. If we waste and neglect this resource, if we allow it to dwindle and grow soft then we will destroy much of our ability to meet the great and vital challenges which confront our people. We will be unable to realize our full potential as a nation." Kennedy believed that America's "softness" was a security threat. "Thus the physical fitness of our citizens is a vital prerequisite to America's realization of its full potential as a nation, and to the opportunity of each individual citizen to make full and fruitful use of his capacities." He vowed to implement a national program to improve the fitness of all Americans including the creation of a White House Committee on Health and Fitness and an expanded role for the Department of Health, Education, and Welfare.[41]

IX

The transition was a fast moving, confusing affair as Kennedy traveled seemingly whimsically from his family's white stucco mansion in Palm Beach to his red brick federal home at 3307 N Street in Georgetown to his family's suite at the Carlyle Hotel in Manhattan. Salinger sometimes told reporters that he didn't know when the next Kennedy trip would be or for what purpose. Jackie Kennedy later recalled that her husband was running "back and forth all the time" during the transition. That restlessness would not cease. She vividly described the chaos of their Palm Beach trips with family members coming and going and the press strolling from the patio through the house before and after press conferences. Evelyn Lincoln said there were so many houseguests that the family's maids scurried about the Kennedy mansion "like barnyard chickens at feeding time" as they cleaned rooms and made beds.[42]

Life at the Kennedy house in Georgetown was scarcely more tranquil as lawmakers, job applicants, and Kennedy staff moved from room to room. The phones rang nonstop, there always seemed to be someone at either the front or back door, crowds gathered outside the house, and cars and motorcycles sped by regardless of the hour. Curiosity seekers hoped to get a glance at the incoming first lady or the president-elect. Jackie complained that it was impossible to get a good night's sleep because of the noise. She had also just had their second child, John. F. Kennedy Jr., in late November, just a few weeks after the election. Reporters kept a vigil outside the house and came to rely on the generosity of Kennedy neighbor Helen Montgomery, who allowed them to use her phone and bathroom and offered them coffee.

Tom Wolfe, then a young reporter for the *Washington Post*, was assigned to stake out the Kennedy home in Georgetown. He chronicled the N Street ritual, describing himself and other reporters as "that shivering, shambling, bedraggled clump of men waiting for handouts from 3307 N Street." Reporters, he wrote, wore "raggedy surplus-store ponchos, boots and mittens" as they waited to see Kennedy and hear his announcements. "To hear these fateful words, the reporters seem only too glad to wait out the Arctic ice of the sidewalk from dawn on, shivering, shuffling, and numbing . . . Our next president doesn't take the old, easy way of making his announcements about new cabinet ministers, the fate of the new frontier, etc. from his office on Capitol Hill—where, if one need edit, the corridors have steam heat. He just steps right out on the old front porch at 3307 N St. NW and starts talking. And disappears back into the manse."[43]

Kennedy flew 15,000 miles during the transition and seemed in perpetual motion, even leaving his very pregnant wife in D.C. on Thanksgiving Day to return to Florida—only to learn when he landed that she had just delivered a son by C-section. "I'm never there when she needs me," Kennedy admitted to an aide. He immediately flew back to Washington to see his wife and meet John F. Kennedy Jr.

The president-elect gained fifteen pounds over these ten weeks, and joked that he would have to call off the inauguration unless he lost some weight. He also had difficulty adjusting to the substantial increase in security that surrounded him. Observing a coast guard cutter patrolling the water in front of his family's Florida home, Kennedy grumbled, "Are they expecting Castro to invade Palm Beach?"

No day was typical during the transition, but Evelyn Lincoln's diary for December 13, 1960, captures some of the craziness of this time. Kennedy had a breakfast meeting with labor leader George Meany, took a call from Chicago Mayor Richard Daley, reviewed an inaugural sculpture, approved an inaugural photo, and examined two memos from Richard Goodwin and discussed them with him by phone. Then Kennedy met for half an hour with the president of the Illinois Farm Bureau about secretary of agriculture candidates, had a half hour meeting with Congressman Harold Cooley of North Carolina, and lunch with Senator Joe Clark of Pennsylvania. He then met with Robert McNamara and learned he would agree to be his secretary of defense, talked by phone with his father, met with the president of the Missouri Farm Bureau, conferred with his brother Robert, had a conference with his budget director David Bell, got a flu shot in an upstairs bedroom, met with Shriver and his personnel team, stopped by journalist Ben Bradlee's house for a drink, and then attended a dinner at his friend Charlie Bartlett's house. In her detailed chronology, Lincoln does not even mention the major public event of the day: Kennedy's outdoor press conference announcing McNamara as his secretary of defense.

In many respects the emotional pivot of the transition was Kennedy's trip to Boston on January 9 when he gave his farewell address to the Massachusetts legislature. The event was hastily organized. Kennedy was scheduled to be in Boston that day to attend a meeting of Harvard's Board of Overseers and to confer with several people about potential White House positions. The day before the speech Salinger told reporters that Kennedy might talk extemporaneously rather than from prepared remarks. However, Sorensen quickly drafted a speech that used some material that was being considered for Kennedy's inaugural address.

Though only three dozen sentences long, Kennedy's farewell was poignant and powerful. He obsrerved that he would soon "assume new and broader responsibilities," and was preparing for "that high and lonely office to which I now succeed." He insisted he had not come to bid farewell to Massachusetts but to pay tribute to its best traditions and challenge all its public officials to meet high standards. "For those to whom much is given, much is required. And when at some future date the high court of history sits in judgement on each one of us—recording whether in our brief span of service we fulfilled our responsibilities to the state—our success or failure, in whatever office we hold, will be measured by the answers to four questions." Each would have to say whether he or she was a person of courage, of judgment, of integrity, and of dedication. These, Kennedy declared, were "the historic qualities of the Bay Colony and the Bay State—the qualities which this state has consistently sent to Beacon Hill here in Boston and to Capitol Hill back in Washington. And these are the qualities which, with God's help, this son of Massachusetts hopes will characterize our government's conduct in the four stormy years that lie ahead."[44]

EIGHT

PASSING THE TORCH

I

A s Inauguration Day neared, Washington grew electric with anticipation. Visitors flocked to the city, arriving by car, plane, bus, and
train. Edward Foley, head of the Inaugural Committee, predicted
the largest crowd ever in Washington and estimated that up to a half million people would watch or participate in the festivities. Scores of special
trains teeming with visitors lumbered into Union Station that week; twelve
special trains arrived on January 17; twenty-two on the 18th; thirty-two
on the 19th; and forty-nine on Inauguration Day itself, January 20. David
Halberstam, then a young reporter for the *New York Times*, wrote that
arriving trains packed with inaugural revelers transformed Washington's
Union Station into a Pullman city. Some trains remained in the station,
serving as hotels for the week.[1]

Washington's hotels filled up and spilled over, sending visitors to Annapolis and Baltimore in search of rooms. *Time* magazine quipped that it was "easier to get a cabinet job than a bed" in Washington. More than two hundred Democratic Party volunteers set up welcome booths at Washington National Airport, Baltimore's Friendship Airport, Union Station, and at forty-five hotels and motels in Washington. Volunteers dispensed maps, guidebooks, and information on how to pick up tickets for the various events. The Washington Metropolitan Police Department was stretched to the point that all of its officers had to work long hours in the days leading to the inauguration. The police even formed a special five-person unit to monitor the city's hotels "in search of confidence men and other shady characters who could ruin someone's festivities," the *Washington Post* reported.

Political activists, curiosity seekers, ordinary citizens, and school children arrived at the nation's capital city to witness history. There was a palpable sense of change in the air, a feeling that one chapter was ending and another beginning, that one generation was yielding power to its successor. Kennedy's relative youth and apparent vigor and energy were surely part of the appeal. The contrasting, even clashing, images and histories of the outgoing and incoming presidents added to the mood of a new era being born.[2]

Plenty of VIPs were scheduled to be in town, including three former presidents, four former vice presidents, four former first ladies, thirty-eight governors, Kennedy's nine surviving crewmates from the boat he commanded in the South Pacific, and even Gunji Hosono, the commander of the Japanese destroyer that sliced Kennedy's PT-109 in half in August of 1943 and helped transform a restless navy lieutenant into a celebrated war hero.

Kennedy's inauguration also brought some of America's leading intellectuals to Washington. The president-elect, signaling his desire to sweep away the perceived cultural mustiness of the Eisenhower years, invited more than 150 arts and sciences luminaries to his inauguration. A dazzling array of novelists, poets, composers, diplomats, musicians, museum directors, jurists, and political scientists were sent special invitations. Ernest Hemingway, Pearl Buck, William Faulkner, John Steinbeck, Robert Frost, Archibald MacLeish, e. e. cummings, Arthur Miller, Thornton Wilder,

Tennessee Williams, Edmund Wilson, Edward Hopper, and Leonard Bernstein all received telegrams of invitation and many eagerly came to Washington.[3]

Arriving celebrities and political leaders required formal wear and limousines and, with demand far exceeding supply in Washington, tuxedos and Rolls-Royces arrived from Chicago and New York to take advantage of the shortage. The owner of a New York–based fleet of Rolls-Royces dispatched seven of his thirty-six cars to Washington and said he could have generated enough business there to justify sending his entire fleet.

Washington was buzzing with dances, luncheons, buffets, dinners, receptions, and cocktail parties. The streets were scrubbed clean, American flags flew everywhere, and photos of John Kennedy and Lyndon Johnson were displayed in downtown businesses. Visiting hours were extended for the Washington Monument, Lincoln Memorial, and Jefferson Memorial, and a number of embassies held special open houses.

Not surprisingly, tickets to inaugural events were in huge demand. About sixty thousand bleacher seats were erected along the parade route, with prices ranging from $3.00 to $15.00 per seat depending on location. Scalpers took advantage of the demand, selling tickets at five times their face value. Kennedy wanted the parade route crowded with excited people but he also ordered the briefest parade in recent history. Impatient and restless, Kennedy could not imagine himself spending most of his inaugural day at the reviewing stand, waving at floats. Event planners said the inaugural parade would run exactly two hours and forty-six minutes, far shorter than the four hours and thirty-nine minutes of Eisenhower's first inaugural parade. Still it was no small affair with 33,000 marchers, 275 horses, two mules, and a burro. Army organizers assembled an eighty-three page briefing book that resembled a military battle plan and scripted the parade in exquisite detail. Units that fell behind schedule were warned they would be pulled out of the parade.

While the parade would be shorter than in previous years, Democratic organizers proudly declared that more people would be attending the inaugural ball than ever before. To accommodate the 25,000 attendees, each paying $25.00 per ticket, the inaugural ball would be stretched out over five venues: the Statler Hilton, Shoreham, Mayflower, and Sheraton Park hotels, and the Washington Armory. To put everyone at ease, Democratic officials pledged that Kennedy and Johnson would visit each venue on inaugural night.

As Inauguration Day neared, final touches were underway to spruce up Washington and complete its makeover. The National Park Service sprayed green dye on the lawns near the Washington Monument to create a springlike appearance, and also applied a concoction called Roost No More to discourage starlings from gathering in trees along the parade route and disrupting festivities with their droppings.

Renovations at the U.S. Capitol, which had begun three years earlier, had recently been completed. The east façade was extended more than thirty feet and the deteriorating sandstone was replaced with white marble. The project was undertaken for both aesthetic and utilitarian purposes. The expansion gave lawmakers two additional acres of floor space and sixty-five new rooms, including dining rooms on the first floor, reception rooms on the second floor, and committee rooms and offices on the third floor. The Capitol dome now gleamed; thirty-two coats of old paint were removed and fresh coats of Oyster White were applied.[4] Following the formal transfer of presidential power at noon Friday, January 20, on the east front of the Capitol, the new president would speak to the nation and the world.

In an apparent celebration of the election of the first Catholic president of the United States, Washington's Archbishop Patrick O'Boyle announced that all Catholics who were in Washington on Inauguration Day would receive dispensation from the Friday fast that prohibited meat. Due to the kindness of the Washington archbishop, Catholics didn't even have to attend inaugural events to enjoy a hamburger or steak that Friday.

Democrats were euphoric as Inauguration Day 1961 neared. They were poised to regain power after what seemed to them eight long years of the phlegmatic Eisenhower administration. Their jubilant mood was compared to that of 1933 and the arrival of Franklin Roosevelt and his New Deal. However this time the incoming president was young, seemingly vigorous, and brought a young wife and two small children to the executive mansion. Emmet John Hughes, an Eisenhower speechwriter, said that for Democrats and Kennedy admirers, "the sloth of age had been replaced by the vigor of youth, superficiality by profundity, shallowness by intellectuality, irresolution by certitude, timidity by boldness, sheer weakness by sheer strength."[5]

Meanwhile, Republicans were gloomy as they braced to hand over the keys to the White House and control of the executive branch. Party stalwarts organized a "transition ball" a week before the inauguration where nine hundred Republicans gathered at the Statler Hilton to lament the impending loss of power with songs and skits. Small campaign posters of Eisenhower and Nixon hung from the ballroom's walls and party loyalists, administration officials, and Republican lawmakers braced for the Democratic era. Their battle hymn for the occasion had a hopeful refrain: "Glory, glory we'll be back in '64: when we'll rise again." The rules for the ball were clearly stated: "no crying allowed." The crowd broke into applause when a skit ended with the quip that Kennedy had won with the smallest landslide in history. The organizers of the GOP ball displayed a sardonic humor. One of the ballroom bars was named "Going Out of Business" while another was called "New Front Here," a playful dig at Kennedy's much celebrated New Frontier campaign slogan. This bar served some cleverly named drinks: "Apple Jackie Cider," "Pink Lady Bird," and "Old Fitzgerald on the Rocks."[6]

As January 20 approached, Vice President Nixon presided over the Senate for the final time in his constitutional capacity as its president. He won bipartisan praise for his eight years of dutiful service. Senate Republican leader Everett Dirksen called Nixon one of the nation's greatest vice presidents and noted that none of his parliamentary rulings had been overruled. Democratic leader Mike Mansfield thanked Nixon for his fairness and courtesy, and Senator Clinton Anderson, also a Democrat, praised Nixon as a "seasoned statesman." Senators from both parties offered Nixon good-natured thanks for trying to enforce Senate rules and keep morning speeches to three minutes.

On a symbolically discordant note, Senate Republicans decided in a private meeting they would wear business suits to the inauguration rather than the formal attire that Kennedy would be wearing, with a cutaway coat, striped trousers, and a silk top hat. Dirksen said Republicans wanted to "keep close to the people" by wearing regular business suits. A *Washington Post* reporter questioned if the Senate Republican decision was motivated more by political sour grapes than sartorial modesty. Ben Gingiss, the president of a formal menswear company, assured the paper that a Nixon victory "would have found all the Republican senatorial recalcitrants in the vanguard of those wearing cutaways and striped trousers for the inauguration."[7]

II

The two dominant figures in the days leading up to the inauguration were, of course, President Eisenhower and President-Elect Kennedy. Their schedules and activities during this stage of the transition could not have been more different.

Eisenhower spent the last weekend of his presidency at Camp David with his wife, Mamie. They left Washington Friday afternoon and returned to the White House Sunday afternoon. By then the city was consumed with preparations to receive his successor.

Eisenhower's waning days in the White House were deeply emotional as he said goodbye to associates, friends, and staff and prepared to end one of the most remarkable public service careers in American history. The intensifying preparations for the inaugural only made his looming departure more poignant and bittersweet. Eisenhower could insist that he was eager for a tranquil and restful retirement but he was, in truth, deeply ambivalent about leaving center stage and handing the White House to a man who had repudiated his administration on the campaign trail.

III

President-Elect Kennedy was at his Florida home and appeared to be in no particular hurry to arrive in Washington, even as his family, friends, and supporters streamed into the city. His family rented various homes in Georgetown that were within blocks of Kennedy's residence. Ted Reardon, a Kennedy aide, kept in constant touch with the Inaugural Committee about its many preparations and updated the president-elect in Florida. But in the days leading up to the inauguration, Kennedy and his wife remained in Palm Beach with their two young children and an array of helpers. Kennedy had a light schedule of meetings. He basked in the sunshine, darkened his tan, and fine-tuned his inaugural address.

Kennedy understood his inaugural address would be one of the defining moments of the transition and his presidency. "JFK knew that an inaugural address stamps a brand on a new president that can last for years, both nationally and globally, as either a warrior or a peacemaker, a bore or a source of inspiration, as first rate or mediocre," Ted Sorensen later wrote.[8]

Kennedy first mentioned the address to Sorensen, his chief speechwriter, in November, and directed its preparations. He instructed Sorensen to study past inaugural addresses so they both understood which speeches endured and which were immediately forgotten. Kennedy also had Sorensen read the Gettysburg Address, which to Kennedy remained the gold standard for eloquence and concision. Kennedy told Sorensen to solicit ideas from an assortment of people including Adlai Stevenson, Chester Bowles, John Kenneth Galbraith, and journalist Joseph Kraft. Kennedy wanted his speech to be brief and focused on foreign policy. "He did not want it to sound partisan, pessimistic, or critical of his predecessor," Sorensen recalled. "And he wanted it to set a tone for the era about to begin."[9]

The inaugural address was on the back burner for Kennedy and Sorensen throughout much of November and December. Kennedy was focused on staffing his administration and Sorensen was busy with other projects including overseeing transition task forces, assembling a policy agenda, and crafting messages to be sent to Congress in the first weeks of the administration. He also was charged with drafting Kennedy's farewell speech to Massachusetts, albeit at the last minute.

Sorensen wrote a memo in November about possible themes for the inaugural address but most of these never made it in the final draft.

When preparing a major speech, Kennedy typically outlined to Sorensen the central points he wanted to make and Sorensen would then prepare a draft for Kennedy to review. Always an active editor, Kennedy would mark up the draft and then often dictate a new version based on his revisions. That draft would then be edited by Kennedy and Sorensen until it was acceptable. This was how Kennedy's inaugural was written. After preliminary conversations with Kennedy and reviewing the ideas of others, Sorensen wrote a draft and gave it to Kennedy on January 10 as the president-elect was flying to Palm Beach. Kennedy reviewed it during the flight and then summoned his secretary Evelyn Lincoln to his cabin. "He dictated and dictated and dictated," Lincoln recalled. She then typed up a fresh draft, which she handed to Kennedy as the plane landed in Florida.[10]

Kennedy continued to work on the speech in Palm Beach. Jackie Kennedy recalled draft pages from the speech scattered on their bedroom floor and on her husband's desk. "I had heard it in bits and pieces many times while he was working on it in Florida. There were piles of yellow paper covered with his notes all over the bedroom floor," she said.[11]

Sorensen flew to Palm Beach on January 15 and worked on the speech with Kennedy over the next few days. Some revisions were done sitting on the patio of the Kennedy home facing the Atlantic Ocean. Sorensen returned to the Palm Beach Towers Hotel and typed up a new draft while sitting by the pool. "No Kennedy speech ever underwent so many drafts. Each paragraph was reworded, reworked, and reduced," Sorensen said.[12] On January 17 Kennedy and Sorensen flew back to Washington on Kennedy's private plane and continued to work together on the inaugural address. But it was nearly done.

IV

Kennedy arrived in Washington from Palm Beach about 6:00 P.M., went to his home, watched Eisenhower's farewell address on TV alone, and then attended a party hosted by his sister Jean. The gathering was an intriguing if not an entirely successful blend of people from Boston, Washington, New York, and Hollywood. Kennedy's family and political luminaries mingled with Hollywood and New York celebrities. The atmosphere at the Smith home was like a movie premiere with neighbors looking on as political and entertainment personalities arrived to flashing cameras, blazing TV lights, and a police cordon. More than two hundred onlookers scrambled to get a glimpse of Frank Sinatra, Tony Curtis, and other celebrities. Kennedy arrived late and seemed uneasy. He rarely enjoyed large parties; his tendency was to buttonhole the most interesting guests and spend the evening talking to them privately in a secluded corner.

Kennedy left his sister's home around 10:00 P.M. and briefly stopped by another party at the Statler Hilton hosted by Bart Lytton, a California businessman and Democratic fundraiser. Kennedy's appearance there caused bedlam among the six hundred partygoers. He stayed only twelve minutes and then headed to the airport to fly to New York City.

The reason for his eighteen-hour visit to New York City left even his press secretary, Pierre Salinger, confounded. "Off the record, it beats me," he told reporters who asked the reason for the trip to New York just hours after returning to Washington.

Kennedy stayed at his family's seven-room suite on the thirty-fourth floor of the Carlyle Hotel. According to one biographer, Kennedy had an amorous liaison that night with a woman who had flown in from Paris. The next day he conducted an odd smattering of meetings including with former New York governor Averell Harriman, Puerto Rico's governor Luis Muñoz Marín, and the leader of the British Labor Party, Hugh Gaitskell. He also saw his dentist, his tailor, and his hat fitter before returning to Washington that afternoon. The pace was about to quicken.

The formal inaugural events began that afternoon, Wednesday, January 18, with an event at the National Gallery of Art honoring the "first ladies of the New Democratic administration." Several members of the Kennedy and Johnson families were on the receiving line as were the wives of cabinet nominees, Democratic female members of Congress, and the wives of congressional leaders. Kennedy did not attend this reception, nor did Jackie, who arrived that night from Palm Beach. Later that evening, Kennedy stopped briefly at a reception honoring Lyndon and Lady Bird Johnson at the Statler Hilton Hotel. He then went home, spent some time with Jackie, apparently grew restless, and left for a Georgetown party hosted by Florence Mahoney. He arrived late, was greeted with a standing ovation, and sat between former president Harry Truman and poet Robert Frost.

V

The day before the inauguration, January 19, was loaded with activity and consequential for both Kennedy and Eisenhower. Kennedy was woken at 6:45 A.M. by a motorcycle racing by his Georgetown house. He reportedly expressed his displeasure at the driver by yelling out his bedroom window. Two hours later Kennedy left for the White House and his final meeting with Eisenhower before the inauguration. He sat in the back seat of his

car, browsed through his briefing books, and brushed his hair. Wilton
Persons, Eisenhower's chief of staff, met Kennedy outside the West Wing
and ushered him into the Oval Office.

Kennedy and Eisenhower first met privately and were later joined by
one of Eisenhower's closest aides, Andrew Goodpaster. The purpose of
the meeting was to review emergency evacuation and military procedures
including how to operate the nation's nuclear codes. Eisenhower also
showed Kennedy how to quickly summon a helicopter. They then went to
the Cabinet Room and conferred with outgoing and incoming secretaries
of state, defense, and treasury, and the two transition coordinators, Persons
and Clifford. The meeting primarily reviewed the situations in Laos and
Cuba and the balance of payments problem. The wisdom of Eisenhower's
advice on Laos and Cuba would continue to be the subject of sharp contention among politicians and historians.

As the session ended, Kennedy thanked Eisenhower for his generous
and statesmanlike handling of the transition. Eisenhower said it was his
responsibility and pleasure. The president-elect then stepped outside to the
driveway near the West Wing and spoke with reporters as snow began to
fall. He once again publicly praised the president and his team for their
cooperation during the transition. "I don't think there is anything we asked
for they haven't done," Kennedy said, adding that Eisenhower pledged to
be available for future consultations.[13]

From the White House Kennedy headed to the Georgetown home of
his friend, William Walton, where he took refuge as Jackie prepared for
the coming days' events. Kennedy took over the front room of Walton's
house where he held a busy afternoon of appointments. Walton welcomed
visitors to his home and kept them comfortable in his dining room until
Kennedy was ready to see them. Kennedy met with Ted Sorensen and his
family who had arrived from Nebraska; General Lyman Lemnitzer, the
chairman of the Joint Chiefs of Staff; Arthur Goldberg, the incoming labor
secretary; journalist William White; and Najeeb Halaby, whom he would
soon appoint to head the Federal Aviation Agency. Journalist Rowland
Evans stopped by and shared a lunch of chipped beef and baked potatoes
with Kennedy and Walton. Kennedy wanted a post-lunch cigar that Walton
pilfered from a reporter waiting outside his house. The president-elect then
regaled Evans and Walton with off-color jokes and political stories.

Snow continued to fall in Washington and Kennedy canceled the meeting with the members of his PT-109 crew, ostensibly because of the weather. He was driven to a session with labor leaders and then attended the Governors' Reception at the Park Sheraton Hotel. As Kennedy worked the receiving line he saw Harry Truman, spoke with him for a few minutes, and then the two went back to Kennedy's house on N Street. They sat before a fire in Kennedy's library and chatted for more than half an hour. As Kennedy bid Truman goodnight they were met by a bevy of reporters and photographers at the front door. The former president took that opportunity to lavish praise on Kennedy saying he was brilliant and a "nice, decent young man . . . He knows the history of government as well as anyone I've ever met and that includes me."

By that evening, snow was falling hard and Washington was descending into chaos. "Traffic stopped. The city was paralyzed. It was almost as though an H bomb had struck," a news report said. Bridges across the Potomac River connecting Washington to Virginia were blocked, as were highways from Washington into Maryland. Thousands of cars were abandoned across the city, hundreds of them along the next day's parade route. Washington-area hotels, already filled to capacity, offered respite to the stranded as best they could. Cots were set up in banquet halls and conference rooms, couches in offices and clubs became beds. Washington's airport closed. "Confusion we have seen before. But this was gilt edged, mink lined, silk hatted, 10 gallon, 100 proof, classic and absolutely capital chaos," wrote Wolfe in the *Washington Post*. "It snowed sideways. The traffic was bedlam."[14] That evening, Defense Secretary Tom Gates called on several thousand troops to help clear roads when Washington's snow removal manager concluded the situation was "absolutely hopeless" as nearly eight inches of snow draped the city.

Kennedy and Jackie were driven to a reception hosted by Philip and Katharine Graham, owners of the *Washington Post*, where they made only a brief stop. Then they were off to the inaugural concert at Constitution Hall, but not many others made it. When the concert began only a few hundred were in the auditorium rather than the 3,500 expected. Many of the musicians from the National Symphony Orchestra also failed to get there by the start of the concert. Kennedy was asked how he managed to make his way through the snow. "I had a little help," he quipped.

The Kennedys and William Walton left the concert at intermission and were driven to the National Guard Armory for one of the big events of the week, a special fundraising gala hosted by Frank Sinatra and Peter Lawford, the actor who also was Kennedy's brother-in-law. Kennedy ordered his limousine's interior light turned on as they traveled across the city so people could see Jackie and so he could read some selections from Thomas Jefferson that were in the earlier concert's program. "Better than mine," he quipped of Jefferson's writings.

Rose Kennedy recalled her trip across Washington that night to the gala as both beautiful and harrowing. Visibility was limited to a few yards and their car inched down the streets. "In the front seat, with the driver, was a man with a snow shovel. Every now and then, when the drifts and the churned up snow slush had us in jeopardy, he would put on his gloves, hunch his coat collar up, seize the shovel, and go out and extricate us. I was so amused by the situation and preoccupied with wondering whether we would actually get to our destination that I didn't learn his name or anything else about him. Yet in my memory he remains one of the heroes of the evening," she recalled.[15]

The gala organizers hoped it would raise more than a $1 million to help pay down the Democratic National Committee's $3 million debt. Stars from Hollywood and Broadway were the featured entertainment. In addition to Sinatra and Lawford, Sammy Davis Jr., Nat King Cole, Tony Curtis, Janet Leigh, Bette Davis, Ella Fitzgerald, Gene Kelly, Leonard Bernstein, Milton Berle, Ethel Merman, and Laurence Olivier performed.

Because of the storm, the gala started ninety minutes late. The official entrance of the incoming first couple was marked by a rendition of "Anchors Aweigh." While billed as one of America's great entertainment shows, the event had an ad hoc, improvised feel. The sound quality was poor and most of the audience was cold and wet. While all 12,000 seats had been sold at $100 per ticket, at least half of the audience didn't make it to the Armory. But there were some signature moments, including Sinatra revising his rendition of "That Old Black Magic" into "That Old Jack Magic," Ethel Merman's stirring "Everything's Coming up Roses," and Gene Kelly's remarkable dancing. "The gala was excellent, though a bit disjointed because half the performers had been stuck or delayed in the snow and arrived at random times," Rose Kennedy recalled. Jackie Kennedy said the show was "alright," but added some of the comedy acts were in poor taste because they ridiculed marriage.

Her husband concluded the show, commending the audience for braving the elements and thanking the entertainers for donating their time and talent to help launch his presidency. "There's an old saying that only in winter can you tell which trees are evergreen. Only when the winds of adversity blow can you tell which individual, which party, which country has the qualities of character and steadfastness, and the fact that there was, in the worst storm of the year, hardly an empty seat in this great hall shows what kind of party we're members of," he said, apparently oblivious to the many empty chairs. Then Kennedy grew lyrical about the convergence of the political and artistic worlds. "The happy relationship between the arts and politics which has characterized our long history, I think reached culmination tonight."[16]

After the gala, Kennedy's father Joe hosted a party for three hundred guests at Paul Young's restaurant on Connecticut Avenue, attended by the show's cast, the Kennedy family, and their friends. Kennedy fully enjoyed himself and was in no hurry to leave, telling his friend Paul Fay that he would not be able to sleep even if he were at home and in bed. Kennedy did not get home until almost 3:30 A.M.—just about eight hours before he was to be sworn in as the thirty-fifth president.

Eisenhower's final full day in office was lightly scheduled, aside from his morning meeting with Kennedy. In the afternoon he spent about a half hour saying goodbye to his West Wing staff. He met for a few minutes with his legislative aide, Bryce Harlow, and then went up to the residence around 6:00 P.M. John Eisenhower went through the West Wing that afternoon gathering his father's personal documents, collecting materials that would fill eight safes. Some of Eisenhower's White House staff were unable to get home due to the bad weather. They slept in meeting rooms in the mansion, enjoying their final night in power and mourning its impending end. The mood was a peculiar blend of festivity and sadness.

VI

On the most momentous day of his political life, John Kennedy got up at 8:00 A.M. after about four hours of sleep. "Not the amount of sleep I recommended for his Inauguration Day," his mother would later write disapprovingly.[17] He had breakfast with Jackie on a tray that was set on a luggage rack in front of the fireplace. Kennedy attended 9:00 A.M. Mass at the nearby Holy Trinity Church, sitting close to the front, watched closely by reporters at the rear of the church. His mother, bundled up against the snow and cold, with a scarf over her head babushka-style, walked to the same Mass by herself. She arrived before her son and sat near the back of the church and was pleasantly surprised to see him enter. It appears that Kennedy did not see his mother during the service. Embarrassed by her disheveled appearance and not wanting it memorialized it in a photograph in the next day's newspapers, she did not speak to her son after Mass. But she did approach a Secret Service agent, introduced herself as the president-elect's mother, and requested a ride back to the house she was renting. "He nodded," Mrs. Kennedy later wrote. "But no car came. Evidently, he thought I was either an imposter or demented—because I certainly didn't look like a president's mother."[18]

Just before Kennedy returned to his house, he stopped across the street to present a plaque to his neighbor, Helen Montgomery, and her eighty-six-year-old father. During the transition the Montgomerys had provided reporters waiting outside Kennedy's house with coffee and allowed them to use their phone and utilize their front window as an observation post. "In the cold winter of 1960–61 this house had an important role in history," it read. "From it was flashed to the world news of preinaugural announcements by President John F. Kennedy. Presented by the grateful newsmen who were given warm haven here by Miss Helen Montgomery and her father Charles."

Helen was deeply touched by Kennedy's visit. "Oh Senator, I am overcome. I mean president-elect, forgive me. I am overcome. This is simply wonderful," she said.[19]

Kennedy went home after Mass to dress for the big event. Since he had gained weight during the transition he needed a special collar for his shirt. The entire household rummaged through drawers. He even called his father to check his supply but to no avail. Kennedy finally found a collar that would work. "It was an ordeal to get him ready," recalled Mary Gallagher, a Kennedy aide who was at the house that morning. The Kennedy house was not a tranquil place, Gallagher recalled. "The phone rang incessantly, and throughout the entire household every pair of hands moved swiftly. The president-elect rehearsed his speech behind closed doors in the downstairs library."[20]

The congressional escort committee arrived at the Kennedy home at 10:30 led by Senator John Sparkman, head of the Congressional Inaugural Committee, and House Speaker Sam Rayburn. Their job was to take the Kennedys to the White House for coffee with the Eisenhowers. Jackie was not ready; her frustrated husband paced in the house. "Please hurry," he said. "C'mon Jackie. For God's sake. Let's go." Finally, the Kennedys left their home just before 11:00, and were driven to the White House. Jackie later lamented that she never had a chance to say goodbye to her house.

Eisenhower's final half day as president began when he got up at 6:15 A.M.—less than three hours after Kennedy had gone to bed. Eisenhower had breakfast and then strolled toward his office. Since the Oval Office was being repainted for its new occupant, Eisenhower worked out of the Cabinet Room. "The morning of the inauguration the atmosphere in the West Wing was eerie," recalled Eisenhower's son John. "With no papers to sign or examine, we simply idled away the time. Dad spent a good deal of the morning leaning on a safe talking with Ann Whitman (his secretary) and others."[21] Eisenhower thanked various staffers for their help over the years including those who worked in the White House mess.

The president had invited the Kennedys for coffee at 11:00, a half hour before the official party was to head to the Capitol. Eisenhower met them at the North Portico. The two families were joined by Vice President Nixon, his wife, Pat, and Vice President–Elect Johnson and his wife, Lady Bird. They all gathered in the Red Room for a rather awkward conversation. Jackie Kennedy and Pat Nixon sat on the same sofa but reportedly did not speak to each other.

The official party was driven to the Capitol in a carefully choreographed procession of cars. Eisenhower, Kennedy, Sparkman, and Rayburn were in the lead car, followed by Mamie, Jackie, and Senator Styles Bridges in the second car. Richard Nixon, Lyndon Johnson, Senator Carl Hayden, and House Majority Leader John McCormack were in the third car while Pat Nixon, Lady Bird Johnson, and House Minority Leader Charlie Halleck rode in the fourth car. Ed Foley, the chairman of the Inaugural Committee, and Franklin Dryden, the director of the Joint Congressional Committee, traveled in the fifth car.

Eisenhower and Kennedy bantered during the trip down Pennsylvania Avenue from the White House to the Capitol but they were not always on the same page. Kennedy asked Eisenhower if he had read *The Longest Day* by Cornelius Ryan, about the D-Day invasion, perhaps thinking this would spark an interesting conversation. Eisenhower said he had not, probably thinking that since he had organized and led the historic invasion he did not need to read about it. Kennedy later said he was surprised Eisenhower had not read the book.

While the official party's drive went smoothly, travel was not easy for everyone else in snow-battered Washington. Joe and Rose Kennedy were on their way to one of the great events of their lives with their son Ted and his wife Joan when their car got stuck in the snow. Joe angrily got out of the car, barked orders to the driver, and then helped push the car out of a snow bank. "It was classic Joe Kennedy," recalled Ted Kennedy. "Take charge and do it right, even if it means having to do it yourself. We made it to the inauguration."[22]

The snow and cold and biting wind discouraged many from attending the inauguration. The temperature was in the twenties and the wind chill made it feel only in the single digits. According to the *Washington Post*, about 50,000 gathered on the east side of the Capitol. Interestingly, the *New York Times* estimated the crowd at 100,000.[23] Those in attendance and those watching at home on TV saw a ceremony with palpable majesty and probably did not notice, or even suspect, the behind-the-scenes chaos and disarray. The ceremony began thirty minutes late due to the weather and a lack of chairs on the inaugural platform. As Boston's Cardinal Richard Cushing proceeded with a lengthy prayer, smoke rose from the base of the podium. "Looks like you got a hot speech," Eisenhower quipped to Kennedy who seemed more amused than alarmed. Secret Service and Capitol maintenance workers crawled down to fix the overheated motor that adjusted the height of the podium. After the delay and with a fire averted, the ceremony finally began, and riveted the nation and the world. Opera singer Marian Anderson provided a stirring rendition of the national anthem and Robert Frost, unable to read his new poem due to the brightness of the sun and the glare of the snow, recited another poem from memory that stirred the crowd and prompted Kennedy to lead a standing ovation.

Finally, at 12:51, Chief Justice Earl Warren administered the oath of office to Kennedy. He placed his hand on a family Douhay Bible, an English version created for Roman Catholics in the sixteenth century. He chose not to have the Bible opened to any particular verse, which had been the practice of many past presidents.

To assure an impressive delivery of his inaugural address, Kennedy wrote an assortment of reminders to himself in sections of his reading copy: "Slow . . . Deep . . . Quietly . . . Very Quietly and Slow." He also made more than thirty slight revisions from the version that had been distributed to the press the previous day. Kennedy then delivered a speech for the ages. "Let the word go forth from this time and place, to friend and foe alike, that the torch has been passed to a new generation of Americans—born in this century, tempered by war, disciplined by a hard and bitter peace, proud of our ancient heritage—and unwilling to witness or permit the slow undoing of those human rights to which this Nation has always been committed, and to which we are commited today, at home and around the world," he said. The new president also offered a stern statement of resolve. "Let every nation know, whether it wishes us well or ill, that we shall pay any price, bear any burden, meet any hardship, support any friend, oppose any foe to assure the survival and success of liberty." Kennedy concluded by challenging Americans to work for the good of their country. "And so my fellow Americans, ask not what your country can do for you—Ask what you can do for your country."[24]

As Kennedy delivered his inaugural address in the biting January cold, Eisenhower looked on, shivering in his overcoat and scarf, gazing at his successor, applauding several times. Several of Eisenhower's longtime assistants watched the ceremony in anguish from the Jefferson Hotel in downtown Washington, several miles from the Capitol. "The world was coming to an end," one later recalled. Eisenhower's grandson, David, reported that Ike's now former aides "drowned their sorrow and remorse with martinis."[25]

At the end of the ceremony, Kennedy and Eisenhower shook hands and parted ways.

The new president entered the Capitol to sign documents officially nominating the members of his cabinet. Then the first couple attended a hurried lunch for eighty special guests and senior lawmakers in the Capitol's Old Supreme Court Chamber. The meal included cream of tomato soup with crushed popcorn, deviled crabmeat imperial, New England boiled stuffed lobster, and prime Texas ribs of beef au jus. More than one hundred friends and members of Kennedy's extended family who attended the inauguration boarded three buses labeled KENNEDY FAMILY and were taken to the Mayflower Hotel for lunch.

The new president and first lady left the Capitol after 2:00 P.M., thirty minutes later than the official schedule called for, and were driven to the White House and then walked to the nearby reviewing stand to watch what one observer called "that gloriously martial, touchingly corny, deliciously cockeyed, all-American spectacle: the Inaugural Parade." The parade included "a motley assemblage of Indians, cowboys, beauty queens, and Eskimos; horses, mules, dogs, and a beguiling buffalo; middle aged men bulging in fussy Old Guard Regiment uniforms and scores of pretty girls shivering in flimsy fancy costumes." The float that received the most applause was a replica of Kennedy's PT-109 carrying the nine surviving crewmen and Lieutenant Edward Thom, whose father served on Kennedy's boat and died in an accident shortly after the war.[26]

The parade's 33,000 marchers walked the two-and-a-half-mile route in about three and a half hours, an hour longer than scheduled. Everyone was on good behavior, having been warned by the Secret Service not to engage in "horseplay." This probably referred to the cowboy who playfully lassoed President Eisenhower during the 1953 inaugural parade. Kennedy remained in the reviewing stand for the entire parade, sipping coffee and soup to keep warm. Jackie Kennedy left after an hour to rest in her new home. Family members and friends kept the new president company, moving about the reviewing stand in a way that some likened to musical chairs.

Eisenhower left the Capitol after the inauguration and was driven to a private lunch with members of his former administration in downtown Washington. He told waiting reporters that Kennedy's speech had been "fine, very fine." Asked about being a private citizen now, Eisenhower said, "Wonderful, fine." As he entered the 1925 F Street Club an accordionist played "For He's A Jolly Good Fellow." Guests raised champagne glasses and sang. The accordionists then played "Old Soldiers Never Die."

Toasts were raised during the two-hour-plus gathering that was warm and sentimental.

And then it was time for Dwight and Mamie Eisenhower to travel the eighty miles from Washington to Gettysburg. Their car was driven by Secret Service agent Dick Flohr, who had been Eisenhower's chauffeur since 1952 and would stay with the family for the next month.

As they headed home, Dwight and Mamie were greeted by groups of people lining the highway between Washington and Frederick, Maryland. Students and nuns from Mount St. Mary's and St. Joseph's colleges gathered along the route holding "Welcome Home" signs. The Eisenhower party reached their farm at close to 6:00 P.M. and entered by the south gate because the main gate was still blocked by snow. "There was an eerie loneliness about the absence of motorcycle escorts and caravans of Secret Service and press cars," wrote David Eisenhower, vividly imagining the trip from Washington to Gettysburg in the 1955 Chrysler Imperial that Mamie had bought her husband for his sixty-fifth birthday. "A single Secret Service vehicle with driver and agent led the Chrysler. When the Eisenhowers approached the entrance to their Gettysburg farm, the Secret Service honked the horn and made the U turn, heading back to Washington."[27]

That evening the Eisenhower family gathered for dinner at the Gettysburg home of John, who affectionately toasted his father. "Leaving the White House will not be easy at first. But we are reunited as a family and this is what we have wanted. I suppose that tonight we welcome back a member of this clan who has made us proud," he said. The former president choked up and said only "Hear, Hear."

In Washington, the new president was the toast of the town. Kennedy rested briefly after the parade, then attended a dinner hosted by Mr. and Mrs. George Wheeler at their elegant home on Foxhall Road. Just as Kennedy was settling in, Edward Foley, the chairman of the Inaugural Committee, told him they needed to return to the White House, pick up Jackie, and begin making the round of the inaugural balls. Kennedy snapped, "Ed, you've pushed me around all day. Stop it! This is the first time I've had warm food in front of me since morning. I'm going to sit here another fifteen minutes." Foley said, "I'll give you five." The new president was afforded a few additional minutes of downtime as he and Foley waited for Jackie at the White House. The two men chatted over wine and cigars before the Kennedys headed to the Mayflower Hotel for the first ball venue and then to the Armory. By that time Jackie was exhausted and was taken home. Kennedy continued on to the celebrations at the Statler Hilton, Shoreham, and Sheraton Park.

But even after five receptions, Kennedy was not quite ready to call it a night—or morning. He had learned that his friend, the columnist Joe Alsop, was hosting a small informal gathering at his Georgetown home, a place Kennedy knew well. He stunned Alsop and his party when he arrived at the front door to join the festivities. "Exhilaration always rejuvenated him and he had been greatly exhilarated by his inauguration and all that surrounded it," Alsop recalled. Kennedy stayed until almost 3:30. Alsop offered Kennedy champagne and a bowl of Maryland terrapin soup. "He took the wine, but needed not more than a glance to reject what had formerly been the greatest delicacy in the United States. It hardly mattered. I soon observed that what he really wanted was one last cup of unadulterated admiration, and the people crowding my living room gave him that cup freely, filled to the brim."[28]

NINE

RISING STAR, SETTING SUN

I

The American people were, for the most part, uplifted and reassured by the ten-week transition from Dwight Eisenhower to John Kennedy, culminating in the stirring inaugural ceremony on January 20, 1961.

There was broad agreement that the transition had been executed amicably and professionally. Kennedy and Eisenhower were both pleased with their efforts. The day after he was sworn in, Kennedy sent his predecessor a warm note. "My dear Mr. President: On my first day in office I want to send to you a note of special thanks for your many acts of cordiality and assistance during the weeks since the election. I am certain that your generous assistance has made this one of the most effective transitions in the history of our Republic. I have very much enjoyed personally the association which we have had in this common effort."[1] A few days later,

Eisenhower graciously responded. "It was good of you to inform me of your appreciation of such help as my associates and I were able to give the new Administration in its takeover of Executive Responsibility. We are happy that the cooperation of the 'Old' and the 'New' may possibly have set a record for smoothness in such an operation." Eisenhower added he hoped that under Kennedy's leadership, "the country will be peaceful, prosperous and happy."[2]

The American public and the political class applauded. "It may well have been the most cordial and cooperative exchange in history between American Presidents of different parties," *Newsweek* reported, noting that the friendliness between Eisenhower and Kennedy was evident from their animated conversation even after they had been seated on the inaugural platform. James Reston of the *New York Times* was also impressed. "The changing of the guard in Washington has been achieved with more civility and common sense this time than ever in living memory. There has been less friction and less personal bitterness, despite the closeness of the election, than anybody expected, and this says a great deal for the essential unity of the American people and the stability of their political institutions." Reston praised Eisenhower for being "a model of courtesy and generosity" and Nixon for conducting himself "with dignity and even good humor." Kennedy, he said, had "moved with great sensitivity to bind up the wounds of the campaign."[3] As the transition was ending, the *New York Times'* editorial page saw much to celebrate. "Rarely if ever before has there been so much concentration and so much effort, accompanied by so much cooperation on both sides, as has been currently apparent in the handling over of the reins of government and of power in Washington from the Administration of one party to that of another. The strength of American institutions and the depth of the democratic idea could not be better illustrated than by the relative ease and apparent goodwill by which this massive shift is being accomplished."[4]

But not everyone celebrated the transition. David Lawrence, a columnist for the *Washington Evening Star*, said the demands of the modern world required a major rethinking of the concept of transitions and inaugurals. "The inaugural ceremony itself is reminiscent of a coronation of a king," he groused. But Lawrence was most concerned about national security threats during the ten-week transition period. "Continuity in government is purely theoretical. Transition is being described as 'smooth,' but this is mostly because it is accomplished without personal rancor or ill will and in a spirit of cooperation and helpfulness," he wrote. He argued that transition "really means confusion" because there is sweeping changeover of senior government officials. Lawrence argued that the way the United States changed administrations was not suitable for the nuclear age because there were inevitably weeks of confusion and drift. "It may take a disaster some day to awaken public opinion to the dangers of the present slipshod system of 'transition,'" he concluded.[5]

But while Lawrence was grumpy others were ecstatic, especially Kennedy supporters who saw Inauguration Day as the start of a new chapter in American life. "The Kennedy Presidency began with incomparable dash," Arthur Schlesinger Jr. declared. "The young president, the old poet, the splendid speech, the triumphant parade, the brilliant sky and the shining snow: it was one of the most glorious inaugurals. And the new President himself obviously savored every moment of it."[6] Eisenhower's graciousness and professionalism during the transition was widely noted and broadly applauded. Most attributed his constructive actions as being rooted in his deep sense of duty and responsibility. Some wondered if he might have felt some remorse for his role in the frosty and even bitter transition he participated in eight years earlier as President Truman prepared to hand over power to him.

II

The departure of Dwight Eisenhower from Washington after more than a half century of public service was profoundly poignant. Even the most partisan Democrat had to find Eisenhower's quiet journey from Washington to Gettysburg deeply moving. His eighty-mile trip over snowy roads past waving school children in a modest two-car motorcade illustrated the fleeting nature of power. Emmet John Hughes, his former speechwriter, captured the elegiac quality of Eisenhower's return home. The former president, Hughes said, reached his Gettysburg farm "in the frosty and fading sunlight of this late January afternoon . . . The winter sky was clean and icy-bright and the crooked thrusts of trees and shrubs whitely glinted in the sun. But the hour of the day was late. And, this time, the sun was setting."[7]

The day after Eisenhower returned to Gettysburg he was officially welcomed at a ceremony hosted by sixty civic groups that drew two thousand people to the floodlit Lincoln Square on a bitterly cold night. The Gettysburg High School band played "The Battle Hymn of the Republic" and town leaders extolled Eisenhower's service to America. Many then went indoors for a special banquet with music by the Gettysburg College Choir, more speeches, and a special presentation to the Eisenhowers. They received a sterling silver plaque inscribed with the words Eisenhower spoke in 1959 when asked what he hoped Soviet leader Nikita Khrushchev would experience during his trip to the United States. "I want him to see a happy people . . . doing exactly as they choose, within the limits that they must not transgress the rights of others."

After a few days in Gettysburg, Ike traveled to Albany, Georgia, for a quail hunting vacation at the estate of his friend W. Alton Jones. Then he and Mamie took a train across the country to Indian Wells, California, for a lengthy vacation at the Eldorado Country Club. There the Eisenhowers remained for several months, in the company of friends, for rest and relaxation. The former president fell into a new routine with plenty of golf, meals, naps, shopping, and bridge. Eisenhower's trip to Indian Wells that year was the first of seven winter vacations in the Southern California desert that became an important feature of his post-presidential life.

While Eisenhower was in Indian Wells his son John and a small staff set up the former president's new office at Gettysburg College. John sorted through his father's presidential papers, reviewed newspaper accounts of the Eisenhower presidency as it was unfolding, and wrote a draft outline for his father's two-volume presidential memoirs.

When Eisenhower returned to Gettysburg in April of 1961 he turned his attention to these memoirs. He envisioned a chronological and issue-oriented account of his presidency. Unlike his World War II memoirs, which he largely wrote by himself and which fully engaged him, Eisenhower approached his presidential memoirs as a chore. He saw it as both a duty and responsibility to set the record straight about his eight years in the White House. He wanted to ensure that the American people, both now and in the future, understood what he set out to do and what his administration accomplished. He may have believed that the recently concluded presidential campaign and its result obscured the full scope of his administration's achievements.

John Eisenhower and William Ewald, a former White House aide, divided research and drafting responsibilities for the memoir. Ewald focused on domestic issues and John concentrated on foreign policy. They sent draft chapters to Eisenhower, who wielded a fierce editing pen. "These drafts the Boss would cut down, lacerate, and redo time and time again," John said, recalling that some chapters went through five or six drafts. John spent three months researching the Eisenhower administration's policies in Indochina and sent his father a one-hundred-page draft chapter. Ike slashed it in half. He resisted the pleas of his editors to focus more on personalities, or acknowledge his own mistakes, or candidly address controversial topics such as his relationship with Joseph McCarthy. Doubleday, the publisher, wanted conflict, drama, and personalities. Eisenhower wanted a fair and accurate account of his presidency. However, he was not above fudging. According to John, his father once attempted to alter a memo about Vietnam that he had written during his presidency. John reminded him of his obligation to history to be truthful. "What's the matter? Can't I misquote myself?" Ike groused.[8]

Mandate for Change, the first volume of his presidential memoirs, was released on November 9, 1963, nearly three years after he took that long car ride to Gettysburg, and it quickly rose to second place on the *New York Times* bestseller list. However, Kennedy's assassination less than two weeks later dramatically consumed national attention and rendered Eisenhower as ancient history. It's unclear if Eisenhower was ever struck by the irony that his memoir, which was largely written to respond to Kennedy, got shoved aside in the national obsession with the slain president. His second volume, *Waging Peace*, was published in 1965. In both books, Eisenhower made a vigorous case that his presidency was consequential and his governing style was active and engaged, if not showy. However, unlike his riveting account of World War II, his presidential memoirs were too detailed and dense to ever seize the public's imagination. They are valuable to historians, not casual readers. Eisenhower later dictated a memoir about growing up in Kansas and his early military career. *At Ease*, published in 1967, was Eisenhower at his warmest and most nostalgic, with vivid stories of his family and friends, and striking emotion. He described a return visit to Abilene that was strangely sad. "Something is missing. What is it? Well of course, it is my family. We are gone, scattered, and we can never put the pieces together again."[9]

Eisenhower struggled to determine the political role he should play during Kennedy's presidency. Wounded by the press's lavish praise of Kennedy and the unfavorable contrasts that were frequently made to his administration, Eisenhower initially considered leading a Republican shadow government that actively opposed most of his successor's policies. He consulted with congressional Republicans and his former cabinet members but ultimately decided to take a different approach. "As emeritus I must be silent," he said. However, he was hardly silent. He gave interviews, wrote articles, and spoke extensively to express his views on policy issues and current events. Shortly after America's botched role in the Bay of Pigs invasion in which fifteen hundred Cubans, supported by the U.S., were routed by Fidel Castro's army, Eisenhower was invited to Camp David by Kennedy. The new president wanted to explain to Eisenhower what happened and secure at least a general statement of public support from his predecessor. Eisenhower warily attended the meeting, apprehensive that Kennedy might try to link Eisenhower, and his administration, to Kennedy's mistakes. Eisenhower listened carefully to his successor's briefing, asked several questions, and offered advice when it was solicited. He made it clear that Kennedy needed a more organized and disciplined staffing system. "Mr. President, before you approved this plan, did you have everybody in front of you debating the thing so you got the pros and cons yourself and then made the decision or did you see people one at a time?"[10] Kennedy's response indicated the latter was the case. Eisenhower had one overriding suggestion for his successor. "There is only one thing to do when you get into this kind of thing: make sure it succeeds." Eisenhower then dictated a lengthy memo for his files about the meeting. Several years later when he believed some in the Kennedy administration were shifting some of the blame for the disaster on his administration, Eisenhower told his side of the story to a sympathetic reporter who faithfully reported Ike's view of the Bay of Pigs debacle. This was in response to the recently published memoirs of two stalwart Kennedy aides, Ted Sorensen and Arthur Schlesinger Jr., who suggested that Kennedy inherited a flawed plan from Eisenhower and was more the victim than the cause of the debacle.

Eisenhower tried to support Kennedy on foreign policy initiatives but he usually did so in a general way. He made it clear he opposed many aspects of Kennedy's agenda, most notably his willingness to substantially increase federal spending for both domestic and international programs. He derided the "fantastically expensive" investment in space and often said the Kennedy administration was fiscally irresponsible. Ike was sometimes hurt when his administration did not get the credit he thought it deserved, such as its initial efforts to launch the space program. Eisenhower thought his administration's approach to space was thoughtful, measured, and strategic, not the crash spending approach he believed Kennedy embraced. He was disappointed that his administration's contributions were ignored when Americans celebrated John Glenn's first orbit around the earth on February 20, 1962.[11]

During the run-up to the 1962 congressional midterm elections Eisenhower grew far more critical of the Kennedy administration. At a Republican campaign dinner that June, Eisenhower accused the Kennedy administration of incompetence, declaring that "to list all the examples of political mal-administration, mal-functioning, and mal-adjustment in Washington" would take too much time. "Quite obviously, this administration is floundering—thrashing aimlessly and a bit desperately about," he charged. The former president derided the Kennedy team for its supposed intellectual prowess. "One cannot doubt the principal figures in official Washington today are academically proficient. As the Administration modestly asserts, it is sophisticated. But it has started the whole nation to question its ability to comprehend."[12]

During an October campaign speech for Republicans in Boston, Eisenhower compared his administration's competence in foreign policy with Kennedy's "dreary foreign record," which he dismissed as "too sad to talk about." Ike cited his accomplishments in Korea, the Middle East, Europe, and elsewhere. "In those eight years, we lost no inch of ground to tyranny. We witnessed no abdication of international responsibility. We accepted no compromise of pledged word or withdrawal from principle. No walls were built. No threatening foreign bases were established. One war was ended and incipient wars were blocked. I doubt that anyone can persuade you that in the past twenty-one months there has been anything constructive in the conduct of our foreign relations to equal any part of that eight-year record."[13] *Time* called this Eisenhower attack of Kennedy "the most succinct and devastating paragraph" of the 1962 campaign.

Eisenhower gave Kennedy modest credit for his handling of the Cuban Missile Crisis in October of 1962, but believed his earlier missteps during the Bay of Pigs set the stage for the Soviet Union's insertion of nuclear missiles in Cuba. Even while the crisis was unfolding, Eisenhower was campaigning for congressional Republicans for the impending midterm elections. He said all Americans should support the president's international positions, but added that his domestic policies remained appropriate targets for criticism.

However, for the most part the two presidents were publicly restrained toward each other and their private communications were civil, even with flashes of kindness. Kennedy sent Eisenhower periodic notes, provided him with foreign policy briefings, and invited him to special Washington ceremonies. He offered Eisenhower government transportation whenever needed and signed legislation that reinstated Eisenhower's rank as a five star general. He also sent Eisenhower a set of golf balls with the presidential seal that he had received as a gift but could not use because of his bad back. Kennedy hoped his predecessor could put them to work. "Since I am trying my best to play at least five days a week, I assure you that your gift is not only a useful one, but most welcome," Eisenhower responded.[14]

Kennedy visited Eisenhower in Palm Desert in March 1962 while he was in Southern California on a political and personal trip. He briefed Eisenhower on foreign policy issues and agreed to support Eisenhower's request for promotions for several military officers who had worked with him over the years. In keeping with his tradition of sending personal notes, Eisenhower wrote to his successor when Kennedy's father suffered a serious stroke in December 1961 and again when Jack and Jackie Kennedy lost their infant baby in 1963. "Mrs. Eisenhower joins me in profound sympathy on the death of your infant son and we trust that Mrs. Kennedy is doing well," Ike wrote from Caen, France. Kennedy responded graciously. "Dear General: You and Mrs. Eisenhower were kind indeed to think of us at this very difficult time. Your message was a comfort to me and my family and we are very grateful to you."[15]

David Eisenhower, the former president's grandson, said Eisenhower and Kennedy maintained a surface cordiality but shared "a natural antagonism" because Kennedy had won the presidency campaigning as a fierce critic of the Eisenhower presidency. David speculated the nature of their relationship changed after the October 1962 Cuban Missile crisis, which raised Kennedy's stature and gave him confidence as a world leader. "In hindsight, the Cuban crisis marks a demarcation between the Eisenhower and Kennedy eras," David wrote.[16]

Eisenhower was shaken by a 1962 survey of historians that ranked the American presidents. The survey, created by Arthur Schlesinger Sr. of Harvard, was published in the *New York Times Magazine*. The results placed Eisenhower near the bottom of the "Average" category, ranking him twenty-eighth of the thirty-three presidents. Eisenhower feigned indifference but was stung by the findings. "The old man was wounded by the thing," recalled his son John. Kennedy delighted in the poll, especially its elevation of Truman to "Near Great" status and its low marks for Eisenhower. He mused that the poll later propelled Eisenhower to get more involved in the 1962 midterm elections. "Eisenhower has been going along for years, basking in the glow of applause he has always had. Then he saw the poll and realized how he stood before the cold eye of history—way below Truman; even below Hoover. Now he's made to save his reputation," Kennedy told Arthur Schlesinger Jr.[17]

III

Dwight Eisenhower was in New York City, attending a Columbia University event, on November 22, 1963, when he learned of Kennedy's assassination. He was stunned by the killing. He told reporters that he felt a sense of shock and dismay at the despicable act. He attended Kennedy's funeral in Washington and reached a partial reconciliation with Harry Truman. The two former presidents and their wives stayed at Blair House and shared drinks one evening as they pondered the tragedy. Eisenhower admitted to close friends that he was puzzled by the nation's intense and prolonged grief for Kennedy, especially as his successor ascended to near martyr status for millions of Americans. During his long military career Eisenhower had seen much killing, often the death of young men in war. With so many young Americans killed during World War II he came to view death as a deeply sad but inexorable reality.

Eisenhower was well acquainted with the newly sworn-in president, Lyndon Johnson, who had been the Senate Democratic leader during most of Eisenhower's presidency. Johnson assiduously and relentlessly cultivated

Eisenhower, lavishing praise on him, seeking his advice and, especially, his support on foreign policy. He wanted Eisenhower's endorsement for America's participation in the war in Vietnam. Eisenhower publicly backed Johnson on Vietnam, but was privately critical about his incremental approach to increasing American troop levels there. His deeply held belief—and advice to Kennedy after the Bay of Pigs—was that when the United States committed its military forces it must ensure the operation is successful. Eisenhower believed Johnson should make a decisive commitment to either prevail in Vietnam or not commit American troops at all. He was sharply critical of Johnson's Great Society domestic agenda, describing it as wildly expensive and fiscally irresponsible. David Eisenhower said his grandfather was personally fond of Lyndon Johnson, but had reservations about his ability to handle the presidency.[18]

Eisenhower struggled with retirement. "He was sorry giving up the Presidency," his former secretary Ann Whitman said. "Dad was not a happy ex-president," added his son John. While Eisenhower had hobbies and friends, he was perpetually restless, even well into his seventies and with declining health. A career of relentless, if not always overt, striving was hard to shut down. Mamie sought the help of Eisenhower's former aides and family members to divert his attentions. "Take him off my hands. Alone here he just goes wild," she told one secretary. David Eisenhower said his grandfather was an unsettled man during his retirement years. "When alone, he prowled the Eldorado cottage [in Indian Wells] like a caged lion. Mamie's difficulties were not unlike those of any military wife accustomed to a husband being gone for long stretches of time. Even in Gettysburg, Mamie had never really regained the ability to pacify and entertain her husband. The difficult hours were the inactive ones."[19]

Ike remained a revered figure in the United States and around the world. In four of his postpresidential years, Gallup polls identified him as the most admired man in America. Republicans eagerly sought his advice and solicited his support. Eisenhower spoke extensively, often to business and civic groups. He typically focused on patriotic themes and pleaded for fiscal responsibility. He urged Republicans to back a moderate agenda that he called progressive. Eisenhower viewed the 1964 Republican presidential nomination of Senator Barry Goldwater, an archconservative, as a sharp repudiation of his own more centrist policies. Though

Eisenhower supported his former vice president Richard Nixon as the 1968 Republican presidential nominee he did not make the endorsement until a month before the Republican convention. His backing may have been encouraged by the fact that his grandson David and Nixon's daughter Julie were engaged to be married. Eisenhower addressed the August 1968 Republican Convention from his hospital room at Walter Reed Hospital via closed circuit TV. These were his last remarks to a Republican convention and among his last public remarks.

Eisenhower's health was declining sharply as a result of a heart attack in 1965 and two heart attacks in 1968. He died of congestive heart failure at Walter Reed Army Medical Center on March 28, 1969, at the age of seventy-eight. In his final hours, Eisenhower ordered the venetian blinds to be lowered in his room and that he be pulled into a sitting position on his hospital bed. "Higher," he commanded. And then he turned to his son and said, "I want to go. God take me."[20] As word of his passing spread, bells tolled throughout Washington and flags were lowered to half-staff. The former president was buried in a standard issue $80.00 Army coffin in Abilene, Kansas, on April 2, 1969. America and the world grieved the passing of one of the iconic leaders of the twentieth century.

IV

Kennedy used the transition to cultivate an image of a strong, idealistic, energetic leader who was determined to propel the United States in a new direction. He projected confidence, optimism, and youth and seemed to be a man of ideas and of action.

President Kennedy took Washington by storm. Syndicated columnist Joe Alsop described the early days of the Kennedy administration as "a breathless time, full of promise and energy and, oddly enough, glamour, which is not usually a quality associated with Washington . . . The truth is that after the staid Eisenhower years, the Washington that was invaded by members of the Kennedy administration was suddenly enormously festive and gay."[21]

Arthur Schlesinger Jr., the Harvard historian and Kennedy staffer, said a seismic jolt hit Washington with the onset of the Kennedy presidency. "The capital city, somnolent in the Eisenhower years, had come suddenly alive," he wrote. "The air had been stale and oppressive; now fresh winds were blowing. There was the excitement that comes from an injection of new men and new ideas, the release of energy, which occurs when men with ideas have a chance to put them into practice. Not since the New Deal more than a quarter century before had there been such an invasion of bright young men. Not since Franklin Roosevelt had there been a President who so plainly delighted in innovation and leadership." Schlesinger depicted a time of drive and purpose. "The pace was frenetic. Everyone came early and stayed late . . . Telephones rang incessantly. Meetings were continuous. The evenings too were lively and full. The glow of the White House was lighting up the whole city. Washington seemed engaged in a collective effort to make itself brighter, gayer, more intellectual, more resolute. It was a golden interlude . . . The excitement in the White House infected the whole executive branch. A new breed had come to town, and the New Frontiersman carried a thrust of action and purpose wherever they went."[22] While the term New Frontier was more of a campaign slogan and marketing strategy than a detailed governing agenda, it was based on the premise that the Eisenhower years has been listless and reactive and America had regressed. Kennedy's program promised to bring drive and energy and purpose to American public life, propelled forward by an activist federal government.

Kennedy's first three months in office indeed featured a blizzard of activity. A cascade of proposals poured from the White House. Kennedy sent more than three dozen special messages and letters to Congress calling for legislation, ten prominent world leaders visited Washington, Kennedy held nine televised press conferences, and he launched signature programs including the Peace Corps and the Alliance for Progress for Latin America.

Kennedy's initial messages to Congress focused on economic recovery and growth, gold and the balance of payments deficit, health and hospital care, education, natural resources, the federal highway program, the Peace Corps, foreign aid, fiscal policy, the defense budget, regulation, and taxation. In 1961, Kennedy made more than 350 legislative requests in 66 separate messages. About half were approved by Congress, but several major initiatives stalled. There was more activity than accomplishment, but the overarching message was clear: a bold new president and administration were now in charge.

Kennedy's first press conference was held on the evening of January 25 at the State Department auditorium and was the first presidential press conference to be televised live. Americans saw a young leader who seemed confident, well briefed, and witty. Kennedy assumed a sterner visage when he appeared before a Joint Session of Congress a few days later to deliver his State of the Union address. He sketched out an agenda that could only be read as a stark repudiation of the Eisenhower years. "I speak at an hour of national peril and national opportunity. Before my term has ended, we shall have to test anew whether a nation organized and governed such as ours can endure. The outcome is by no means certain. The answers are by no means clear," he began. Kennedy said the economy he inherited was weak, the federal budget had already moved out of balance, America's cities "are being engulfed in squalor," and even the water supply was dwindling. "But all these problems pale when placed beside those which confront us around the world. No man entering this office, regardless of party, regardless of his previous service in Washington, could fail to be staggered upon learning—even in this brief ten-day period—the harsh enormity of the trials through which we must pass in the next four years. Each day the crises multiply. Each day their solution grows more difficult. Each day we draw nearer the hour of maximum danger, as weapons spread and hostile forces grow stronger . . . The tide of events has been running out and time has not been our friend." Kennedy vowed aggressive plans to revive the economy and strengthen national defense. He prepared Americans for tough challenges. "Life in 1961 will not be easy. Wishing it, predicting it, even asking for it, will not make it so. There will be further setbacks before the tide is turned. But turn it we must. The hopes of mankind rest upon us," he declared.[23]

As part of his plan to energize the executive branch, Kennedy dismantled key national security entities that Eisenhower had so carefully created. In the spring of 1961 Kennedy killed Eisenhower's prized Operations Coordinating Board within the National Security Council, a body that was designed to coordinate and implement security policy. But Kennedy saw that board as usurping the role of the State Department. Kennedy's executive order that ended what his predecessor had so painstakingly constructed was devastatingly brief and banal. "The Board was used in the last administration for work which we now plan to do in other ways. This action is part of our program for strengthening the responsibility of the individual departments," the order read.[24]

Kennedy conspicuously departed from other defining features of Eisenhower's government. He rarely held cabinet or staff meetings, both of which were regular features of Eisenhower's presidency. Kennedy celebrated operating outside of regular bureaucratic procedures, famously seeking information from government officials well below the cabinet secretary level. This would have been anathema to Ike. Eisenhower's carefully thought-out procedures and methodical deliberations were replaced by Kennedy's frenzied pace and informal, even ad hoc, approach to decision making. But his energy and élan captivated Washington. "He did everything today except shinny up the Washington Monument," James Reston wrote approvingly in a column about Kennedy early in his presidency. "The deadline for everything is the day before yesterday," quipped his labor secretary, Arthur Goldberg.

In late May Kennedy again went before a Joint Session of Congress to deliver a special message on "Urgent National Needs." He described formidable foreign policy and domestic challenges. America, he said, needed to understand revolutionary changes occurring in Asia, Latin America, Africa, and the Middle East. He called these the "lands of the rising peoples," adding, "Their revolution is the greatest in human history." On the domestic front, Kennedy said his administration was working to turn the recession into a recovery. But he also had grander plans in mind. "I believe that this nation should commit itself to achieving the goal, before this decade is out, of landing a man on the moon and returning him safely to earth," he declared. Kennedy said it would require an enormous investment of energy and national treasure, and the nation should go all in—or not at all. "If we are to go only half way, or reduce our sights in the face of difficulty, in my judgment it would be better not to go at all."[25]

Americans liked their new president. Kennedy's approval ratings were sky high, reaching 72% after his first month in office and 83% by the end of April, and this was even after the Bay of Pigs debacle. "I'm like Ike," Kennedy quipped in private. "The worse I do the more they like me." He was also convinced his predecessor was rooting for him to fail. During a crisis with the Soviet Union over Berlin in the summer of 1961, Kennedy envisioned Ike enjoying his struggles. "He probably glories in my failures," Kennedy quipped.[26]

But Kennedy was careful to speak respectfully about Eisenhower in public and to keep in touch with him. He sent his predecessor notes, called him periodically, and sought his support on foreign policy, trade, and civil rights. He knew Eisenhower still enjoyed the strong support of Republican leaders in Congress and millions of other Americans, and sometimes asked Eisenhower to support his administration's initiatives on foreign policy and trade. When there were news reports in May 1962 about friction between the two, Kennedy sent Eisenhower an almost obsequious letter. "As you perhaps know, I have been a great admirer of yours since our first meeting in Frankfurt, in 1945, when I accompanied Secretary Forrestal on a trip to Europe. I agree with your view concerning the differences that could easily arise between us and will certainly do everything in my power to prevent any misunderstandings of thoughts, actions, or motive from eroding our association," Kennedy wrote. He thanked Eisenhower for his support during a tense period between the U.S. and the Soviet Union over Berlin in the summer and fall of 1961. He also thanked Eisenhower for his support of free trade and foreign aid reform initatives. "Your continued interest in our national security problems, and your ready acceptance of intelligence and operational briefings concerning Southeast Asia, leads me to feel that your important support and judgment are readily at the nation's command, for which I am truly grateful," he wrote.[27]

Even as Kennedy grew more confident with his mastery of the presidency, by 1963 he still kept in touch with his predecessor. He was certain that Eisenhower would never be his enthusiastic ally, but he wanted to make sure that Eisenhower was never an overt adversary.

V

So how should we regard the transition from Dwight Eisenhower to John Kennedy?

Eisenhower transferred the presidency to Kennedy in an organized and efficient way, with a minimum of public rancor or ill will. Eisenhower's commitment to an orderly transition coupled with Kennedy's tact and professionalism were evident and important during these ten weeks. The press generally described the transition as smooth and successful. "This transition has the unharnessed energy of summer skeet lightning, the intensity of an Alfred Hitchcock murder thriller, and the passion of a political revolution. It is a mixture of superficial chaos and studied purpose," John Steele, a *Time* magazine reporter, said in a dispatch several days before the inauguration. "It is clear that never before in the nation's history have men of good will cooperated so intimately or so effectively in transferring governmental responsibility. It is a high water mark in the practice of responsible and free government, a lesson which should be long remembered at home and marked by free men everywhere."[28] The two men appointed ideal representatives to oversee the transition: Wilton Persons, Eisenhower's chief of staff, and Clark Clifford, Kennedy's liaison. Persons and Clifford were experienced and skilled operatives who understood politics, power, and people. They knew and respected each other and were determined to honorably fulfill their responsibilities.

The Eisenhower-Kennedy transition revealed flaws in a system that was informal and ad hoc. At that time, transition procedures were reinvented with every change of administration. There was no institutional structure nor established procedures and the costs of standing up a new government were primarily the responsibility of the incoming president's political party. The Kennedy transition was a larger-scale operation than its predecessors, partly because of its ambitious agenda, myriad task forces, and lack of a command center. Kennedy traveled extensively between Washington, New York, and Palm Beach during this ten-week period. The Democratic National Committee spent more than $350,000 in transition costs between November 1960 and January 1961. Kennedy's private resources and his Senate office funds paid for some additional expenses. However, many of his appointees had to use their own funds to pay for trips to Washington, lodging, and other work-related expenses as they prepared for their new responsibilities.

Once in office President Kennedy created a bipartisan commission to examine the larger issue of campaign costs. One of its recommendations was that the federal government should pay for the costs of the presidential transition. That provision was included in legislation that Kennedy proposed to Congress. The 1963 Transition Act was ultimately approved in March 1964, about four months after Kennedy was killed.[29] The law has served as the framework for transitions ever since. Initially, Congress allocated $900,000 for the transition. By 2017 the federal government's allocation for transition expenses was $7 million.

While the Eisenhower-Kennedy transition was mechanically successful, the first months of the Kennedy administration were very uneven, despite the public perception of his success and high approval ratings. Kennedy inherited a struggling economy and difficult foreign problems, specifically regarding Laos and Cuba. Both foreign situations vexed Kennedy. He managed to find a reasonable short-term arrangement in Laos in 1961 but never developed a sound long-term strategy for Southeast Asia. He eventually sent more than 10,000 advisers to Vietnam, a significant escalation in America's commitment to that country. The Kennedy administration's role in the Bay of Pigs invasion by Cuban rebels trying to oust Castro was a fiasco of the first order. Kennedy publicly assumed responsibility for the debacle but his team quietly tried to shift some of the blame to Eisenhower, confirming some of the worst fears Eisenhower had harbored as he started his retirement. During his first half year in the White House, Kennedy also faced mounting tension with the Soviet Union, especially over the fate of Berlin which resulted in the erection of the Berlin Wall. It's hard to blame the transition itself for these problems. It is possible that if America's electoral and political calendar had been arranged differently, Eisenhower, with more time, would have handed Kennedy less formidable challenges.

The Eisenhower-Kennedy transition is remembered as a singular moment in American history—the oldest serving president gave way to the youngest elected president, the former five star general handed power to the former junior naval officer. Kennedy consciously sought to build his administration around this generational motif. He openly acknowledged that he was a "generational chauvinist" and was far more comfortable around people of his age and with similar experiences. "Never before in American history had an incoming administration dismissed a generation from the corridors of power," wrote historian David Fromkin.[30]

The most memorable aspects of the transition are the two statements that remain the rhetorical capstone of the change in power: Dwight Eisenhower's farewell address and John Kennedy's inaugural address. Undoubtedly, these are two of the great speeches in American history—delivered in the same city, only three days apart. Initially, Eisenhower's farewell address was received respectfully, but most political leaders and the public did not linger over his departing admonishments about frugality, prudence, and stewardship. He was damned with faint praise. But as time passed, many have come to regard Eisenhower's remarks as unusually wise. These quiet warnings have become more fully appreciated by politicians, scholars, and even the public over the last half century. "Eisenhower delivered a message of stunning prescience, but it took some time for its full weight to impress itself on the American public," wrote historian Jim Newton. "Just as with Washington, some of Eisenhower's message was lost, distorted, or selectively read in ways that tell more about the interpreter than about the message."[31] By contrast, Kennedy's vivid and compelling inaugural address immediately captivated America and the world, as analysts made favorable comparisions to Abraham Lincoln's and Franklin Roosevelt's historic addresses. House Speaker Sam Rayburn even judged that Kennedy had exceeded Lincoln. The allure of Kennedy's speech continues; generations of Americans can recite his signature phrases from memory. It is routinely referred to as one of the great inaugural addresses in American history. However, some now question whether Kennedy's triumphant and triumphal speech paved the way for the reckless and expensive foreign policy ventures that occurred in subsequent years.

It's impossible to conclude this story without contemplating several striking historical ironies.

In January 1961 John Kennedy was the rising star and Dwight Eisenhower the setting sun. The underlying drama of this transition of power was captured in a now-famous photo of the youthful Kennedy on the inaugural platform. As the new president spoke confidently and gestured forcefully to his mesmerized audience, a frigid-looking, almost cowering, Eisenhower is in clear view off to the side, looking attentive but stern. At that moment it seemed certain that Kennedy would dominate American politics for the decade of the 1960s and Eisenhower would withdraw into an obscure retirement. No one could then have imagined that Kennedy would be dead in less than three years or that Eisenhower would survive him by almost six years and would remain an important political force during both the Kennedy and Johnson presidencies.

Eisenhower and Kennedy were linked in the sequence of history, the elderly thirty-fourth president followed by the youthful thirty-fifth. But the reputational balance between them has shifted over the decades.

Kennedy remains a singular figure in American history and popular culture—the young martyred leader, killed at the height of his powers. Historians today give Kennedy's presidency a mixed assessment, but his public esteem remains steady and high. He will always be an icon.

As the years have passed, however, Eisenhower's stature has risen steadily among historians. The unsealing of documents related to his administration and the perspective granted by subsequent events have given Eisenhower's presidency a respect that was not conferred on him during his lifetime. A 2017 poll of historians that ranked American presidents placed Eisenhower fifth, behind only Abraham Lincoln, George Washington, Franklin Roosevelt, and Teddy Roosevelt. Kennedy was rated eighth. Interpretations will change and rankings will likely shift in the coming decades but Eisenhower seems safely ensconced in the top tier of American presidents, something that would have confirmed Eisenhower's self-assessment and assuaged some of the hurt he felt when Kennedy swept into office and was celebrated for being his opposite. Kennedy's standing is elevated by his large but unrealized potential and the tragedy of his passing.

The intimate association between the thirty-fourth and thirty-fifth American presidents that began during those ten fateful weeks continues to this day. Dwight Eisenhower and John Kennedy are destined to stride together, in a remarkable pairing, throughout the long march of American history.

Bibliography

MAIN BOOKS CONSULTED

Adams, Sherman, *Firsthand Report*: *The Story of the Eisenhower Administration*. New York: Harper & Brothers, 1961.

Alsop, Joseph W., with Adam Platt, *"I Have Seen The Best of It"*: *Memoirs*. Mount Jackson, VA: Axios Press, 1992.

Ball, George, *The Past Has Another Pattern: Memoirs*. New York: W.W. Norton, 1982.

Beschloss, Michael, Introduction and Annotations. *Jacqueline Kennedy: Historic Conversations on Life with John F. Kennedy*. New York: Hyperion, 2011.

Bishop, Jim, *A Day in the Life of President Kennedy*. New York: Bantam Book, 1964.

Bradlee, Benjamin, *Conservations with Kennedy*. New York: W.W. Norton & Company, 1975.

Bradlee, Benjamin, *A Good Life: Newspapering and Other Adventures*. New York: Simon & Schuster, 1995.

Brauer, Carl, *Presidential Transitions: Eisenhower Through Reagan*. New York: Oxford University Press, 1986.

Brownell, Herbert, with John P. Burke, *Advising Ike: The Memoirs of Attorney General Herbert Brownell*. Lawrence, KS: University Press of Kansas, 1993.

Burns, James MacGregor. *John F. Kennedy: A Political Profile*. New York: Brace & World, 1961.

Campbell, Kurt, and James Steinberg, *Difficult Transitions: Foreign Policy Troubles at the Outset of Presidential Power*. Washington: Brookings Institution Press, 2008.

Clarke, Thurston, *Ask Not: The Inauguration of John F. Kennedy and the Speech That Changed America*. New York: Henry Holt and Company, 2004.

Cohen, Andrew, *Two Days in June: John F. Kennedy and the 48 Hours That Made History*. New York: Penguin Random House, 2014.

Dallek, Robert, *Camelot's Court: Inside the Kennedy White House.* New York: HarperCollins, 2013.

Dallek, Robert, *An Unfinished Life: John F. Kennedy, 1917–1963.* Boston: Little, Brown, 2003.

Divine, Robert, *Foreign Policy and U.S. Presidential Elections, 1952–1960.* New York: New Viewpoints, 1974.

Donaldson, Gary A., *The First Modern Campaign: Kennedy, Nixon, and the Election of 1960.* New York: Rowman & Littlefield, 2007.

Donovan, Robert, *Confidential Secretary: Ann Whitman's 20 Years with Eisenhower and Rockefeller.* New York: E.P. Dutton, 1998.

Donovan, Robert, *Eisenhower: The Inside Story.* New York: Harper & Brothers, 1956.

Drury, Allen, *Advise And Consent.* New York: Doubleday, 1959.

Eisenhower, David, with Julie Nixon Eisenhower, *Going Home to Glory: A Memoir of Life with Dwight D. Eisenhower, 1961–69.* New York: Simon & Schuster, 2010.

Eisenhower, Dwight, *At Ease: Stories I Tell to Friends.* Garden City, NY: Doubleday, 1967.

Eisenhower, Dwight, *Mandate for Change: The White House Years, 1953 to 1956.* Garden City, NY: Doubleday, 1963.

Eisenhower, Dwight, *Waging Peace: The White House Years, 1957 to 1961.* Garden City, NY: Doubleday, 1965.

Eisenhower, John, *Strictly Personal: A Memoir.* Garden City, NY: Doubleday, 1974.

Eisenhower, Milton, *The President Is Calling.* Garden City, NY: Doubleday, 1974.

Evans, Rowland, and Robert Novak, *Lyndon B. Johnson: The Exercise of Power.* New York: Signet Books, 1966.

Ewald, William Bragg, Jr., *Eisenhower The President: Crucial Days, 1951–1960.* Englewood Cliffs, NJ: Prentice-Hall, 1981.

Fay, Paul, *The Pleasure of His Company.* New York: Popular Library, 1964.

Ferrell, Robert H., ed., *The Eisenhower Diaries.* New York: W.W. Norton, 1981.

Frank, Jeffrey. *Ike and Dick: Portrait of a Strange Political Marriage.* New York: Simon & Schuster, 2013.

Gaddis, John Lewis, *The Cold War: A New History.* New York: Penguin Books, 2005.

Gaddis, John Lewis, *Strategies of Containment: A Critical Appraisal of Postwar American National Security Policy.* New York: Oxford University Press, 1982.

Gallagher, Mary Barelli, *My Life with Jacqueline Kennedy.* New York: David McKay, 1970.

Gellman, Irwin F., *The President and the Apprentice: Eisenhower and Nixon, 1952–61.* New Haven: Yale University Press, 2015.

Goldstein, Gordon M., *Lessons in Disaster: McGeorge Bundy and the Path to War in Vietnam.* New York: Henry Holt and Company, 2008.

Goodwin, Richard, *Remembering America: A Voice From the Sixties.* New York: Open Road, 1988.

Graham, Katharine, *Personal History.* New York: Alfred Knopf, 1997.

Greenstein, Fred, *The Hidden-Hand Presidency: Eisenhower as Leader.* Baltimore: Johns Hopkins University Press, 1994.

Halberstam, David, *The Best and the Brightest.* New York: Random House, 1969.

Halberstam, David, *The Fifties.* New York: Villard Books, 1993.

Henry, Laurin, *Presidential Transitions.* Washington: Brookings Institution Press, 1960.

Hughes, Emmet John, *The Ordeal of Power: A Political Memoir of the Eisenhower Years.* New York: Dell Publishing, 1962.

Johnson, Paul, *Eisenhower: A Life.* New York: Viking, 2014.

Jones, Howard, *The Bay of Pigs.* New York: Oxford University Press, 2008.

Kempe, Frederick, *Berlin 1961: Kennedy, Khrushchev, and the Most Dangerous Place on Earth.* New York: Putnam, 2011.

Kennedy, Edward M., *True Compass.* New York: Twelve, 2009.

Kennedy, John F., *Profiles in Courage*. New York: Harper & Row, 1956.

Kennedy, John F., *The Strategy of Peace*. New York: Popular Library, 1960.

Kennedy, Rose, *Times to Remember*. Garden City, NY: Doubleday, 1974.

Krock, Arthur, *Memoirs: Sixty Years on the Firing Line*. New York: Funk & Wagnalls, 1968.

Kumar, Martha Joynt, *Before the Oath: How George W. Bush and Barack Obama Managed a Transfer of Power*. Baltimore: Johns Hopkins University Press, 2015.

Ledbetter, James, *Unwarranted Influence: Dwight D. Eisenhower and the Military-Industrial Complex*. New Haven: Yale University Press, 2011.

Lincoln, Evelyn, *My Twelve Years with John F. Kennedy*. New York: David McKay, 1965.

Logevall, Fredrik, *Embers of War: The Fall of an Empire and the Making of America's Vietnam*. New York: Random House, 2012.

Luce, Henry, foreword, *The National Purpose: America in Crisis: An Urgent Summons*. New York: Holt, Rinehart & Winston, 1960.

Manchester, William, *The Glory and Dream: A Narrative History of the America, 1932–1972*. New York: Bantam Books, 1972.

Manchester, William, *Portrait of a President*. Boston: Little, Brown, 1962.

Maraniss, David, *Rome 1960: The Summer Olympics That Stirred the World*. New York: Simon and Schuster, 2008.

McPherson, Harry, *A Political Education: A Washington Memoir*. Austin: University of Texas Press, 1972.

Nasaw, David, *The Patriarch: The Remarkable Life and Turbulent Times of Joseph P. Kennedy*. New York: Penguin Press, 2012.

Neustadt, Richard E., *Preparing to Be President: The Memos of Richard E. Neustadt*. Washington: AEI Press, 2000.

Neustadt, Richard E., *Presidential Power: The Politics of Leadership*. New York: John Wiley & Sons, 1960.

Newton, Jim, *Eisenhower: The White House Years*. New York: Doubleday, 2011.

Nitze, Paul, with Ann M. Smith and Steven L. Reardon, *From Hiroshima To Glasnost: At the Center of Decision—A Memoir*. New York: Grove Weidenfeld, 1989.

Oakley, J. Ronald, *God's Country: America in the Fifties*. New York: Barricade Books, 1986.

O'Donnell, Kenneth, and David Powers with Joe McCarthy, *"Johnny We Hardly Knew Ye": Memories of John Fitzgerald Kennedy*. Boston: Little, Brown, 1970.

Oliphant, Thomas, and Curtis Wilkie, *The Road To Camelot: Inside JFK's Five-Year Campaign*. New York: Simon & Schuster, 2017.

O'Neill, Tip, with William Novak, *Man of the House: The Life and Political Memoirs of Speaker Tip O'Neill*. New York: Random House, 1987.

Opotowsky, Stan, *The Kennedy Government*. New York: Popular Library Edition, 1961.

Parmet, Herbert S., *Eisenhower and The American Crusades*. New York: Macmillan, 1972.

Parmet, Herbert, *Jack: The Struggles of John F. Kennedy*. New York: Dial Press, 1980.

Parmet, Herbert, *JFK: The Presidency of John F. Kennedy*. New York: Dial Press, 1983.

Pietrusza, David, *1960: LBJ vs. JFK vs. Nixon: The Epic Campaign That Forged Three Presidencies*. New York: Union Square Press, 2008.

Reston, James, *Deadline: A Memoir*. New York: Times Books, 1991.

Rorabaugh, W. J., *The Real Making of the President: Kennedy, Nixon, and the 1960 Election*. Lawrence, KS: University Press of Kansas, 2009.

Rubin, Gretchen, *Forty Ways to Look at JFK*. New York: Ballantine Books, 2005.

Salinger, Pierre, *With Kennedy*. New York: Avon Books, 1966.

Savage, Sean J., *The Senator from New England: The Rise of JFK*. Albany: State University of New York Press, 2015.

Schlesinger, Arthur, *A Thousand Days: John F. Kennedy in the White House*. New York: Houghton, Mifflin Company, 1965.

Sestanovich, Steven, *Maximalist: America in the World from Truman to Obama*. New York: Alfred A. Knopf, 2014.

Sevareid, Eric, ed., *Candidates 1960*. New York: Basic Books, 1959.

Shaw, John T., *JFK in the Senate: Pathway to the Presidency*. New York: Palgrave MacMillan, 2013.

Slater, Ellis, *The Ike I Knew*. Ellis D. Slater Trust, 1980.

Smith, Jean Edward, *Eisenhower in War and Peace*. New York: Random House, 2012.

Snead, David, *The Gaither Committee, Eisenhower, and the Cold War*. Columbus: Ohio State University Press, 1999.

Sorensen, Theodore, *Counselor: A Life at the Edge of History*. New York: HarperCollins, 2008.

Sorensen, Theodore, *Kennedy*. New York: Konecky & Konecky, 1965.

Sorensen, Theodore, ed., *"Let the Word Go Forth": The Speeches, Statements, and Writings of John F. Kennedy, 1947 to 1963*. New York: Dell Publishing, 1988.

Tanzer, Lester, ed., *The Kennedy Circle*. Washington: Luce, 1961.

Thayer, Mary Van Rensselaer, *Jacqueline Kennedy: The White House Years*. New York: Popular Library, 1967.

Thomas, Evan, *Ike's Bluff: President Eisenhower's Secret Battle To Save the World*. Boston: Little, Brown, 2012.

Tofel, Richard, *Sounding the Trumpet: The Making of John F. Kennedy's Inaugural Address*. Chicago: Ivan R. Dee, 2005.

Tye, Larry, *Bobby Kennedy: The Making of a Liberal Icon*. New York: Random House, 2016.

Widmer, Ted, selected and introduced, *Listening In: The Secret White House Recordings of John F. Kennedy*. New York: Hyperion, 2012.

Whalen, Thomas, *Kennedy Versus Lodge: The 1952 Massachusetts Senate Race*. Boston: Northeastern University Press, 2000.

White, Theodore, *The Making of the President 1960*. New York: Atheneum House, 1961.

White, Theodore, *In Search of History: A Personal Adventure*. New York: Warner Books, 1978.

Wicker, Tom, *Dwight D. Eisenhower*. New York: Times Books, 2002.

Wofford, Harris, *Of Kennedys & Kings: Making Sense of the Sixties*. Pittsburgh: University of Pittsburgh Press, 1980.

REFERENCE BOOKS CONSULTED

The Papers of Dwight David Eisenhower, The Presidency: Keeping the Peace XXI, editors Louis Galambos and Daun Van Ee (Baltimore: Johns Hopkins University Press, 2001).

Public Papers of the Presidents, Dwight D. Eisenhower, 1960–61 (Washington: US Government Printing Office, 1961).

Public Papers of the Presidents, John F. Kennedy, 1961 (Washington: US Government Printing Office, 1962).

John Fitzgerald Kennedy: A Compendium of Speeches, Statements and Remarks Delivered During His Service in the Congress of the United States (Washington: US Government Printing Office, 1964).

The Speeches of Senator John F. Kennedy, Presidential Campaign of 1960 (Washington: US Government Printing Office, 1961).

The Speeches of Vice President Richard M. Nixon, Presidential Campaign of 1960 (Washington: US Government Printing Office, 1961).

The Joint Appearances of Senator John F. Kennedy and Vice President Richard M. Nixon, Presidential Campaign of 1960 (Washington: US Government Printing Office, 1961).

Endnotes

INTRODUCTION

1. Theodore C. Sorensen, ed., *Let The Word Go Forth: The Speeches, Statements, and Writings of John F. Kennedy, 1947 to 1963* (New York: Dell Publishing, 1988), 56.
2. Paul B. Fay Jr., *The Pleasure of His Company* (New York: Popular Library, 1977), 65.
3. Richard N. Goodwin, *Remembering America: A Voice from the Sixties* (New York: Open Road Media, 1988), 11.
4. Dwight D. Eisenhower, *Public Papers of the Presidents, Dwight D. Eisenhower, 1960–61*, 1035.
5. John F. Kennedy, *Public Papers of the Presidents, John F. Kennedy, 1961*, 1.
6. Dwight Eisenhower, press conference, January 18, 1961, Eisenhower Presidential Library.
7. James Reston, "The Reassuring Civility of the Transition," *New York Times*, January 15, 1961.

CHAPTER ONE: ELECTION DAY IN AMERICA

1. "Ambulance Carries a Patient to the Polls," *Chicago Tribune*, November 9, 1960.
2. "Man, 95, Casts Vote for Nixon, Then Falls Dead," *Los Angeles Times*, November 9, 1960.
3. "Women, 86, Nervous As She Casts Her First Ballot," *Los Angeles Times*, November 9, 1960.
4. "Clark Gable Able to Vote at Hospital," *Los Angeles Times*, November 9, 1960.
5. "Herbert Hoover Refuses to Predict a Winner," *Los Angeles Times*, November 9, 1960.
6. "Hoover Photo Stays," *New York Times*, November 9, 1960.
7. "Stevenson Waits 40 Minutes to Vote," *New York Times*, November 9, 1960.

8. "Election Aide Dies: Voting Place Moved," *Los Angeles Times*, November 9, 1960.
9. "Flies 3,000 Miles to Register But Can't Vote," *Chicago Tribune*, November 9, 1960.
10. "Woman Drops Ballot into Slot of TV Set," *Chicago Tribune*, November 9, 1960.
11. "US Voting Process Incredible to Envoys," *Washington Post*, November 9, 1960.
12. "Swedish Princesses See City and Learn About Voting," *New York Times*, November 9, 1960.
13. "Times Square Fails to Get Election Night Crowds," *New York Times*, November 9, 1960.
14. "Election Night Signal for Widespread Parties," *Los Angeles Times*, November 9, 1960.
15. "Joy, Gloom Are Polls Apart," *Washington Post*, November 9, 1960.
16. *U.S. News & World Report*, November 14, 1960.
17. *Newsweek*, November 7, 1960.
18. Eric Sevareid, ed., *Candidates 1960* (New York: Basic Books, 1959), 21.
19. *U.S. News & World Report*, November 7, 1960.
20. *Newsweek*, November 21, 1960.
21. *Time*, November 7, 1960.
22. "Video Computers Differ At First, But Then Agree," *New York Times*, November 9, 1960.
23. *Chicago Tribune*, November 9, 1960.
24. "Nixon Unwinds in Dash South of the Border," *Boston Globe*, November 9, 1960.
25. Richard Nixon, *Six Crises* (Garden City, N.Y.: Doubleday & Co, 1962), 378.
26. Ibid, 382.
27. "Democrat Waits: Kennedy Defers Victory Speech," *New York Times*, November 9, 1960.
28. "Longest Hours of My Life, Jacqueline Says of Wait," *Boston Globe*, November 9, 1960.
29. Dwight Eisenhower Presidential Schedule, November 8, 1960, Eisenhower Presidential Library.
30. "Video Computers Differ at First, But Then Agree."
31. Nixon, *Six Crises*, 389.
32. Ibid, 395.
33. Evelyn Lincoln, *My Twelve Years with John F. Kennedy* (New York: Bantam Books, 1965), 157.
34. Pierre Salinger, *With Kennedy* (New York: Avon Books, 1966), 76.
35. Ibid, 76.
36. Benjamin Bradlee, *Conversations with Kennedy* (New York: W.W. Norton, 1975), 32.
37. John Eisenhower, *Strictly Personal: A Memoir* (Doubleday, 1974), 37.
38. Ellis D. Slater, *The Ike I Knew* (Ellis Slater Trust, 1980), 230.

CHAPTER TWO: DAWN OF THE NEW DECADE

1. George Dixon, "Spending New Year's Eve With Secretary Benson," *Washington Post*, January 5, 1960.
2. Red Smith, "Garden Program Has Hub Flavor," *Boston Globe*, January 1, 1960.
3. "Tab for That New Year's Eve Party to Be Higher," *Chicago Defender*, December 31, 1959.
4. "New Year's Eve Black Bear Proves to Be Real Booboo," *Baltimore Sun*, January 7, 1960.

5. "Boys Make Big New Year Bang with Dynamite," *Los Angeles Times*, January 2, 1960.

6. "Holiday Road Toll of 374 Sets Record," *Baltimore Sun*, January 5, 1960.

7. "Polar Bears 'Plunge' into New Year," *Los Angeles Times*, December 31, 1959.

8. *Bulletin of Atomic Scientists*, Doomsday Timeline.

9. "Ike Welcomes New Year at Private Party," *Boston Globe*, January 1, 1960.

10. Mrpopculture.com

11. Evelyn Lincoln Diary, January 1, 1960, Kennedy Presidential Library.

12. J. A. Livingston, "Dynamic Decade Begins with Optimism Rampant," *Washington Post*, January 5, 1950.

13. *New York Herald Tribune*, editorial, January 1, 1960.

14. *New York Times*, editorial, January 1, 1960.

15. *Hartford Courant*, editorial, January 1, 1960.

16. *Washington Post*, editorial, January 1, 1960.

17. J. Ronald Oakley, *God's Country: America In the Fifties* (New York: Barricade Books, 1986), 426.

18. Arnold Toynbee, *New York Herald Tribune*, January 1, 1960.

19. Walter Lippmann, "Second Best," *Washington Post*, January 19, 1960.

20. Eric Goldman, "Good-By to the Fifties—and Good Riddance," *Harper's Magazine*, January 1960.

21. Lawrence Weiss, "Has America Lost The Way—An Appraisal of the National Mood in the Decade of the 1950s," *Denver Post*, December 27, 1959.

22. Ralph Yarborough remarks, "Ceremonies in Honor of Veterans of War Between the States," *Congressional Record*, January 7, 1960.

23. *New York Herald Tribune*, editorials, January 5–January 12, 1961.

24. *Congressional Quarterly Almanac* 1960, 830.

25. *The National Purpose: America In Crisis: An Urgent Summons* (New York: Holt, Rinehart & Winston, 1960), Archibald MacLeish, 37; Billy Graham, 64.

26. "Experts Vision 3 Man Mars Trip in 10 Years," *Los Angeles Times*, January 5, 1960.

27. Dexter Keezer, "Get Set for Happy New Decade," *Baltimore Sun*, January 3, 1960.

28. 1960 Census Report, summary in *The World Book Encyclopedia, 1961 Annual Supplement*, 227–270.

29. *The Gallup Poll: Public Opinion 1935–1971, Volume 3, 1959–71.*

30. William Manchester, *The Glory and The Dream: A Narrative History of America, 1932–1972* (Boston: Little, Brown, 1973), 908.

31. Oakley, *God's Country*, 415.

32. *World Book, 1961 Supplement*, xx.

33. Ibid.

34. Oakley, *God's Country*, 380.

35. *The World Almanac and Book of Facts, 1961* (New York: New York World Telegram, 1961), 510.

36. Ibid, 761.

37. Allen Drury, *Advise and Consent* (New York: Pocket Books, 1959), 593.

38. Richard Neustadt, *Presidential Power: The Politics of Leadership* (New York: John Wiley & Sons, 1960), 10.

39. Clendy Culligan, "Listen to the Mockingbird," *Washington Post*, July 3, 1960.

40. *World Almanac and Book of Facts 1961*, 801.

41. David Maraniss, *Rome 1960: The Summer Olympics That Stirred The World* (New York: Simon & Schuster, 2008), 384.

42. *Los Angeles Times*, January 1, 1960.
43. *World Almanac and Book of Facts 1961*, 781.
44. Ibid.
45. *World Book*, 1961 Supplement, 197.
46. *World Book*, 202.
47. *World Almanac*, 784.
48. *Congressional Directory*, January 1960 (Washington, D.C.: US Government Printing Office).
49. *Congressional Quarterly Almanac 1960*, xxx.
50. Ibid, 65.
51. Walter Lippmann, July 13, 1960.

CHAPTER THREE: THE SHADOW CAMPAIGN
1. Goodwin, *Remembering America*, 108.
2. John F. Kennedy Remarks, *John Fitzgerald Kennedy: A Compendium of Speeches, Statements, and Remarks Delivered During His Service in the Congress of the United States* (Washington, D.C.: United States Government Printing Office, 1964), 1106.
3. James Reston, *New York Times*, January 15, 1960.
4. John F. Kennedy, *Compendium of Speeches*, 992.
5. Sorensen, ed., *"Let The Word Go Forth,"* 83.
6. John F. Kennedy, "A Democrat Looks At Foreign Policy," *Foreign Affairs*, October 1957.
7. John F. Kennedy, *Compendium of Speeches*, 705.
8. John F. Kennedy, *The Strategy of Peace* (New York: Popular Library, 1960), 235.
9. Ibid, 27.
10. Sorensen, ed., *"Let The Word Go Forth,"* 89.
11. John F. Kennedy, *Compendium of Speeches*, 926.
12. Sorensen, ed., *"Let the Word Go Forth,"* 96.
13. John F. Kennedy, *The Speeches of John F. Kennedy, Presidential Campaign of 1960* (Washington, D.C.: US Government Printing Office, 1961), 44.
14. Ibid, 150.
15. Ibid, 95.
16. Ibid, 243.
17. Ibid, 340.
18. Ibid, 433.
19. Ibid, 734.
20. Ibid, 1195.
21. Ibid, 839.
22. Ibid, 620.
23. Dwight Eisenhower, *The White House Years: Waging Peace, 1956–1961* (Garden City, N.Y.: Doubleday, 1965), 8.
24. Nixon, *Six Crises*, 321.
25. Richard Nixon speech, July 28, 1960, The American Presidency Project.
26. Nixon, *Six Crises*, 321.
27. Richard Nixon, *The Speeches of Vice President Richard M. Nixon, Presidential Campaign of 1960* (Washington, D.C.: US Government Printing Office, 1961), 1148.
28. Ibid, 1184.
29. Ibid, 60.
30. Ibid, 1200.

31. Ibid, 265.
32. Ibid, 405.
33. Ibid, 1077.
34. *The Joint Appearances of Senator John F. Kennedy and Vice President Richard M. Nixon, Presidential Campaign* (Washington, D.C.: US Government Printing Office, 1961), 74.
35. Ibid, 76.
36. Ibid, 161.
37. Ibid, 157.
38. Ibid, 220.
39. Ibid, 217.
40. Ibid, 268.
41. Ibid, 264.
42. David Pietrusza, *1960: LBJ vs. JFK vs. Nixon* (New York: Union Square Press, 2008), 386.
43. Eisenhower, *Public Papers of the Presidents*, 144.
44. Ibid, 295.
45. Ibid, 10.
46. Ibid, 142.
47. Ibid, 295.
48. Ibid, 320.
49. Ibid, 590.
50. Ibid, 621.
51. Ibid, 658.
52. Ibid, 695.
53. Ibid, 735.
54. Ibid, 802.
55. Ibid, 820.
56. Ibid, 828.
57. Ibid, 833.
58. Ibid, 838.
59. Ibid, 841.
60. Ibid, 848.
61. Ibid, 854.

CHAPTER FOUR: THE AGE OF EISENHOWER

1. Dwight Eisenhower, *Mandate for Change: The White House Years, 1953 to 1956* (Garden City, N.Y.: Doubleday, 1963), 107.
2. Dwight Eisenhower, *At Ease: Stories I Tell Friends* (New York: Doubleday, 1967), 33.
3. Ibid, 52.
4. Ibid, 93.
5. Jean Edward Smith, *Eisenhower: In War and Peace* (New York: Random House, 2012), 48.
6. Pete Davies, *American Road: The Story of an Epic Transcontinental Journey at the Dawn of the Motor Age* (New York: Henry Holt and Company, 2002). Book jacket copy.
7. Eisenhower, *At Ease*, 165.
8. Ibid, 187.
9. Ibid, 241.

10. Ibid, 213.
11. Paul Johnson, *Eisenhower: A Life* (New York: Viking, 2014), 56.
12. Eisenhower, *At Ease*, 303.
13. Eisenhower, *Mandate*, 5.
14. Herbert Brownell with John P. Burke, *Advising Ike: The Memoirs of Attorney General Herbert Brownell* (Lawrence: University of Kansas Press, 1993), 101.
15. Milton Eisenhower, *The President is Calling* (Garden City, N.Y.: Doubleday, 1974), 246.
16. Brownell, *Advising Ike*, 101.
17. Eisenhower, *Mandate*, 127.
18. Smith, *Eisenhower in War and Peace*, 544.
19. Herbert Parmet, *Eisenhower and the American Crusades* (Piscataway, N.J.: Transaction Publishers, 1972), 169.
20. Emmet John Hughes, *The Ordeal of Power: A Political Memoir of the Eisenhower Years* (New York: Dell Publishing, 1962), 19.
21. Carl Brauer, *Presidential Transitions: Eisenhower Through Reagan* (New York: Oxford University Press, 1986), 3.
22. William Bragg Ewald Jr., *Eisenhower the President: Crucial Days: 1951–1960*, (Englewood Cliffs, N.J.: Prentice-Hall, 1981), 129.
23. Robert Donovan, *Eisenhower: The Inside Story* (New York: Harper & Brothers, 1956), 3.
24. Nixon, *Six Crises*, 161.
25. Eisenhower, *At Ease*, 201.
26. Robert Donovan, *Confidential Secretary: Ann Whitman's 20 Years with Eisenhower and Rockefeller* (New York: Dutton, 1988), 192.
27. Wilton Persons, Oral History, Eisenhower Presidential Library.
28. Ralph Williams, Oral History, Eisenhower Presidential Library.
29. Robert Schulz, Oral History, Eisenhower Presidential Library.
30. John Eisenhower, Oral History, Eisenhower Presidential Library.
31. Eisenhower, *Mandate*, 148.
32. Donovan, *Eisenhower*, 256.
33. Eisenhower, *Mandate*, 148.
34. Oakley, *God's Country*, 154.
35. Eisenhower, *Mandate*, 114.
36. Smith, *Eisenhower*, 580.
37. Eisenhower, *Mandate*, 452.
38. Brownell, *Advising Ike*, 211.
39. Herbert Parmet, *Eisenhower and the American Crusades* (New Brunswick, N.J.: Transaction Publishers, 1972), 28.
40. Eisenhower, *Mandate*, 193.
41. Brownell, *Advising Ike*, 287.
42. Slater, *The Ike I Knew*, 273.
43. Stephen Hess, "What Congress Looked Like From Inside the Eisenhower Administration," [Brookings Institution], January 6, 2002.
44. Tom Wicker, *Dwight D. Eisenhower* (New York: Times Books, 2002), 112.
45. Eisenhower, *Mandate*, 95.
46. Eisenhower, *Waging Peace*, 125.
47. Andrew Goodpaster, interview, "Presidential Transitions and Foreign Policy: Eisenhower and Kennedy."
48. Parmet, *Eisenhower and the American Crusades*, 577.

49. Ibid, 577.
50. Richard Rovere, "Eisenhower and the New President," *Harper's Magazine*, May, 1960.

CHAPTER FIVE: THE JUNIOR SENATOR FROM MASSACHUSETTS
1. Lincoln, *Twelve Years*, 12.
2. David Nasaw, *The Patriarch: The Remarkable Life and Turbulent Times of Joseph P. Kennedy* (New York: Penguin Books, 2012), 12.
3. Ibid, 131.
4. Edward M. Kennedy, *True Compass* (New York: Twelve, 2009), 162.
5. Robert F. Kennedy, foreword to *Profiles in Courage* by John F. Kennedy (New York: Harper & Row, 1964), ix.
6. Nasaw, *The Patriarch*, 225.
7. Ibid, 240.
8. Ibid, 572.
9. Robert Dallek, *An Unfinished Life: John F. Kennedy 1917–1963* (Boston: Little, Brown, 2003), 118.
10. Nasaw, *The Patriarch*, 598.
11. John F. Kennedy in *Listening In: The Secret White House Recordings of John F. Kennedy*, Ted Widmer, ed., (New York: Hyperion, 2012), 48.
12. Kennedy, *Compendium of Speeches*, 971.
13. Kennedy, *Listening In*, 49.
14. Herbert Parmet, *Jack: The Struggles of John F. Kennedy* (New York: Dial Press, 1980), 167.
15. James MacGregor Burns, *John Kennedy: A Political Profile* (New York: Brace & World, 1959), 101.
16. Kennedy, *Listening In*, 33.
17. Kennedy, *Compendium of Speeches*, 138, 181, 220.
18. Ibid, 271.
19. Tip O'Neill with William Novak, *Man of the House: The Life and Political Memoirs of Speaker Tip O'Neill* (New York: Random House, 1987), 90.
20. Paul Douglas, Oral History, June 6, 1964, Kennedy Presidential Library.
21. Ted Sorensen, *Counselor: A Life at the Edge of History* (New York: HarperCollins, 2008), 250.
22. Kennedy, *Compendium of Speeches*, 255.
23. Ibid, 284.
24. Kennedy, *Strategy of Peace*, 91.
25. Kennedy, *Compendium of Speeches*, 511.
26. Ibid, 549.
27. Ibid, 705.
28. Michael O'Brien, *John F. Kennedy: A Biography* (New York: St. Martin's Press, 2005), 352.
29. Executive Sessions of the Senate Foreign Relations Committee, Volume XI, June 9, 1959.
30. Arthur Schlesinger, *A Thousand Days: John F. Kennedy in the White House* (New York: Houghton, Mifflin Company, 19665), 109.
31. Parmet, *Jack: The Struggle of John F. Kennedy*, 355.
32. Kenneth P. O'Donnell and David P. Powers with Joe McCarthy, *"Johnny, We Hardly Knew Ye": Memories of John Fitzgerald Kennedy* (Boston: Little, Brown, 1970), 126.

33. Gretchen Rubin, *Forty Ways to Look at John F. Kennedy* (New York: Ballantine Books, 2005), 52.
34. Clark Clifford with Richard Holbrooke, *Counsel to the President: A Memoir* (New York: Random House, 1992), 303.
35. Burns, *John Kennedy*, 263.
36. Harry McPherson, *A Political Education: A Washington Memoir* (Austin: University of Texas Press, 1972), 41.
37. Schlesinger, *Thousand Days*, 104.
38. Ibid, 115.
39. Goodwin, *Remembering America*, 191.
40. Pierre Salinger, *With Kennedy* (New York: Avon Books, 1966), 93.
41. Kennedy, *Listening In*, 39.
42. Joseph Alsop with Adam Platt, *"I've Seen the Best of It": Memoirs* (Mount Jackson, V.A.: Axios Books, 1992), 471.
43. Theodore Sorensen, *Kennedy* (New York: Konecky & Konecky, 1965), 44.
44. Jacqueline Kennedy interview in *Jacqueline Kennedy: Historic Conversation on Life with John F. Kennedy* (New York: Hyperion, 2011), 19.
45. Kennedy, *Listening In*, 31.
46. Ibid, 42.

CHAPTER SIX: PRESIDENT EISENHOWER TRANSFERS POWER

1. Wilton Persons, Oral History, Eisenhower Presidential Library.
2. Dwight Eisenhower letter to Richard Nixon, November 9, 1960, *The Papers of Dwight David Eisenhower: The Presidency: Keeping the Peace*, Volume XXI, 2156.
3. Slater, *The Ike I Knew*, 230.
4. Dwight Eisenhower, Cabinet minutes, July 1, 1960, Eisenhower Presidential Library.
5. Dwight Eisenhower letter to John Kennedy, November 9, 1960, *Public Papers of Eisenhower*, 857.
6. Dwight Eisenhower, Cabinet paper, CP 60-110/1, Eisenhower Presidential Library.
7. Wilton Persons, Memo for Heads of Departments and Agencies, November 28, 1960, Eisenhower Presidential Library.
8. Dwight Eisenhower, *Public Papers of Eisenhower*, 2189.
9. Dwight Eisenhower, *Public Papers of Eisenhower*, 872.
10. John F. Kennedy remarks, December 6, 1960, Kennedy Presidential Library.
11. Eisenhower, *Waging Peace*, 603.
12. John Kennedy letter to Dwight Eisenhower, December 19, 1960, *Public Papers of Eisenhower*, 2306.
13. Clark Clifford letter to Wilton Persons, December 21, 1960, Eisenhower Presidential Library.
14. Maurice Stans memo, December 12, 1960, Eisenhower Presidential Library.
15. Dwight Eisenhower statement, January 12, 1961, *Public Papers of Eisenhower*, 913.
16. Stephen Ambrose, *Eisenhower: The President* (New York: Simon & Schuster, 1984), 336.
17. Memo of Conference with the President, December 12, 1960, Eisenhower Presidential Library.
18. Memo for the Record, Andrew Goodpaster, December 28, 1960, Eisenhower Presidential Library.

19. Christian Herter memo to Wilton Persons, November 16, 1960, Eisenhower Presidential Library.
20. Dwight Eisenhower statement, January 3, 1961, *Public Papers of Eisenhower*, 891.
21. Eisenhower, *Waging Peace*, 614.
22. Ibid, 62.
23. Eisenhower statement, November 16, 1960, *Public Papers of Eisenhower*, 861.
24. Eisenhower statement, January 17, 1961, *Public Papers of Eisenhower*, 1029.
25. Letter to Eisenhower from Turnpike Land Company, January 3, 1961, Eisenhower Presidential Library.
26. John Eisenhower, *Strictly Personal: A Memoir* (Garden City, N.Y.: Doubleday, 1974), 303.
27. John F. Kennedy letter to Dwight Eisenhower, March 22, 1961, *Public Papers of Kennedy*, 202.
28. Dwight Eisenhower letter to Ambassador Michel Gallin-Douathé, November 14, 1960, *Papers of Dwight Eisenhower*, 2160.
29. Dwight Eisenhower letter to Hastings Lionel Ismay, December 3, 1960, *Papers of Dwight Eisenhower*, 2180.
30. Dwight Eisenhower letter to Clarence Francis, January 4, 1961, *Papers of Dwight Eisenhower*, 2235.
31. Dwight Eisenhower letter to Mohammad Ayub Khan, December 7, 1960, *Papers of Dwight Eisenhower*, 2197.
32. Dwight Eisenhower remarks, January 7, 1961, *Public Papers of Dwight Eisenhower*, 898.
33. Dwight Eisenhower remarks, January 9, 1961, *Public Papers of Dwight Eisenhower*, 904.
34. John Eisenhower, *Strictly Personal*, 285.
35. Malcom Moos interview, Oral History Research Office, Columbia University, 1973, 190.
36. Ralph Williams, Oral History, Eisenhower Presidential Library, January 3, 1988.
37. Dwight Eisenhower remarks, January 17, 1961, *Public Papers of Dwight Eisenhower*, 1035.
38. Jack Raymond, "Military Industrial Complex: An Analysis," *New York Times*, January 22, 1961.
39. *Nation*, editorial, January 28, 1961.
40. Walter Lippmann, "Eisenhower's Farewell Warning," *Boston Globe*, January 19, 1961.
41. Eisenhower, *Waging Peace*, 616.

CHAPTER SEVEN: PRESIDENT-ELECT KENNEDY PREPARES

1. O'Donnell and Powers, *"Johnny We Hardly Knew Ye,"* 242.
2. Sorensen, *Kennedy*, 238.
3. Ibid, 235.
4. Goodwin, *Remembering America*, 206.
5. O'Donnell and Powers, *"Johnny We Hardly Knew Ye,"* 229.
6. White House Pool report, November 17, 1960, by Tom Ottenad.
7. Richard Neustadt, *Preparing to Be the President: The Memos of Richard E. Neustadt* (Washington: Brookings Institution Press, 2000), 144.
8. Clifford, *Counsel to the President*, 319.
9. Clark Clifford, Memorandum of Transition, November 9, 1960, Kennedy Presidential Library.
10. Lincoln, *Twelve Years*, 160.

11. Schlesinger, *A Thousand Days*, 121.
12. Sorensen, *Kennedy*, 230.
13. Clifford, *Counsel to the President*, 333.
14. Clark Clifford interview with Laurin Henry and Dean Mann, February 24, 1961, Kennedy Presidential Library.
15. Clark Clifford, Memorandum of Conversation with Senator Kennedy, November 30, 1960, Kennedy Presidential Library.
16. Clark Clifford notes, December 6, 1960, Kennedy Presidential Library.
17. Clark Clifford letter to John F. Kennedy, December 23, 1960, Kennedy Presidential Library.
18. Clifford, *Counsel to the President*, 344.
19. Adam Yarmolinsky, "The Kennedy Talent Hunt," *Reporter*, June 8, 1961.
20. Margaret Price, "Survey of Major Presidential Appointments of Women To Positions in Government Service," December 8, 1960, Kennedy Presidential Library.
21. Mary McGrory letter to Sargent Shriver, March 2, 1961, Kennedy Presidential Library.
22. Salinger, *With Kennedy*, 106.
23. Sorensen, *Kennedy*, 261.
24. John F. Kennedy, press conference, December 23, 1960, Kennedy Presidential Library.
25. Clifford, *Counsel*, 337.
26. John F. Kennedy, press conference, December 15, 1960.
27. *U.S. News & World Report*, January 30, 1961.
28. Sorensen, *Kennedy*, 256.
29. Clifford, *Counsel to the President*, 334.
30. Goodwin, *Remembering America*, 203.
31. Richard Goodwin memo, "Campaign Promises," undated, Kennedy Presidential Library.
32. Ted Sorensen letter to Jerome Wiesner, December 9, 1960, Kennedy Presidential Library.
33. Paul Samuelson report, "Prospects and Policies for the 1961 American Economy," January 6, 1961, Kennedy Presidential Library.
34. Harris Wofford letter and report, December 30, 1960, Kennedy Presidential Library.
35. Jerome Wiesner letter and report, January 12, 1961, Kennedy Presidential Library.
36. Schlesinger, *A Thousand Days*, 161.
37. Pierre Salinger oral history, July 19, 1965, Kennedy Presidential Library.
38. Sorensen, *Kennedy*, 235.
39. Robert Caro, *The Years of Lyndon Johnson: Passage of Power* (New York: Alfred Knopf, 2012), 169.
40. Salinger, *With Kennedy*, 86.
41. John F. Kennedy, "The Soft American," *Sports Illustrated*, December 26, 1960.
42. Lincoln, *Twelve Years*, 183.
43. Tom Wolfe, *Washington Post*, December 14, 1960.
44. Kennedy in *"Let the World Go Forth,"* 56.

CHAPTER EIGHT: PASSING THE TORCH

1. David Halberstam, "Gay Democrats Jam the Capital," *New York Times*, January 18, 1961.

2. Arthur Krock, "Reminders of '33: Not Since FDR Has the Capital Been So Charged With Excitement," *New York Times*, January 14, 1961.
3. "Kennedys Invite Luminaries in Arts," Associated Press, January 14, 1961.
4. "East Façade of Capitol to Make Debut," *New York Times*, January 19, 1961.
5. Hughes, *Ordeal of Power*, 306.
6. "Transition Ball Staged By GOP," UPI, January 16, 1961.
7. "Are Sour Grapes Showing?" *Washington Post*, January 19, 1961.
8. Sorensen, *Counselor*, 359.
9. Sorensen, *Kennedy*, 240.
10. Lincoln, *My Twelve Years*, 182.
11. Jacqueline Kennedy interview in *Historic Conversations*, March 23, 1964, 146.
12. Sorensen, *Kennedy*, 241.
13. John Kennedy press conference, January 19, 1961, Kennedy Presidential Library.
14. Tom Wolfe, *Washington Post*, January 20, 1961.
15. Rose Kennedy, *Time to Remember* (Garden City, N.Y.: Doubleday, 1974), 383.
16. John Kennedy remarks, Inaugural Gala, January 19, 1961.
17. Rose Kennedy, *Time to Remember*, 384.
18. Ibid, 385.
19. Mary Van Rensselaer Thayer, *Jacqueline Kennedy: The White House Years* (New York: Popular Library, 1967), 66.
20. Mary Barelli Gallagher, *My Life with Jacqueline Kennedy* (New York: Paperback Library, 1970), 93.
21. John Eisenhower, *Strictly Personal*, 287.
22. Edward Kennedy, *True Compass*, 165.
23. *New York Times*, January 21, 1961, *Washington Post*, January 21, 1961.
24. John Kennedy Inaugural Address, January 20, 1961, *Public Papers of John Kennedy*, 1.
25. David Eisenhower with Julie Nixon Eisenhower, *Going Home To Glory: A Memoir of Life with Dwight D. Eisenhower, 1961–69* (New York: Simon & Schuster, 2010), 9.
26. Thayer, *Jacqueline Kennedy*, 81.
27. David Eisenhower, *Going Home To Glory*, 3.
28. Alsop, *"I've Seen the Best of It,"* 480.

CHAPTER NINE: RISING STAR, SETTING SUN

1. John F. Kennedy letter to Dwight Eisenhower, January 21, 1961, Kennedy Presidential Library.
2. Dwight Eisenhower letter to John F. Kennedy, January 30, 1961, Kennedy Presidential Library.
3. James Reston, "Reassuring Civility of the Transition," *New York Times*, January 14, 1961.
4. *New York Times*, editorial, January 18, 1961.
5. David Lawrence, "A Slipshod System," *Washington Evening Star*, January 20, 1961.
6. Schlesinger, *Thousand Days*, 165.
7. Hughes, *The Ordeal of Power*, 282.
8. John Eisenhower, *Strictly Personal*, 307.
9. Eisenhower, *At Ease*, 79.
10. Dwight Eisenhower interview with Malcom Moos, November 8, 1966.
11. David Eisenhower, *Going Home to Glory*, 68.
12. Dwight Eisenhower speech, June 22, 1962, Eisenhower Presidential Library.
13. Dwight Eisenhower speech, October 16, 1962, Eisenhower Presidential Library.

14. Dwight Eisenhower letter to John F. Kennedy, January 13, 1962, Eisenhower Presidential Library.
15. John F. Kennedy letter to Dwight Eisenhower, August 15, 1963, Eisenhower Presidential Library.
16. David Eisenhower, *Going Home to Glory*, 101.
17. Schlesinger, *A Thousand Days*, 675.
18. David Eisenhower, *Going Home to Glory*, 160.
19. Ibid, 59.
20. John Eisenhower, *Strictly Personal*, 336.
21. Alsop, *"I've Seen the Best of It,"* 481.
22. Schlesinger, *A Thousand Days*, 206.
23. John F. Kennedy speech, January 30, 1961, *Public Papers of the Presidents, John F. Kennedy, 1961,* 19.
24. Kennedy statement, February 19, 1961, *Public Papers of the Presidents, John F. Kennedy, 1961,* 104.
25. Kennedy speech, May 25, 1961, *Public Papers of the Presidents, John F. Kennedy, 1961,* 396.
26. Parmet, *JFK: The Presidency of John F. Kennedy,* 73.
27. John F. Kennedy letter to Dwight Eisenhower, May 17, 1962, Eisenhower Presidential Library.
28. Transition memo by John Steele, January 17, 1961, Kennedy Presidential Library.
29. *Congressional Quarterly Almanac 1964,* 425.
30. David Fromkin, *In The Time of the Americans* (New York: Vintage Books, 1996), 6.
31. Jim Newton, *Eisenhower: The White House Years* (New York: Doubleday, 2011), 344.

Acknowledgments

D wight D. Eisenhower and John F. Kennedy were fascinating and consequential leaders. It has been a pleasure and a privilege to study them through the prism of the ten-week transition between Kennedy's election as president on November 8, 1960 and his inauguration on January 20, 1961.

While I have been aided by excellent biographies and narratives, this book relies heavily on primary sources: memoirs, oral histories, contemporary newspaper and magazine articles, and thousands of pages of documents that were generated by the outgoing Eisenhower administration and the incoming Kennedy government. My quest to piece together this story was aided by many skilled and generous people.

The John F. Kennedy Presidential Library in Boston is a remarkable repository for insight into the career of JFK. I am grateful to the staff for their assistance during my visits there. My particular thanks to Stacey Chandler for her good-humored help navigating the archives. Maryrose Grossman, from the Kennedy Library's audiovisual section, was gracious and resourceful as she and her team tracked down dozens of photos from the transition for me to review.

The Dwight D. Eisenhower Presidential Library in Abilene, Kansas is, likewise, an extraordinary institution whose resources I relied on. I am grateful to the Eisenhower Foundation Abilene Travel Grants program which awarded me a grant that allowed me to work at the Library and take in the ambiance of Ike's hometown. Thank you to Kevin Bailey and Tim Rives for help navigating the collection. My gratitude also to Kathy Struss, from the Library's audiovisual department, for assembling photos taken during the transition. My sincere thanks to researcher Sydney Soderberg not only for her tenacity in tracking down documents at the Library but also for inviting me to her home for a wonderful family dinner.

The staff of the U.S. Senate Library was immensely helpful throughout this project. Thanks to Nancy Kervin and Tamara Elliott for their creative and dogged efforts to track down contemporary accounts of this time. Samantha Yeider, in the U.S. Senate Daily Press Gallery, was constantly helpful and cheerful.

My profound thanks go to three people who read the entire first draft of the manuscript and offered perceptive, penetrating, and invaluable advice: Richard Cohen, editor of *The Almanac of American Politics*, Betty Koed, the U.S. Senate Historian, and Ray Mayfield, a former executive in the federal government and private sector. Their comments and questions made this a better book.

My two-decade association with the *Washington Diplomat* magazine has been one of the joys of my professional life and I remain grateful to publisher, Victor Shiblie, and managing editor, Anna Gawel.

While working on the final edits of this book I was given the immense privilege of becoming the director of the Paul Simon Public Policy Institute at Southern Illinois University. I look forward to a long and fruitful career here in Carbondale. America and the world need more leaders like Paul Simon and more universities like SIU.

Jonathan Lyons, my steadfast and supportive agent, believed in this project from the start and found a wonderful home for it at Pegasus Books. My sincere thanks to him, and to Jessica Case, Deputy Publisher at Pegasus, for her exuberance, attentiveness, and boundless energy.

Special thanks are due my family for their support and good humor: my parents, Joe and Terri Shaw, my brothers Dave and Tim Shaw, and my sisters Susan Moller, Pam Mueller, and Marybeth Sheehan.

Much of this book was written in a cottage in Tilghman Island on Maryland's Eastern Shore. Heartfelt thanks to our hosts, first Ray and Jane Mayfield, and then Brenda and Norm Johanson, for their kindness in allowing me and my wife to share their spectacular view of the beautiful Chesapeake Bay. Few places in the world are as inspiring and calming.

This book would not have been possible, or worth doing, were it not for the support of my wife, Mindy Steinman. She sharpened my language, offered creative suggestions, asked penetrating questions, bolstered me during moments of weariness, and shared my passion for rendering this signal moment in American history. And then she packed up our house in Washington and organized our move to Carbondale.

Index